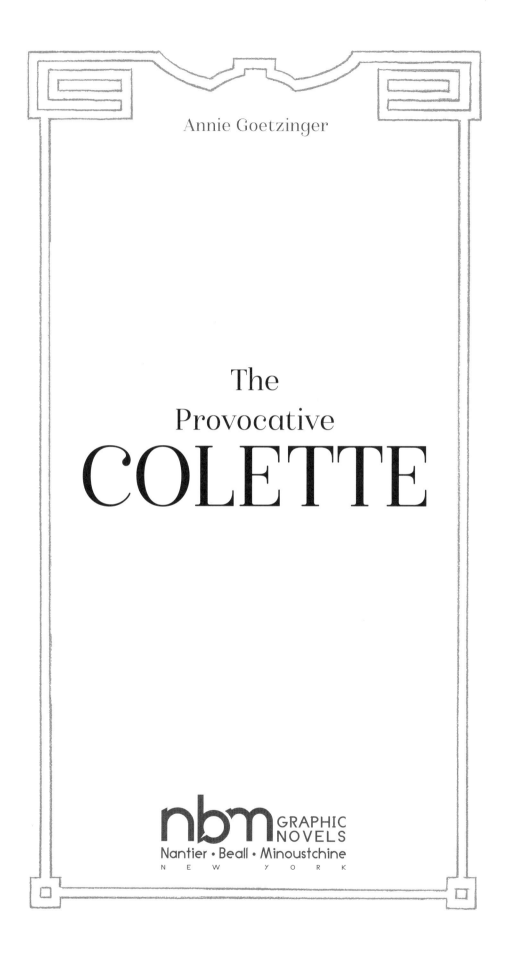

Annie Goetzinger

The
Provocative
COLETTE

nbm GRAPHIC NOVELS
Nantier · Beall · Minoustchine
NEW YORK

ISBN 9781681121703
Initially published in French as Les Apprentissages de Colette
© DARGAUD 2017, by Goetzinger
www.dargaud.com
© 2018 NBM for the English translation
Library of Congress control number: 2018941662
Translation by Montana Kane
Lettering by Ortho
Printed in India
1st printing August 2018

This graphic novel is also available as an e-book

PREFACE

A lauded writer, a revered elder of French letters, an old lady with a sharp eye and a heavy body glued to her "raft-bed" by a protruding belly and crippling arthritis: such is the image of Colette as posterity has frozen her in the collective memory, an image that is eons away from the very young woman Annie Goetzinger has chosen as the heroine of *The Provocative Colette,* a period of education.

In between these two characters, there is a learning process, an education in the sense that the literary genre has given to this term since the eighteenth century: a coming-of-age, an acquisition of knowledge, an experience of the world and, at the end of the road, once the obstacles have been overcome, the first blows received and the disillusions accepted, access to oneself, to one's own dreams and desires.

This is what is at work in this intimate graphic novel by Annie Goetzinger. For young Sidonie-Gabrielle, it's about learning to write, of course, under the abusive mentoring of her Pygmalion-like scribbler of a husband Willy, without whom, nevertheless, she never, but never, would have taken up the pen, as she always maintained, adding: "I wasn't attracted to the idea of writing as a profession. Not in the slightest."

It's an education in the ways of the heart, as well, again via Willy, an impudent husband on whom she later exacts revenge by painting, for the sake of posterity, a portrait of him whose beautiful ferocity is on par with the level of grief he inflicted on her, for "only one's first man causes one to die inside" she wrote–and God knows there was reason enough to die as Willy's naive, loving and neglected young bride.

Lastly, it's an educational journey that teaches her to love freedom, even if it is to come at the price of scandal when, as her bitter conjugal life slowly withers, Colette discovers the sensuous pleasures of dance and mime, of the stage and the audience, and leaves her isolated world in search of new friends and lovers of both the male and female persuasion.

The nuanced portrait of the future author of *Cheri* that Annie Goetzinger paints here reproduces with tremendous finesse the contrasting elements of Colette's personality: she is at once wise and unconventional, sweet and vindictive, steadfast and fickle, natural ("an ardent lover of the purity of the countryside, of wild animals, plants...") and affected. Patience and docility characterize the young woman just as much as her thirst for liberation and her stubbornness. And though, of course, it is always towards greater independence that she makes her way forward in life, month after month and year after year, it would be forcing the issue and distorting reality to make her into a feminist in the modern sense of the term. The struggle for emancipation initiated by Colette is not that of an activist, it is not of a political nature. It is a most personal, individual struggle. While she invests tremendous energy in it, she doesn't do so in the name of some theory, far from it; it is simply a question of her own survival.

This main lesson of freedom that Colette learns over the course of these years is told here in a manner both precise and elliptical, descriptive and dreamy, documentary and fictional.

Colette could not exist or breathe other than free: free, even, if she so wishes, to submit to love, to a man; and equally free to choose solitude when she finds the constraints of love suffocating. In 1904, at the age of 31, as her relationship with Willy is floundering, she authors a book (*Creatures Great and Small*) for the first time under her own name, Colette Willy, and has one of her characters say: "I want to do what I want. I want to perform in pantomimes, even in comedies. I want to dance naked if my garment hinders me. I wish to retire to my island, if I please, or to associate with ladies who live off their charms, provided they are gay, whimsical, even melancholy and wise, as are many ladies of pleasure. I want to write sad and innocent books, in which there are nothing but landscapes, flowers, sorrow, pride, and the candor of the charming animals that are frightened of man... I want to smile at all kind faces, and distance myself from ugly, dirty, and smelly people. I want to cherish he who loves me and give him all that is mine in the world: my rebellious body to share, my sweet tender heart and my freedom!"

Colette's youth fits perfectly into the historical time period known as the Belle Epoque, which Annie Goetzinger is more than familiar with: *The Legend and*

Reality of Goldtop was the first entry in her bibliography back in 1976. In this story, Amélie Élie, aka Goldtop, lived in working class Paris, i.e. the Paris of fortifications and gangs of violent underworld thugs called *Apaches*.

With *The Provocative Colette*, it's as if Annie Goetzinger were taking up the literary saga begun all those years ago in order to expand it, refine it, complete it. Showcasing subtly poetic realism is her specialty regardless of the historical period at play, and here she takes us back to the threshold of the 20th century, only this time it is in other social spheres: the world of the Paris bourgeoisie, the gloomy apartments of the Faubourg Saint-Germain or the Rue Saint-Honoré, and the semi-worldly, semi-artistic salons where the still awkward young woman from the country remains in Willy's shadow ("I was something so unexciting at that time, I was very comfortable with my non-existence," she once said). And then there are the cabarets, the music-hall scenes, the Moulin Rouge and the Ba-ta-clan, where Colette learns to break the shackles of bourgeois mores. And when she does, it is with such sensual grace that Annie Goetzinger draws the young woman's triangular, feline face, the full and slender forms of her naked body draped in veils that expose her more than they cover and conceal her.

Soon, this educational journey reveals a Colette who, in addition to writing her books, leads the frantic life of a journalist, reporter and music-hall critic, and is passionate about the fledgling new art form known as cinema. In fact, Colette– to whom being modern was actually very unimportant– always opened herself up to all that was new, in all fields, with tremendous energy and appetite. She once offered the following piece of advice to Bel-Gazou, her daughter: "I have taken up no habit in life other than the habit of eating, drinking, sleeping. Do not be wary of what is characterized as danger; be wary of routine. It is what makes us cowards and liars."

Nathalie Crom

Do not confuse what I know about myself with what I try to hide,
what I make up about myself with what I guess.

COLETTE

MAY 15, 1893 in CHÂTILLON-COLIGNY in the LOIRET. SIDONIE-GABRIELLE COLETTE is about to marry HENRY GAUTHIER-VILLARS, aka WILLY, after a long, two-year engagement. She's just 20 years old, and he's 34.

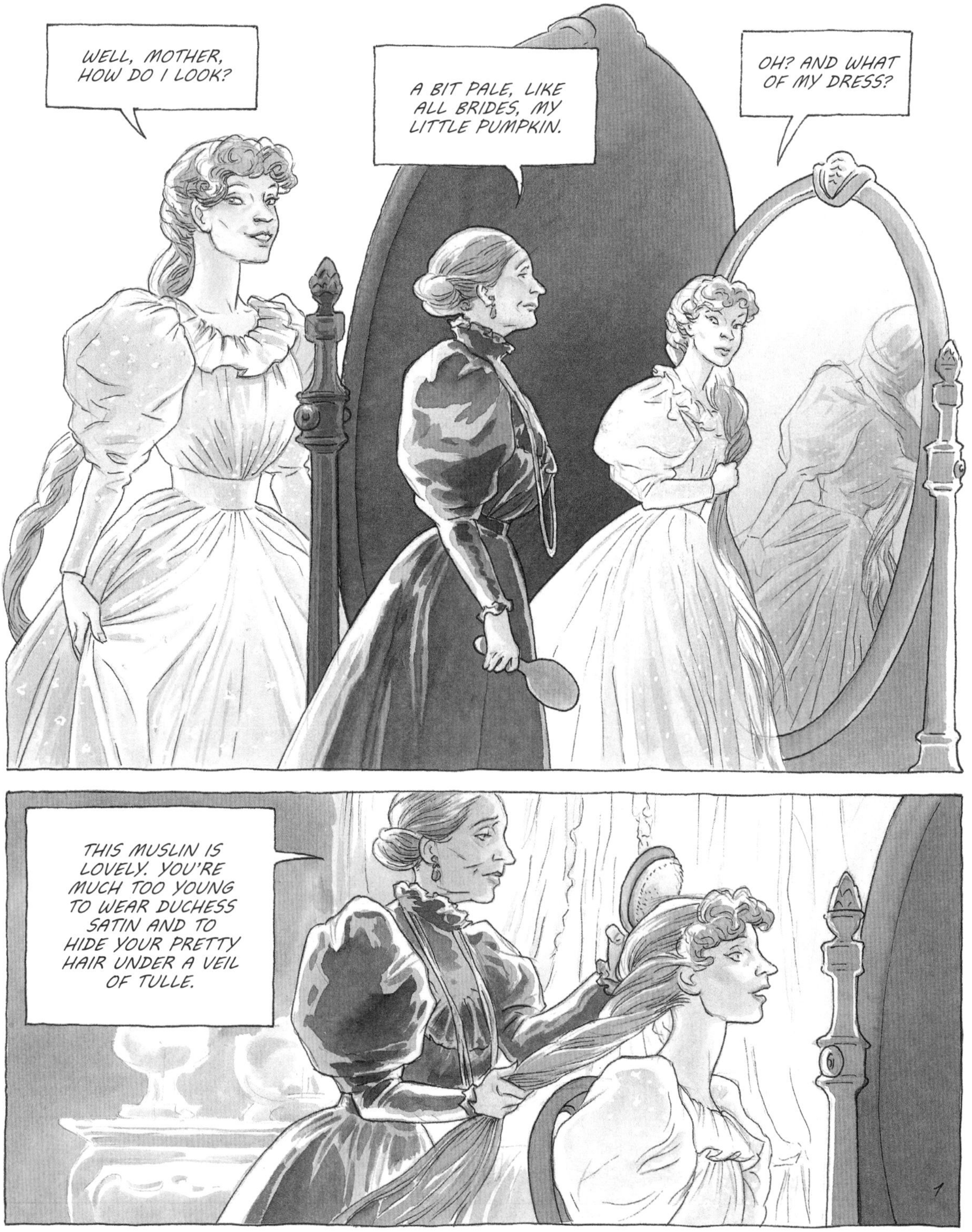
WELL, MOTHER, HOW DO I LOOK?
A BIT PALE, LIKE ALL BRIDES, MY LITTLE PUMPKIN.
OH? AND WHAT OF MY DRESS?
THIS MUSLIN IS LOVELY. YOU'RE MUCH TOO YOUNG TO WEAR DUCHESS SATIN AND TO HIDE YOUR PRETTY HAIR UNDER A VEIL OF TULLE.

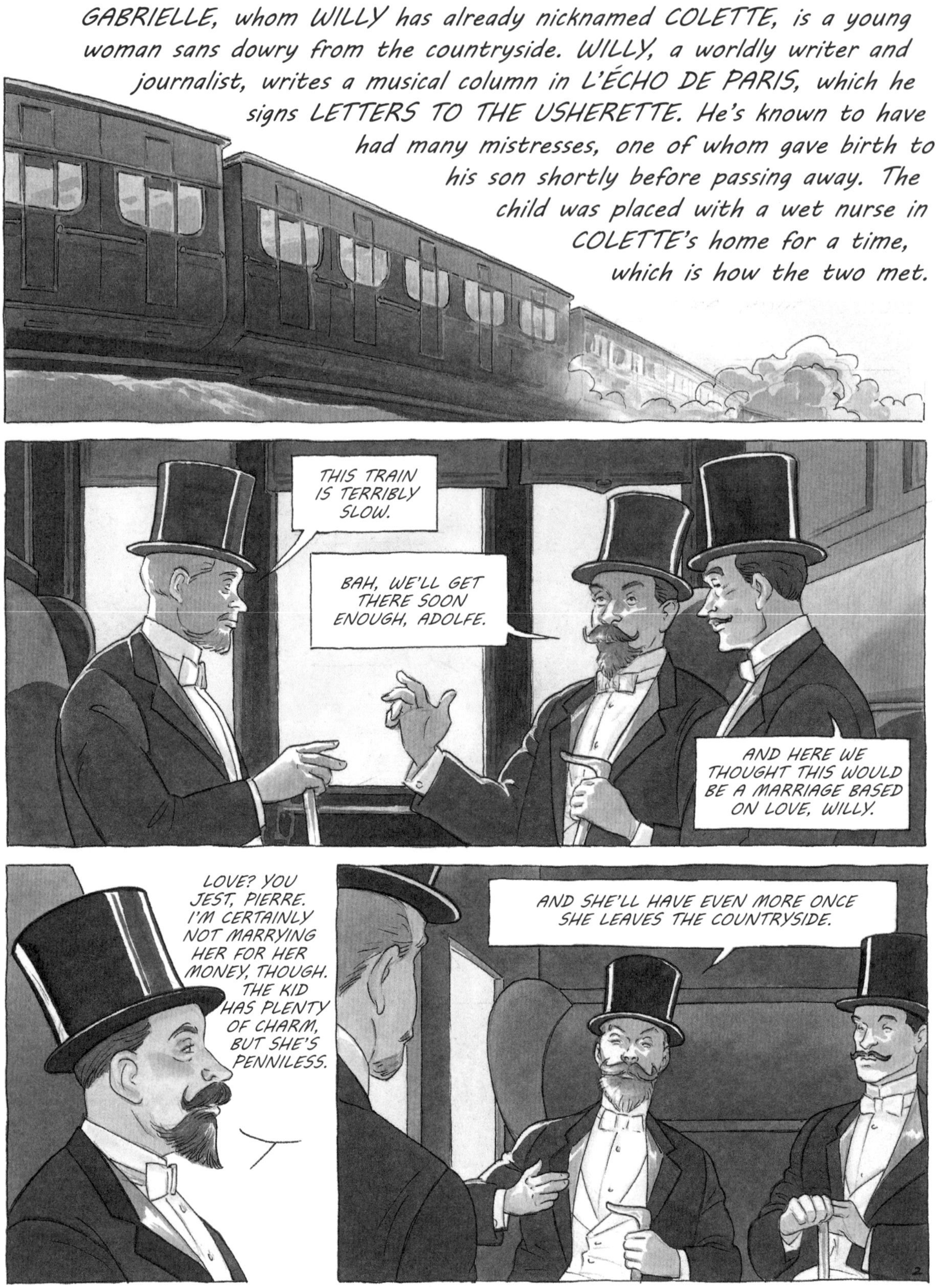
GABRIELLE, whom WILLY has already nicknamed COLETTE, is a young woman sans dowry from the countryside. WILLY, a worldly writer and journalist, writes a musical column in L'ÉCHO DE PARIS, which he signs LETTERS TO THE USHERETTE. He's known to have had many mistresses, one of whom gave birth to his son shortly before passing away. The child was placed with a wet nurse in COLETTE's home for a time, which is how the two met.
THIS TRAIN IS TERRIBLY SLOW.
BAH, WE'LL GET THERE SOON ENOUGH, ADOLFE.
AND HERE WE THOUGHT THIS WOULD BE A MARRIAGE BASED ON LOVE, WILLY.
LOVE? YOU JEST, PIERRE. I'M CERTAINLY NOT MARRYING HER FOR HER MONEY, THOUGH. THE KID HAS PLENTY OF CHARM, BUT SHE'S PENNILESS.
AND SHE'LL HAVE EVEN MORE ONCE SHE LEAVES THE COUNTRYSIDE.

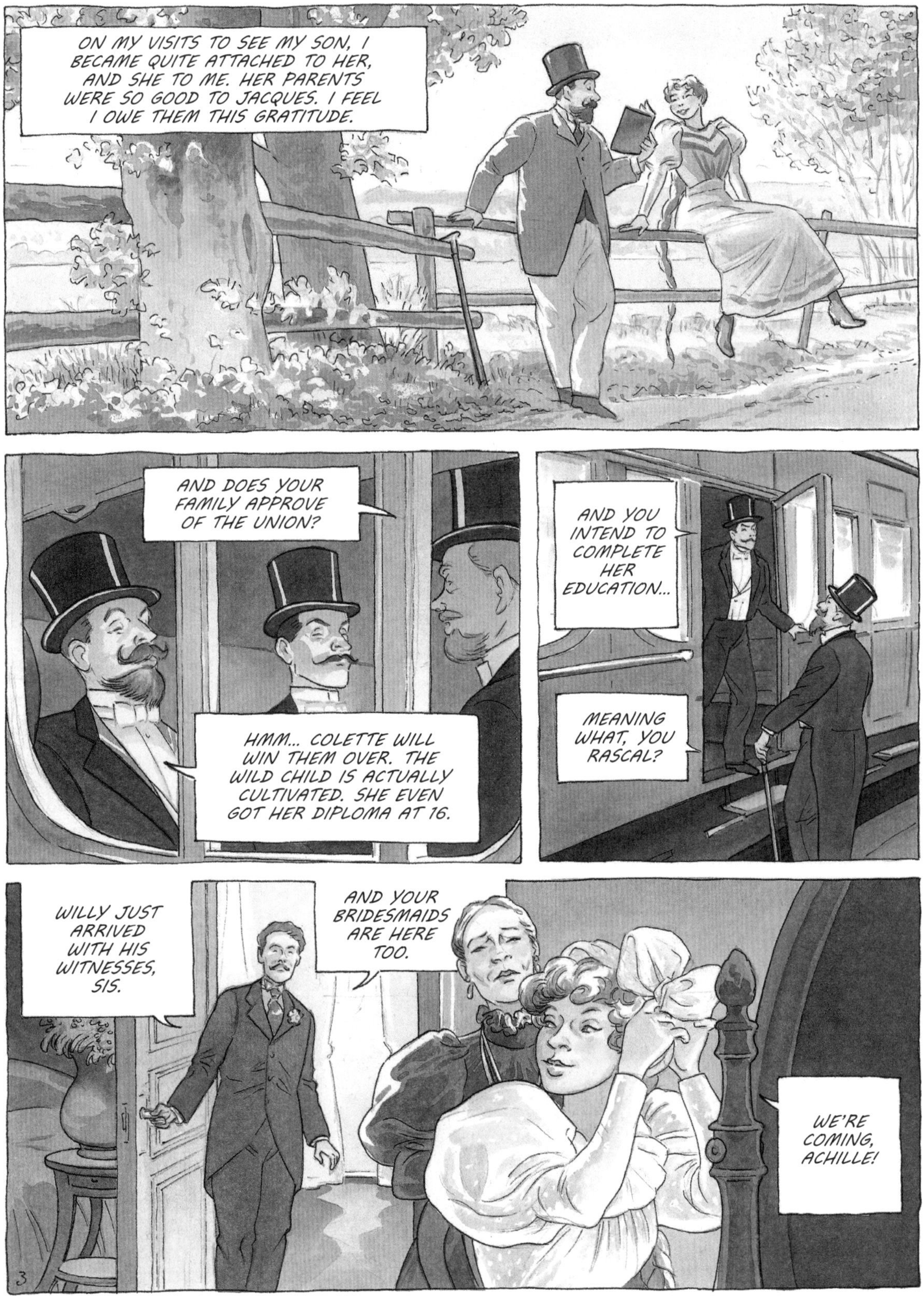
ON MY VISITS TO SEE MY SON, I BECAME QUITE ATTACHED TO HER, AND SHE TO ME. HER PARENTS WERE SO GOOD TO JACQUES. I FEEL I OWE THEM THIS GRATITUDE.
AND DOES YOUR FAMILY APPROVE OF THE UNION?
HMM... COLETTE WILL WIN THEM OVER. THE WILD CHILD IS ACTUALLY CULTIVATED. SHE EVEN GOT HER DIPLOMA AT 16.
AND YOU INTEND TO COMPLETE HER EDUCATION...
MEANING WHAT, YOU RASCAL?
WILLY JUST ARRIVED WITH HIS WITNESSES, SIS.
AND YOUR BRIDESMAIDS ARE HERE TOO.
WE'RE COMING, ACHILLE!

The groom's family does not attend the ceremony, which is but a simple religious blessing at four o'clock in the afternoon...

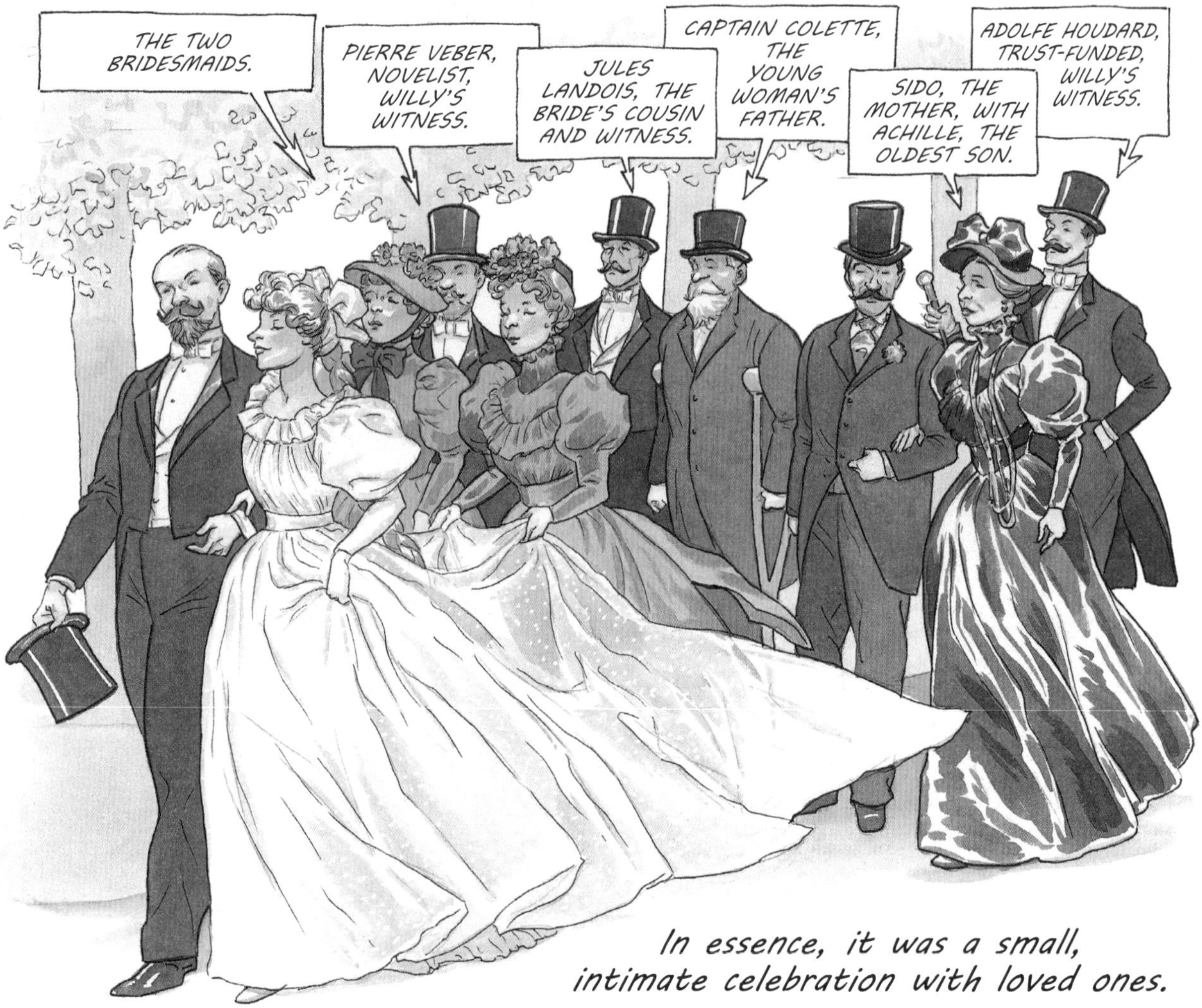
THE TWO BRIDESMAIDS.
PIERRE VEBER, NOVELIST, WILLY'S WITNESS.
JULES LANDOIS, THE BRIDE'S COUSIN AND WITNESS.
CAPTAIN COLETTE, THE YOUNG WOMAN'S FATHER.
SIDO, THE MOTHER, WITH ACHILLE, THE OLDEST SON.
ADOLFE HOUDARD, TRUST-FUNDED, WILLY'S WITNESS.
In essence, it was a small, intimate celebration with loved ones.

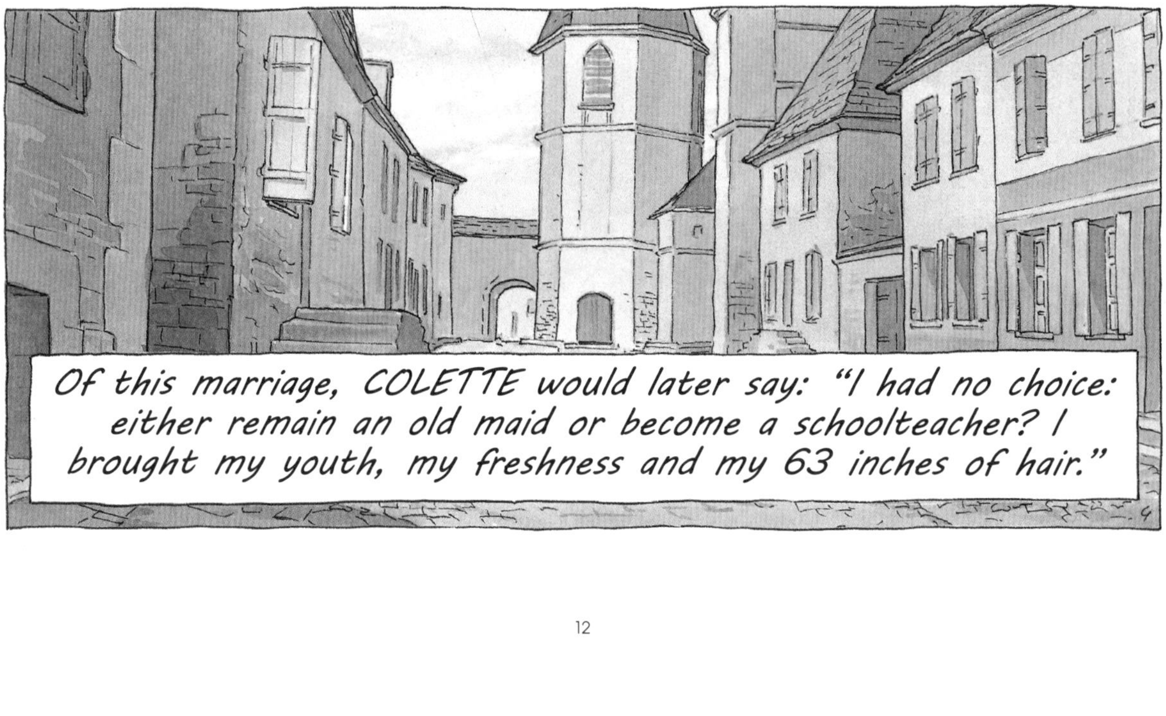
Of this marriage, COLETTE would later say: "I had no choice: either remain an old maid or become a schoolteacher? I brought my youth, my freshness and my 63 inches of hair."

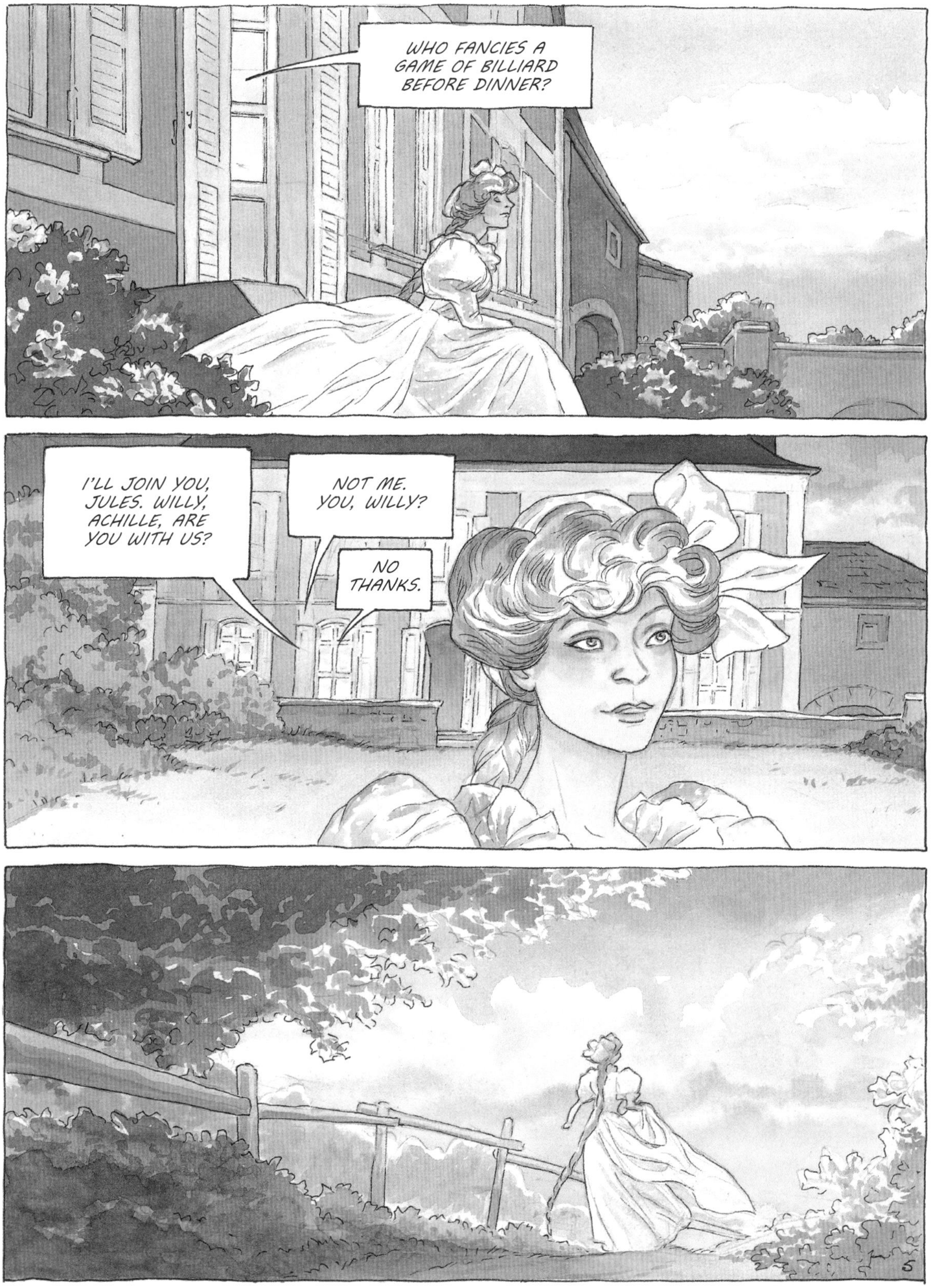
WHO FANCIES A GAME OF BILLIARD BEFORE DINNER?
I'LL JOIN YOU, JULES. WILLY, ACHILLE, ARE YOU WITH US?
NOT ME. YOU, WILLY?
NO THANKS.

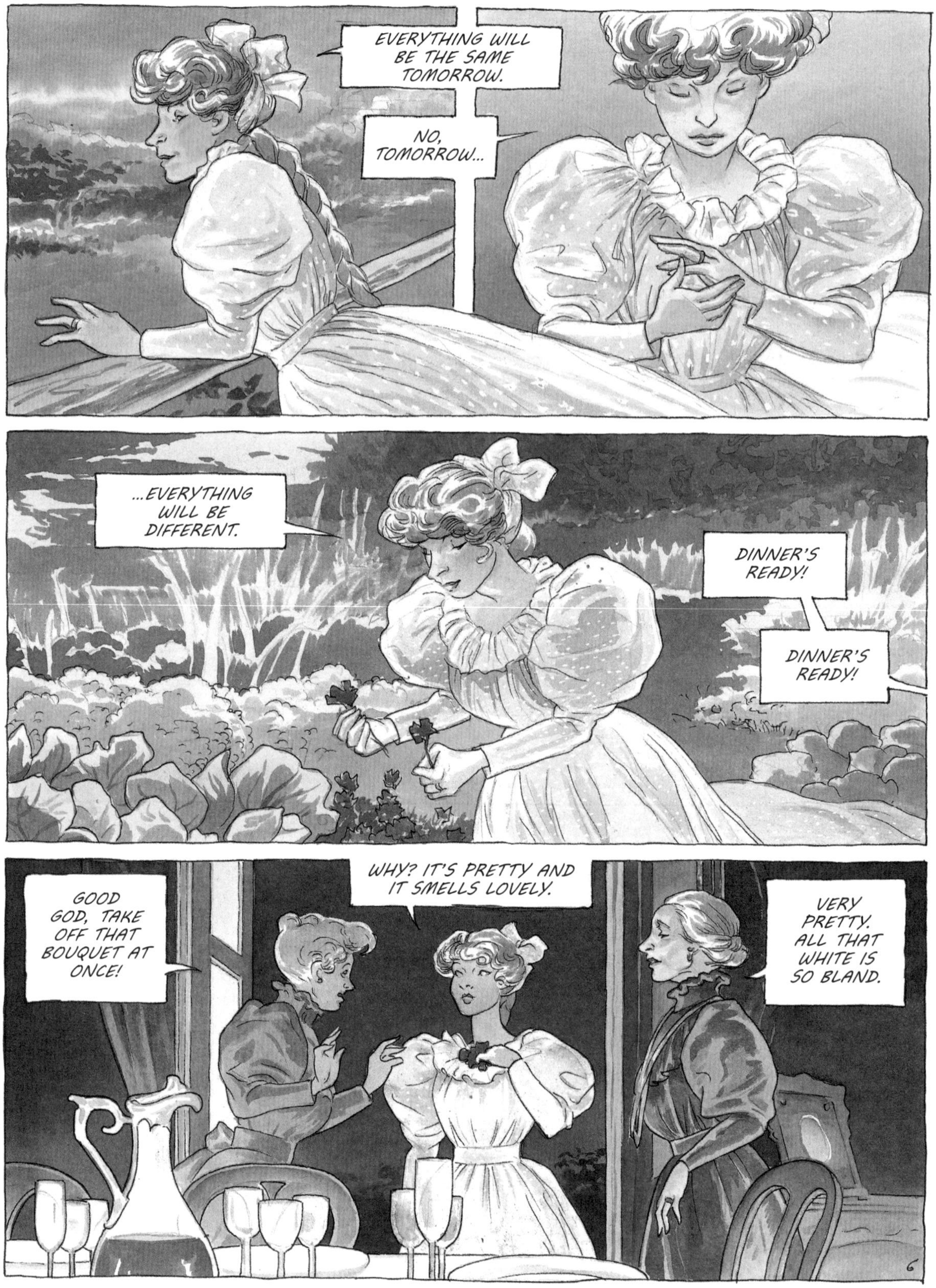
EVERYTHING WILL BE THE SAME TOMORROW.
NO, TOMORROW...
...EVERYTHING WILL BE DIFFERENT.
DINNER'S READY!
DINNER'S READY!
GOOD GOD, TAKE OFF THAT BOUQUET AT ONCE!
WHY? IT'S PRETTY AND IT SMELLS LOVELY.
VERY PRETTY. ALL THAT WHITE IS SO BLAND.
6

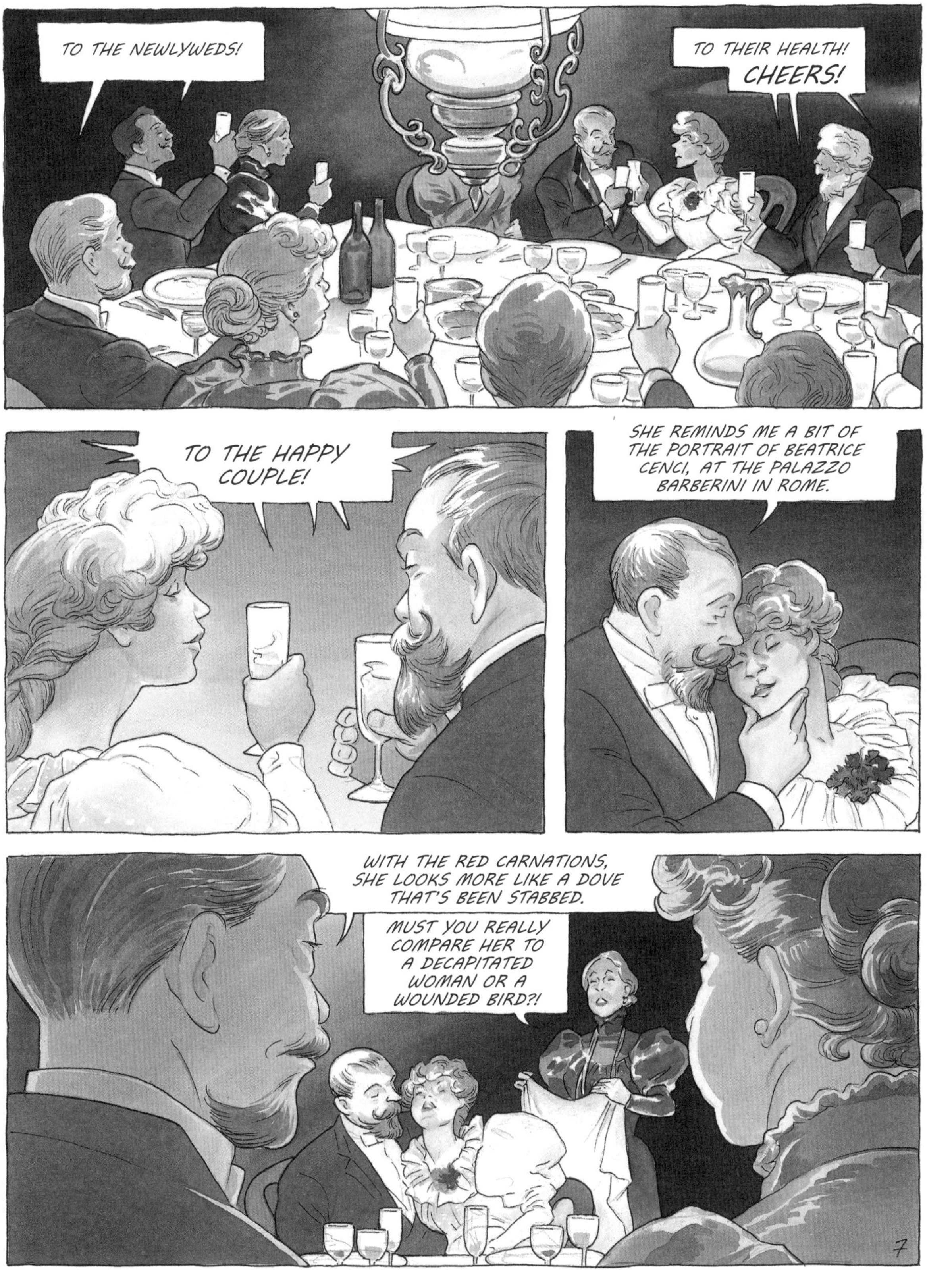
TO THE NEWLYWEDS!
TO THEIR HEALTH! CHEERS!
TO THE HAPPY COUPLE!
SHE REMINDS ME A BIT OF THE PORTRAIT OF BEATRICE CENCI, AT THE PALAZZO BARBERINI IN ROME.
WITH THE RED CARNATIONS, SHE LOOKS MORE LIKE A DOVE THAT'S BEEN STABBED.
MUST YOU REALLY COMPARE HER TO A DECAPITATED WOMAN OR A WOUNDED BIRD?!
7

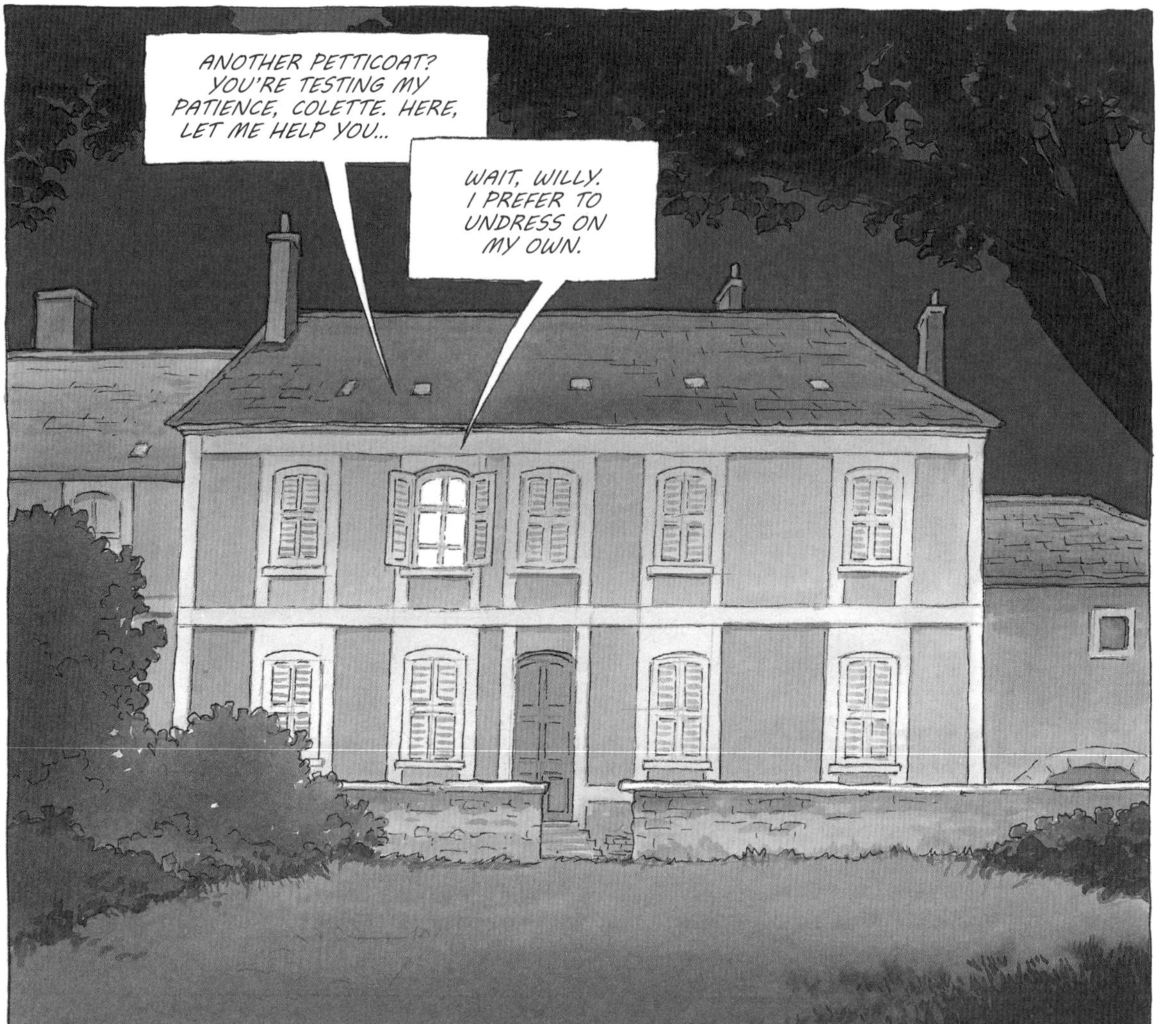
ANOTHER PETTICOAT? YOU'RE TESTING MY PATIENCE, COLETTE. HERE, LET ME HELP YOU...
WAIT, WILLY. I PREFER TO UNDRESS ON MY OWN.

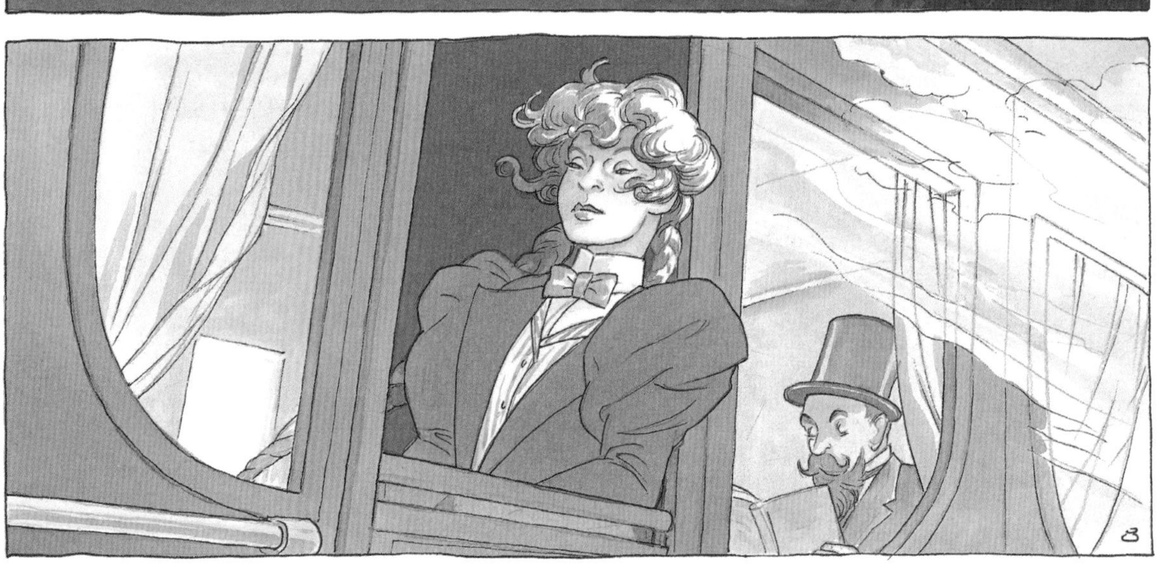

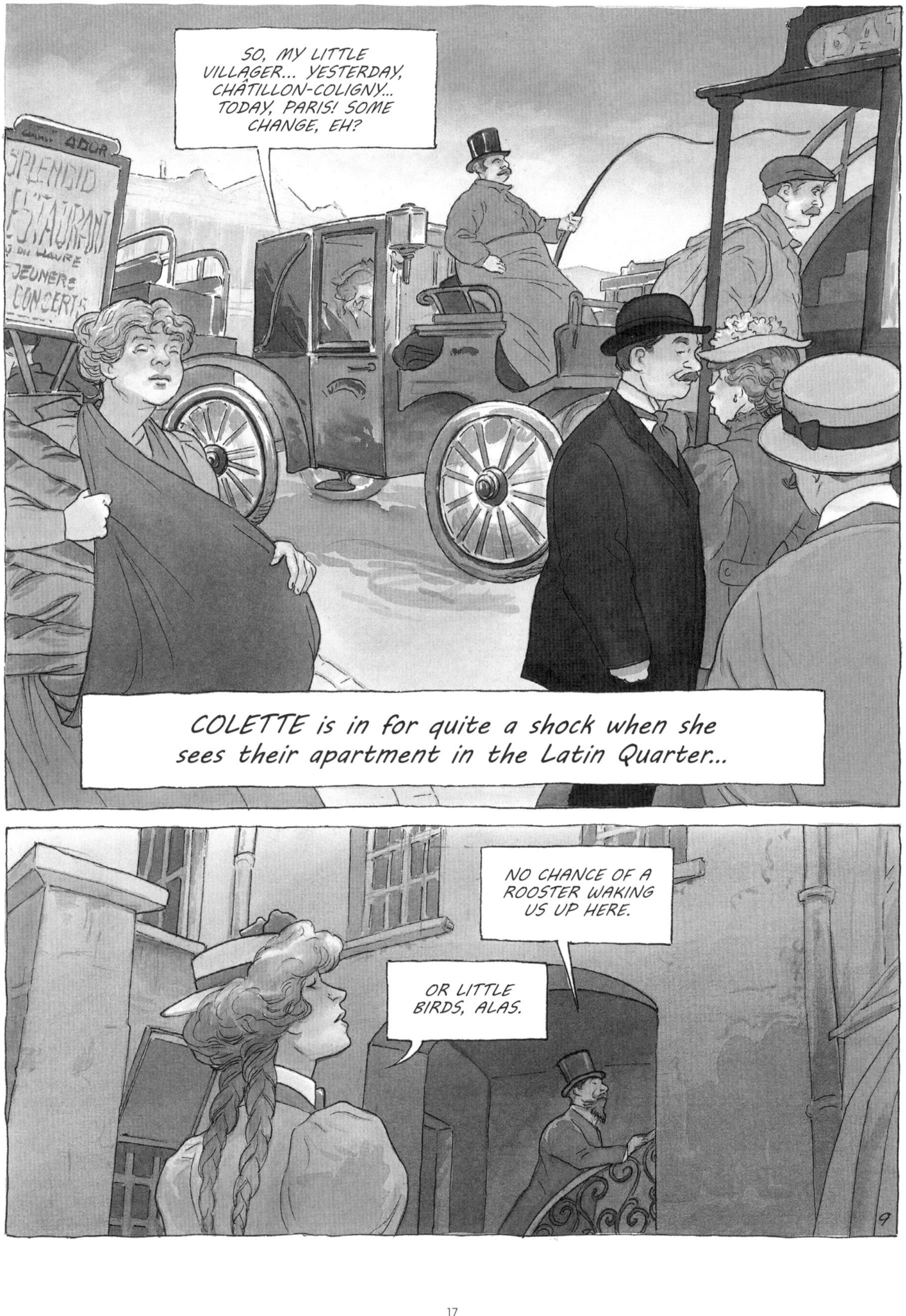
SO, MY LITTLE VILLAGER... YESTERDAY, CHÂTILLON-COLIGNY... TODAY, PARIS! SOME CHANGE, EH?
COLETTE is in for quite a shock when she sees their apartment in the Latin Quarter...
NO CHANCE OF A ROOSTER WAKING US UP HERE.
OR LITTLE BIRDS, ALAS.

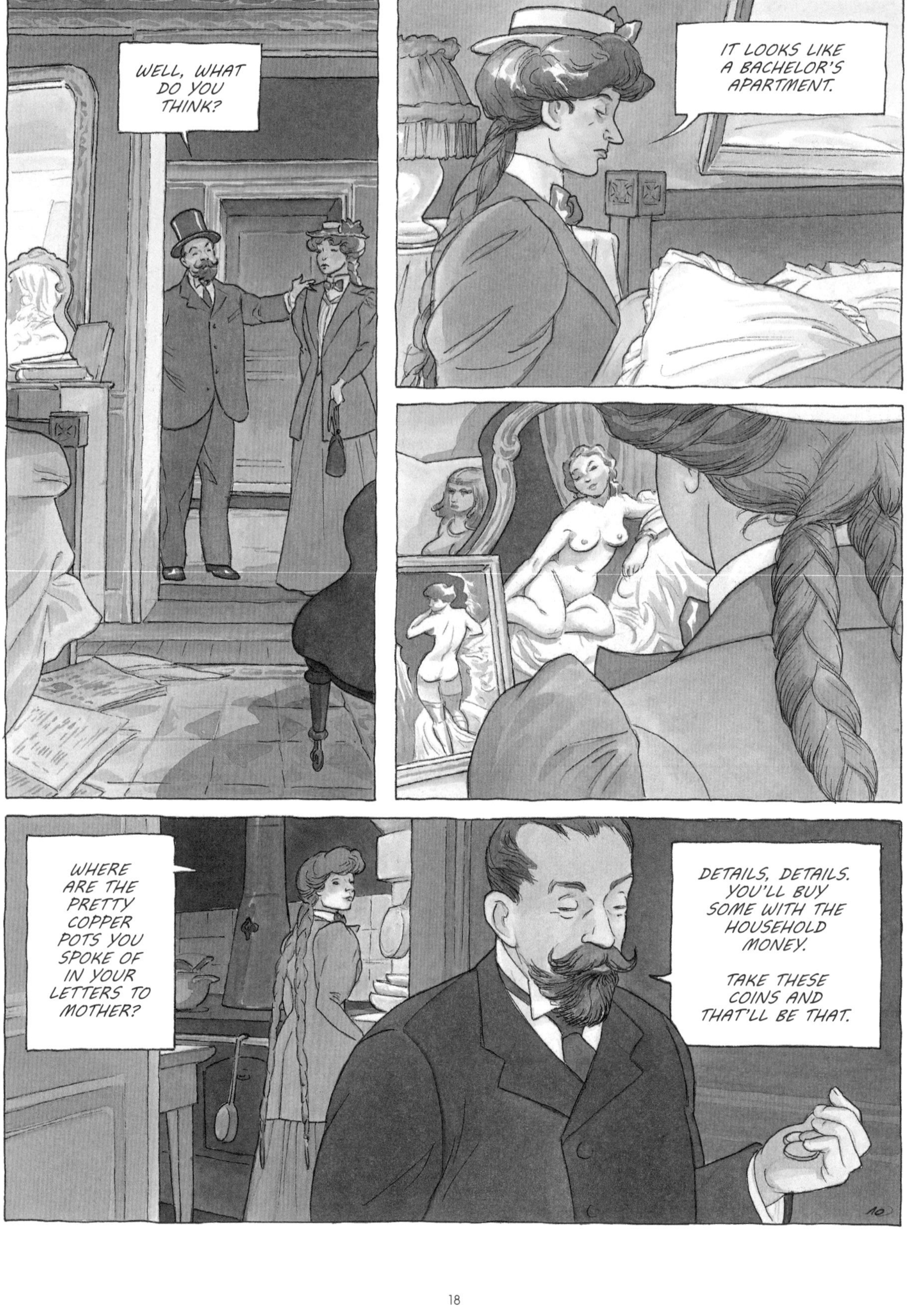
WELL, WHAT DO YOU THINK?
IT LOOKS LIKE A BACHELOR'S APARTMENT.
WHERE ARE THE PRETTY COPPER POTS YOU SPOKE OF IN YOUR LETTERS TO MOTHER?
DETAILS, DETAILS. YOU'LL BUY SOME WITH THE HOUSEHOLD MONEY.
TAKE THESE COINS AND THAT'LL BE THAT.
10

No sooner is he married than WILLY resumes his hold habits, leaving his wife home alone. In the mornings, he rides his horse to the Bois de BOULOGNE, then he lunches with colleagues, and then he goes backstage at the theater to prepare his article.

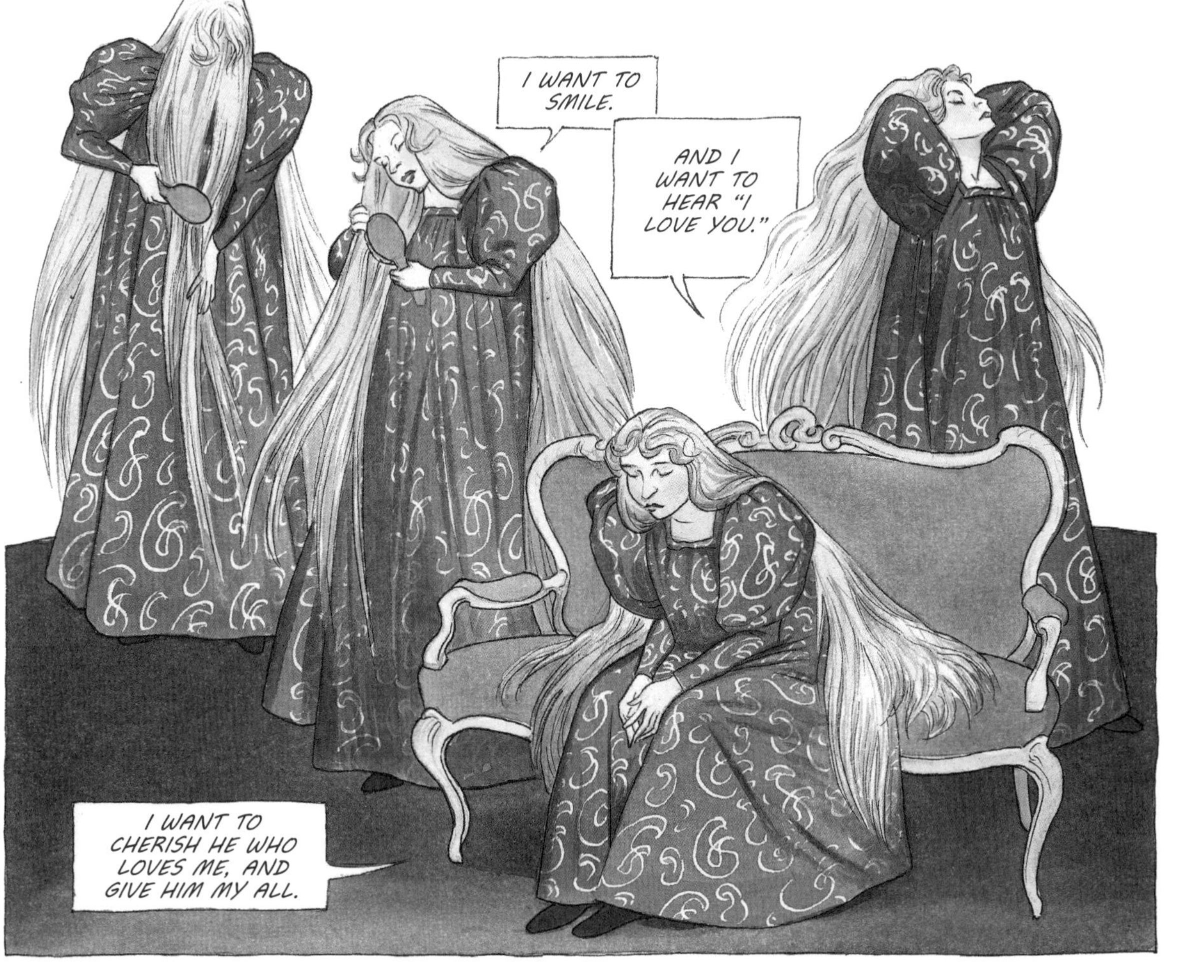

I WANT TO SMILE.
AND I WANT TO HEAR "I LOVE YOU."
I WANT TO CHERISH HE WHO LOVES ME, AND GIVE HIM MY ALL.

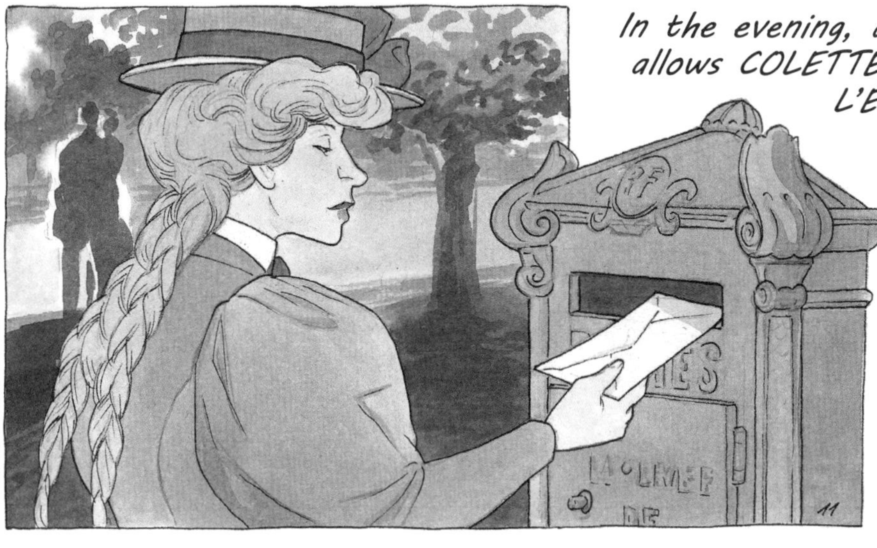

In the evening, and only then, he allows COLETTE to join him at L'ÉCHO de PARIS. She has plenty of time to pen reassuring letters to her mother every day, in which she lies to SIDO and to herself. Out of pride? Out of bravado?

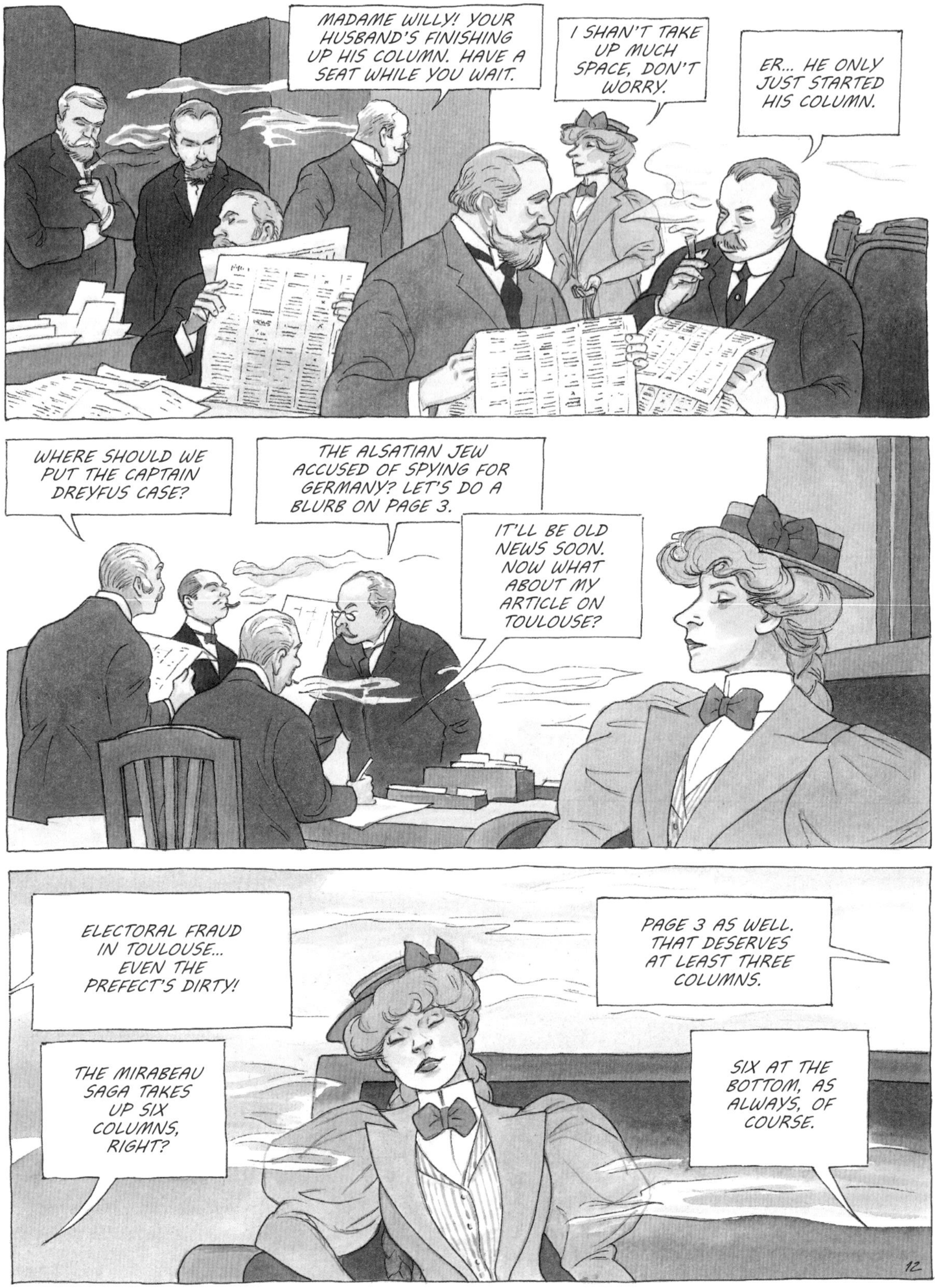
MADAME WILLY! YOUR HUSBAND'S FINISHING UP HIS COLUMN. HAVE A SEAT WHILE YOU WAIT.
I SHAN'T TAKE UP MUCH SPACE, DON'T WORRY.
ER... HE ONLY JUST STARTED HIS COLUMN.
WHERE SHOULD WE PUT THE CAPTAIN DREYFUS CASE?
THE ALSATIAN JEW ACCUSED OF SPYING FOR GERMANY? LET'S DO A BLURB ON PAGE 3.
IT'LL BE OLD NEWS SOON. NOW WHAT ABOUT MY ARTICLE ON TOULOUSE?
ELECTORAL FRAUD IN TOULOUSE... EVEN THE PREFECT'S DIRTY!
PAGE 3 AS WELL. THAT DESERVES AT LEAST THREE COLUMNS.
THE MIRABEAU SAGA TAKES UP SIX COLUMNS, RIGHT?
SIX AT THE BOTTOM, AS ALWAYS, OF COURSE.
12

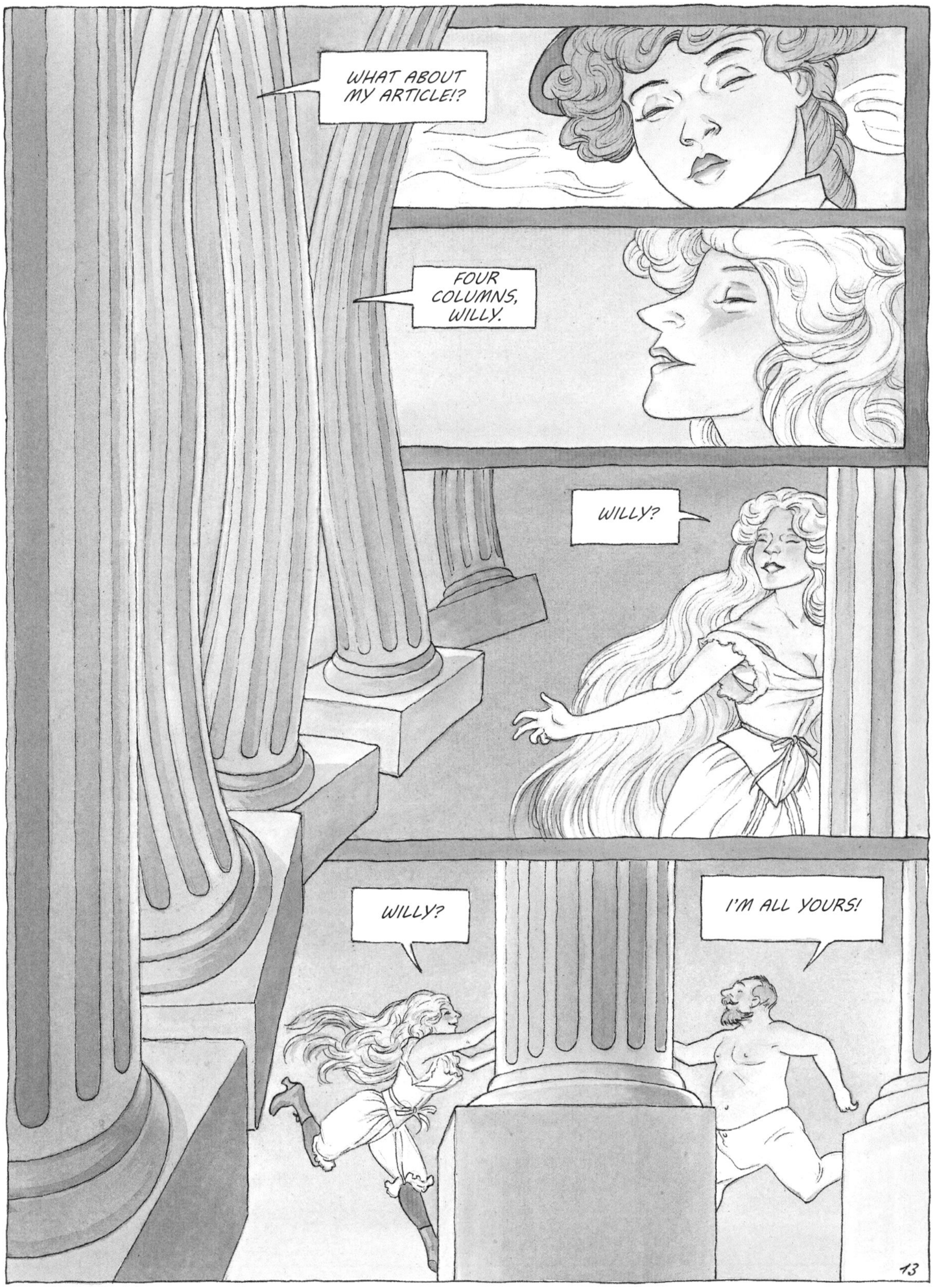
WHAT ABOUT MY ARTICLE!?
FOUR COLUMNS, WILLY.
WILLY?
WILLY?
I'M ALL YOURS!
13

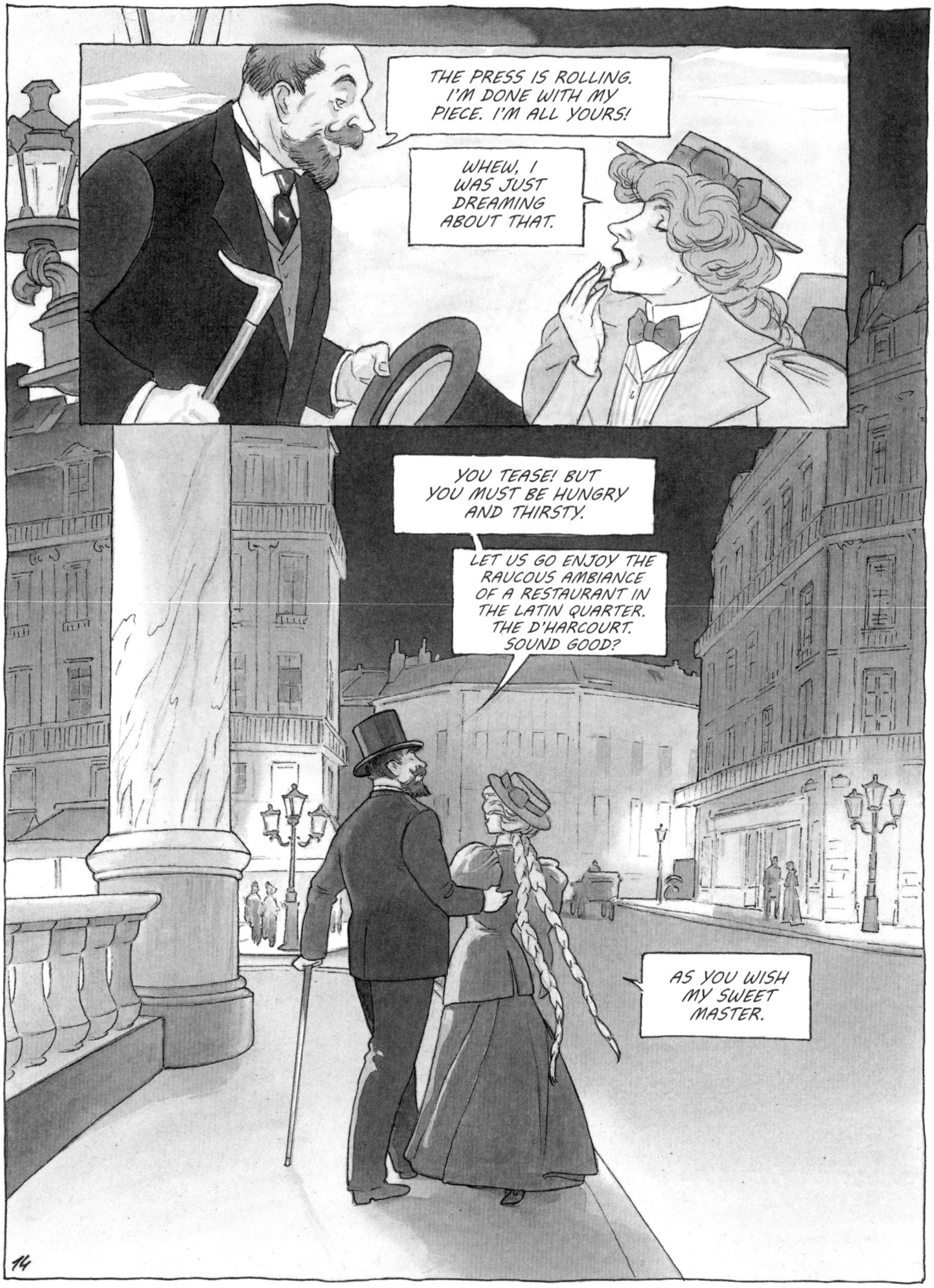
THE PRESS IS ROLLING. I'M DONE WITH MY PIECE. I'M ALL YOURS!
WHEW, I WAS JUST DREAMING ABOUT THAT.
YOU TEASE! BUT YOU MUST BE HUNGRY AND THIRSTY.
LET US GO ENJOY THE RAUCOUS AMBIANCE OF A RESTAURANT IN THE LATIN QUARTER. THE D'HARCOURT. SOUND GOOD?
AS YOU WISH MY SWEET MASTER.
14

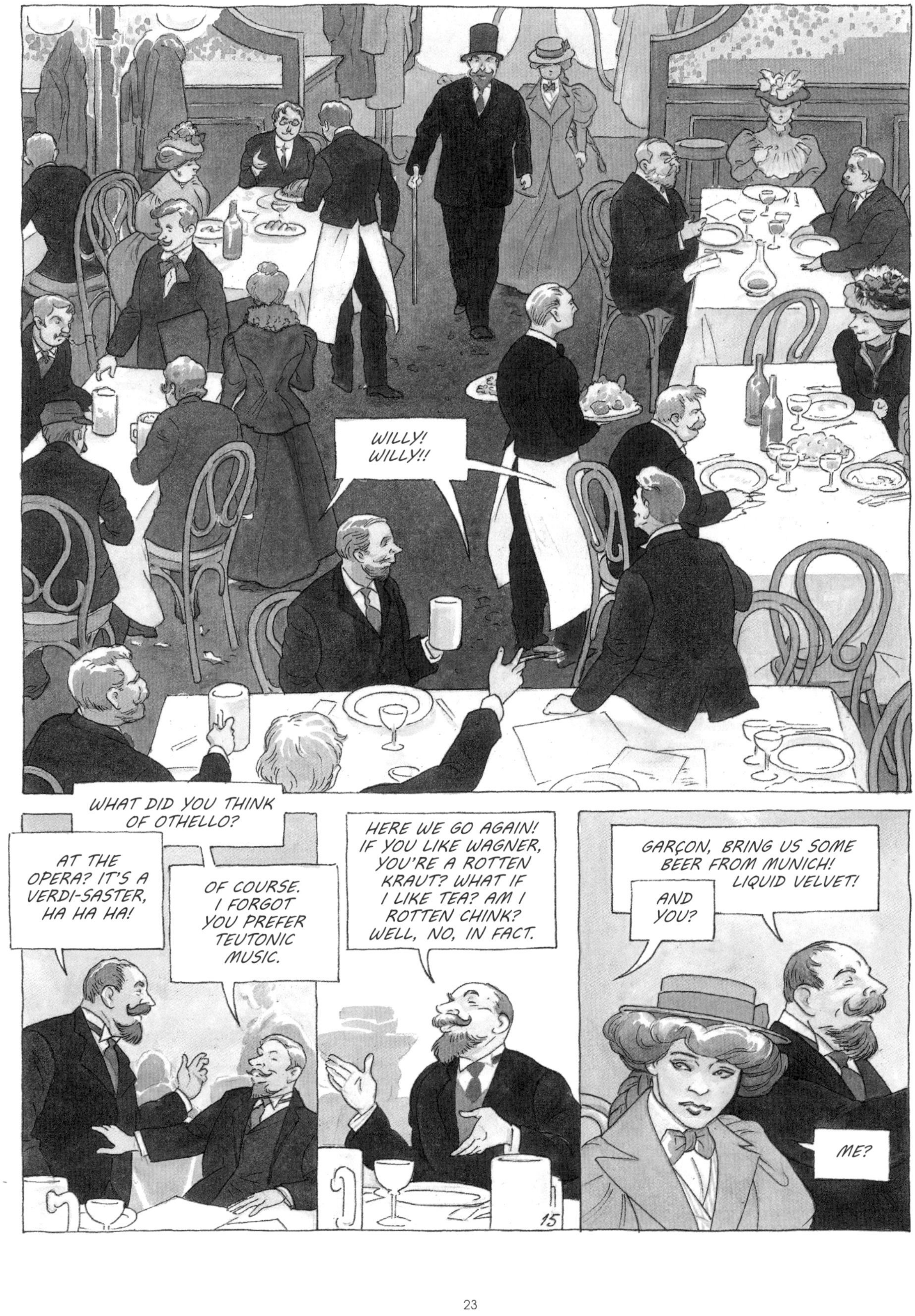
WILLY! WILLY!!
WHAT DID YOU THINK OF OTHELLO?
AT THE OPERA? IT'S A VERDI-SASTER, HA HA HA!
OF COURSE. I FORGOT YOU PREFER TEUTONIC MUSIC.
HERE WE GO AGAIN! IF YOU LIKE WAGNER, YOU'RE A ROTTEN KRAUT? WHAT IF I LIKE TEA? AM I ROTTEN CHINK? WELL, NO, IN FACT.
15
GARÇON, BRING US SOME BEER FROM MUNICH! LIQUID VELVET!
AND YOU?
ME?

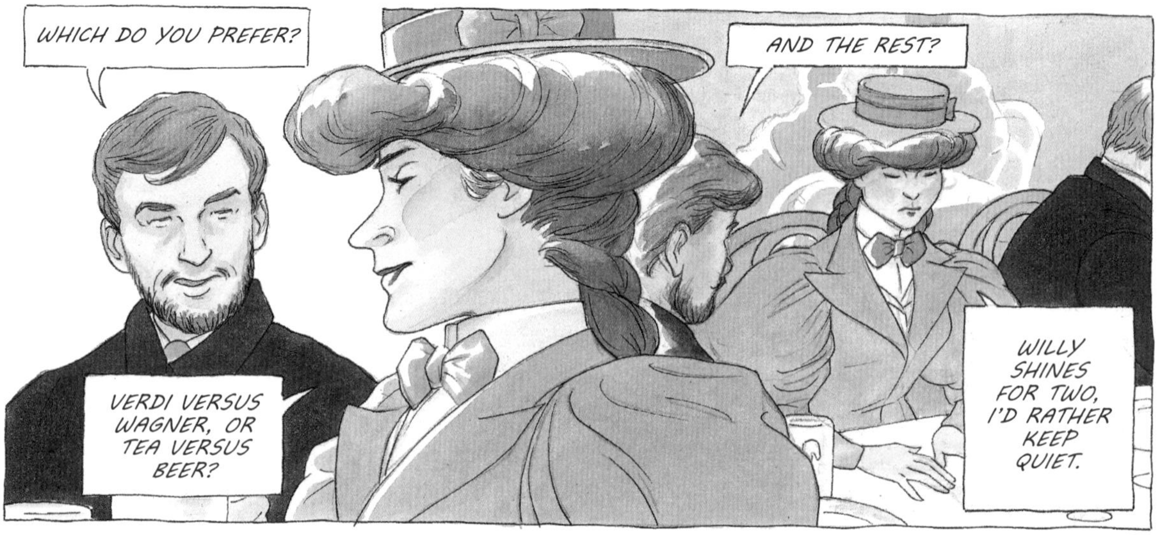
WHICH DO YOU PREFER?
AND THE REST?
VERDI VERSUS WAGNER, OR TEA VERSUS BEER?
WILLY SHINES FOR TWO, I'D RATHER KEEP QUIET.

Self-conscious about her country accent, COLETTE doesn't say much. "They must pity Willy behind his back." In reality, PAUL MASSON, JEAN de TINAN, and PAUL-JEAN TOULET envy the aging newlywed. But WILLY is also their employer. He pays them to pen his novels. They're his ghostwriters, whom he calls associates.

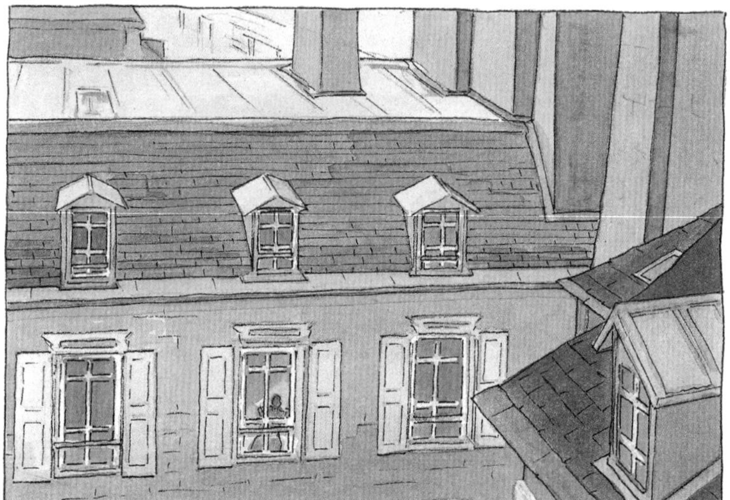

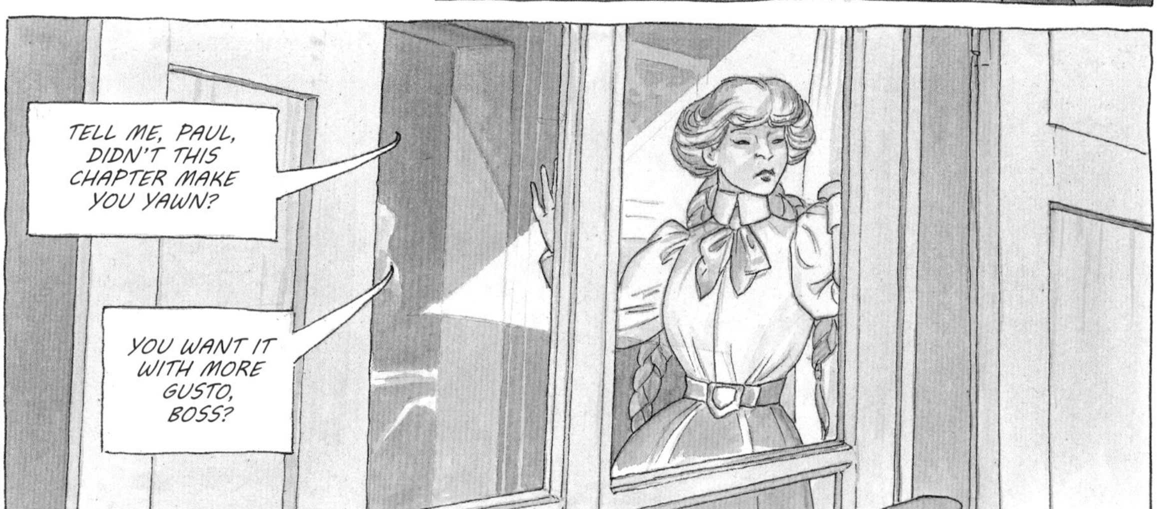
TELL ME, PAUL, DIDN'T THIS CHAPTER MAKE YOU YAWN?
YOU WANT IT WITH MORE GUSTO, BOSS?
16

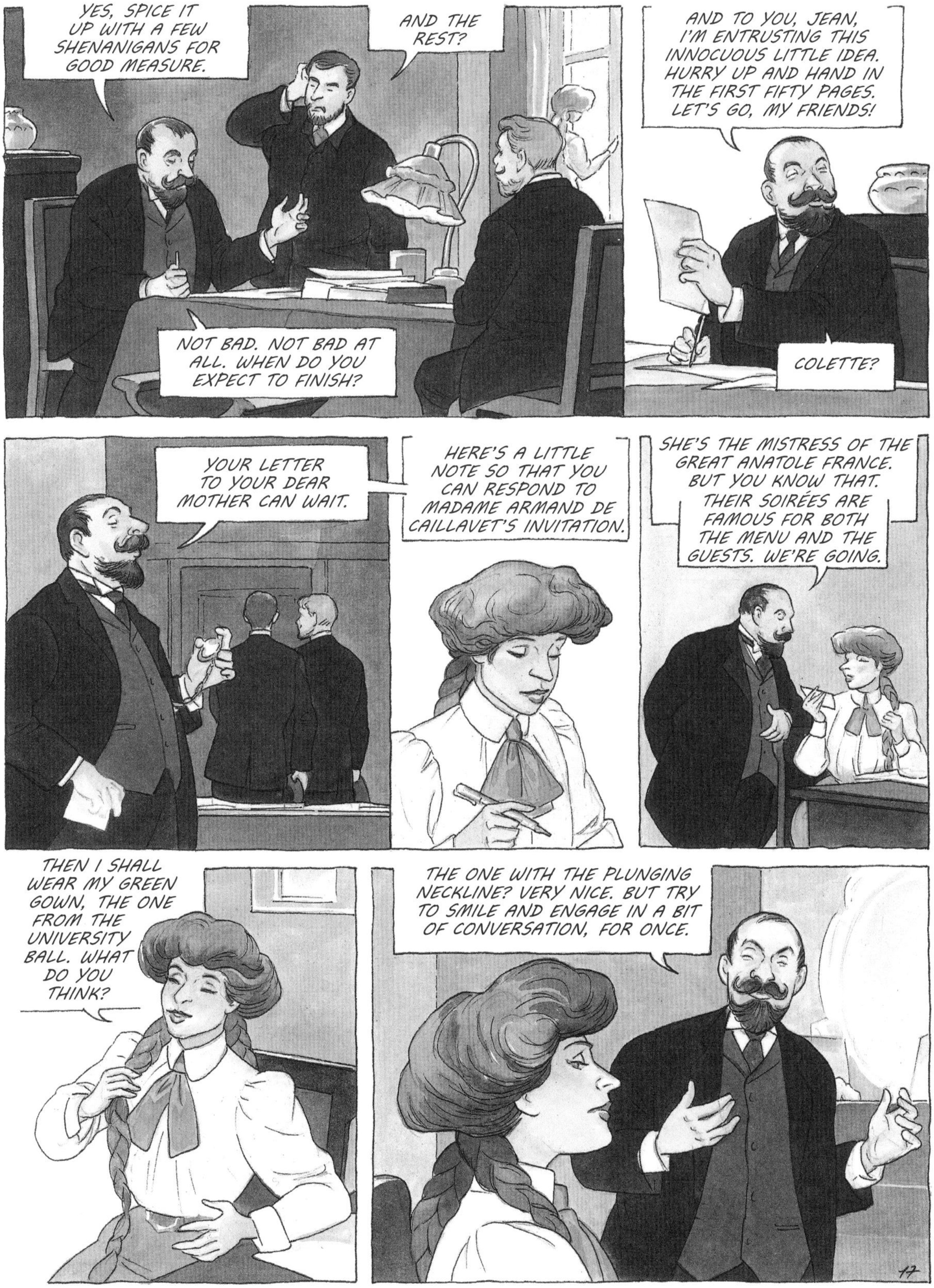
YES, SPICE IT UP WITH A FEW SHENANIGANS FOR GOOD MEASURE.
AND THE REST?
NOT BAD. NOT BAD AT ALL. WHEN DO YOU EXPECT TO FINISH?
AND TO YOU, JEAN, I'M ENTRUSTING THIS INNOCUOUS LITTLE IDEA. HURRY UP AND HAND IN THE FIRST FIFTY PAGES. LET'S GO, MY FRIENDS!
COLETTE?
YOUR LETTER TO YOUR DEAR MOTHER CAN WAIT.
HERE'S A LITTLE NOTE SO THAT YOU CAN RESPOND TO MADAME ARMAND DE CAILLAVET'S INVITATION.
SHE'S THE MISTRESS OF THE GREAT ANATOLE FRANCE. BUT YOU KNOW THAT. THEIR SOIRÉES ARE FAMOUS FOR BOTH THE MENU AND THE GUESTS. WE'RE GOING.
THEN I SHALL WEAR MY GREEN GOWN, THE ONE FROM THE UNIVERSITY BALL. WHAT DO YOU THINK?
THE ONE WITH THE PLUNGING NECKLINE? VERY NICE. BUT TRY TO SMILE AND ENGAGE IN A BIT OF CONVERSATION, FOR ONCE.
17

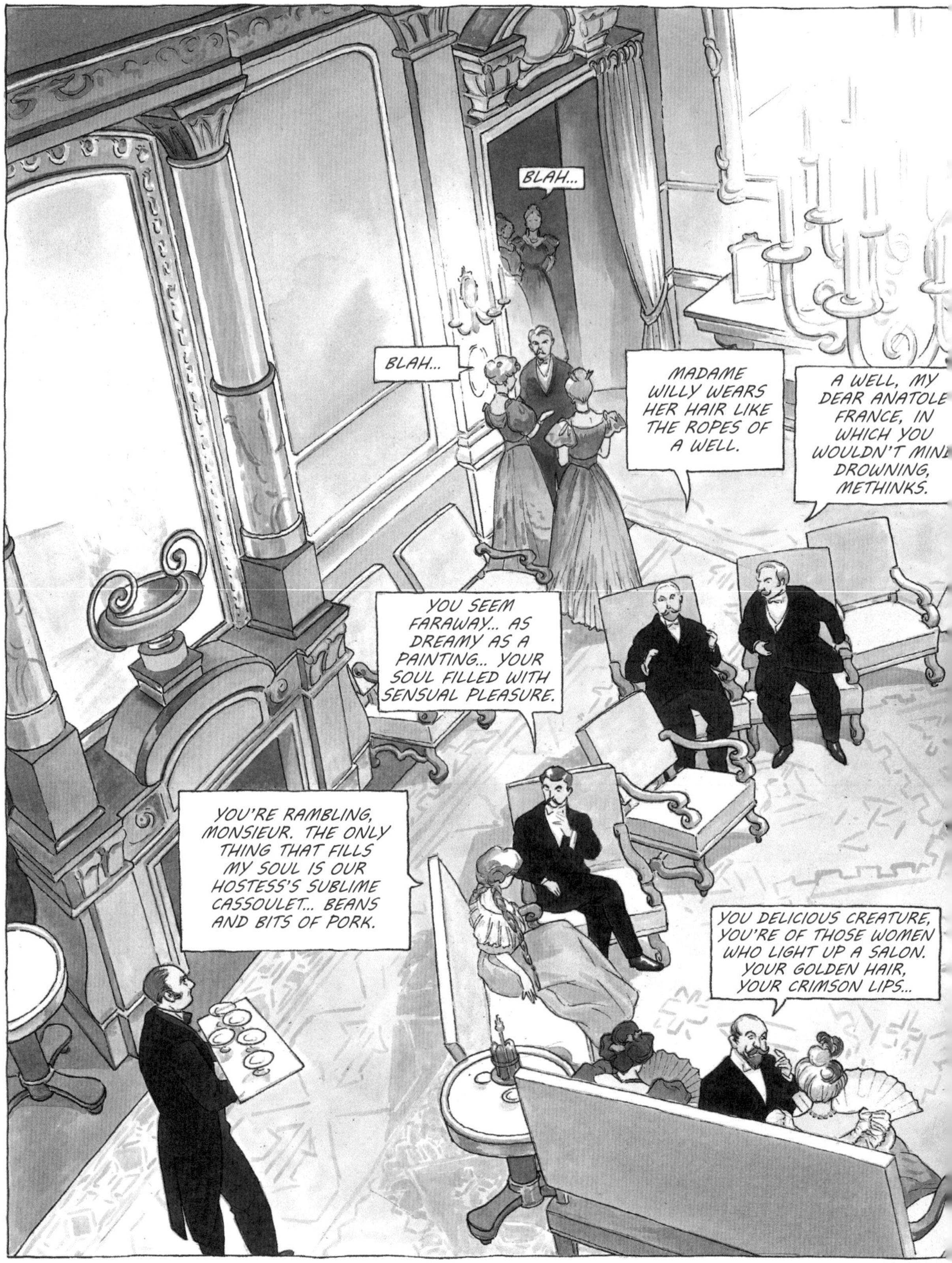
BLAH...
BLAH...
MADAME WILLY WEARS HER HAIR LIKE THE ROPES OF A WELL.
A WELL, MY DEAR ANATOLE FRANCE, IN WHICH YOU WOULDN'T MIN DROWNING, METHINKS.
YOU SEEM FARAWAY... AS DREAMY AS A PAINTING... YOUR SOUL FILLED WITH SENSUAL PLEASURE.
YOU'RE RAMBLING, MONSIEUR. THE ONLY THING THAT FILLS MY SOUL IS OUR HOSTESS'S SUBLIME CASSOULET... BEANS AND BITS OF PORK.
YOU DELICIOUS CREATURE, YOU'RE OF THOSE WOMEN WHO LIGHT UP A SALON. YOUR GOLDEN HAIR, YOUR CRIMSON LIPS...

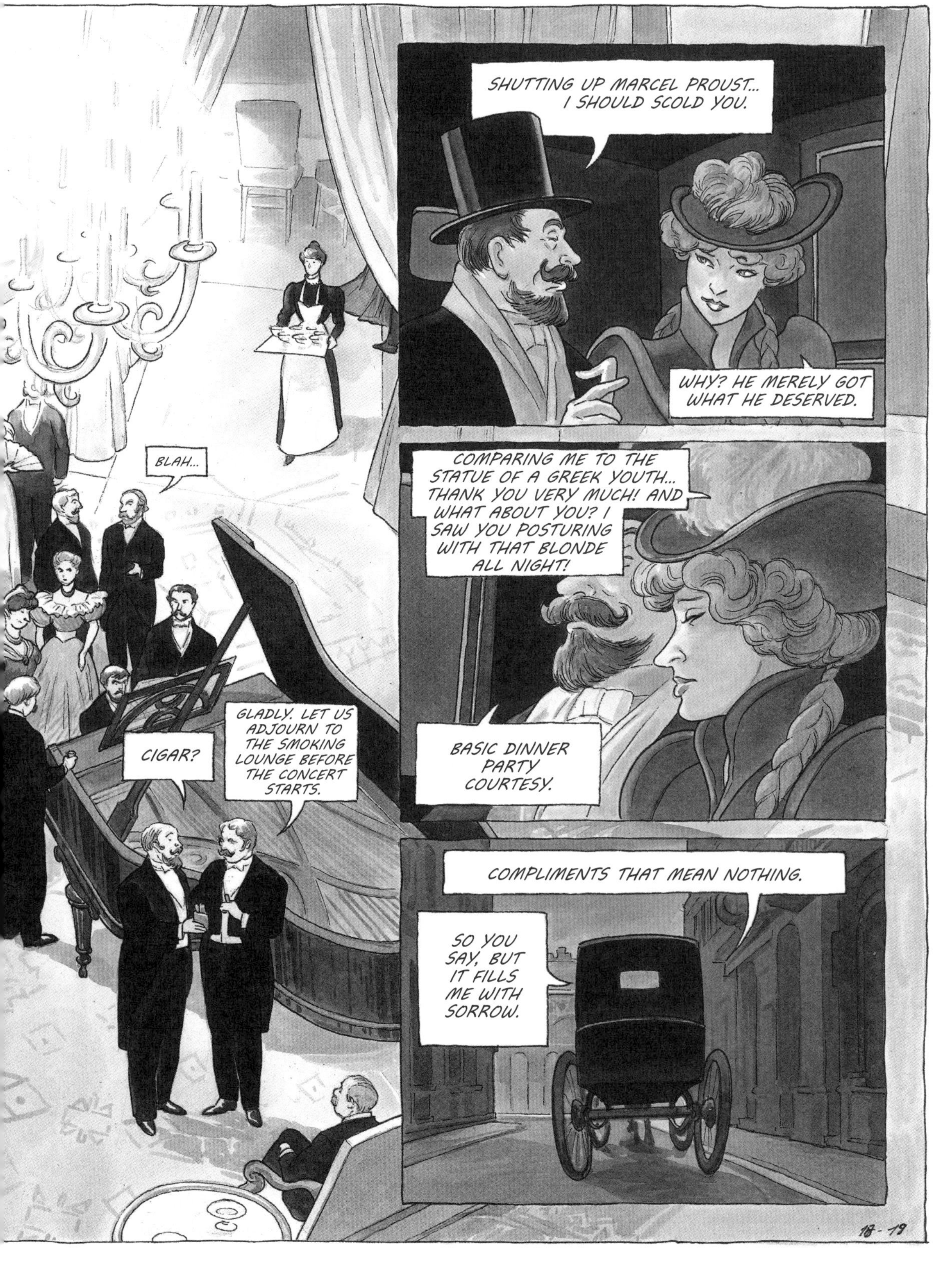
BLAH...
CIGAR?
GLADLY. LET US ADJOURN TO THE SMOKING LOUNGE BEFORE THE CONCERT STARTS.
SHUTTING UP MARCEL PROUST... I SHOULD SCOLD YOU.
WHY? HE MERELY GOT WHAT HE DESERVED.
COMPARING ME TO THE STATUE OF A GREEK YOUTH... THANK YOU VERY MUCH! AND WHAT ABOUT YOU? I SAW YOU POSTURING WITH THAT BLONDE ALL NIGHT!
BASIC DINNER PARTY COURTESY.
COMPLIMENTS THAT MEAN NOTHING.
SO YOU SAY, BUT IT FILLS ME WITH SORROW.
17-19

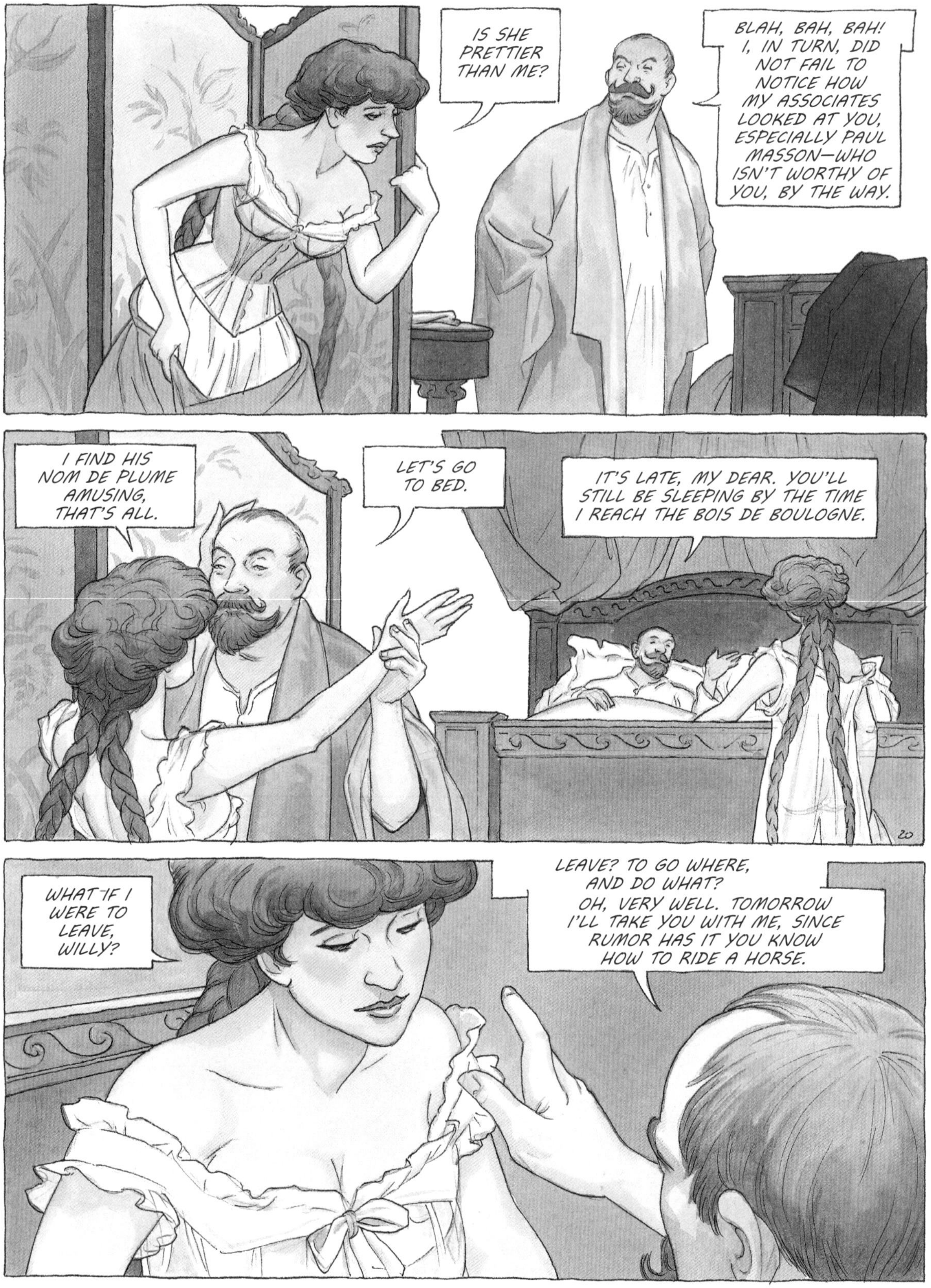
IS SHE PRETTIER THAN ME?
BLAH, BAH, BAH! I, IN TURN, DID NOT FAIL TO NOTICE HOW MY ASSOCIATES LOOKED AT YOU, ESPECIALLY PAUL MASSON—WHO ISN'T WORTHY OF YOU, BY THE WAY.
I FIND HIS NOM DE PLUME AMUSING, THAT'S ALL.
LET'S GO TO BED.
IT'S LATE, MY DEAR. YOU'LL STILL BE SLEEPING BY THE TIME I REACH THE BOIS DE BOULOGNE.
WHAT IF I WERE TO LEAVE, WILLY?
LEAVE? TO GO WHERE, AND DO WHAT?
OH, VERY WELL. TOMORROW I'LL TAKE YOU WITH ME, SINCE RUMOR HAS IT YOU KNOW HOW TO RIDE A HORSE.

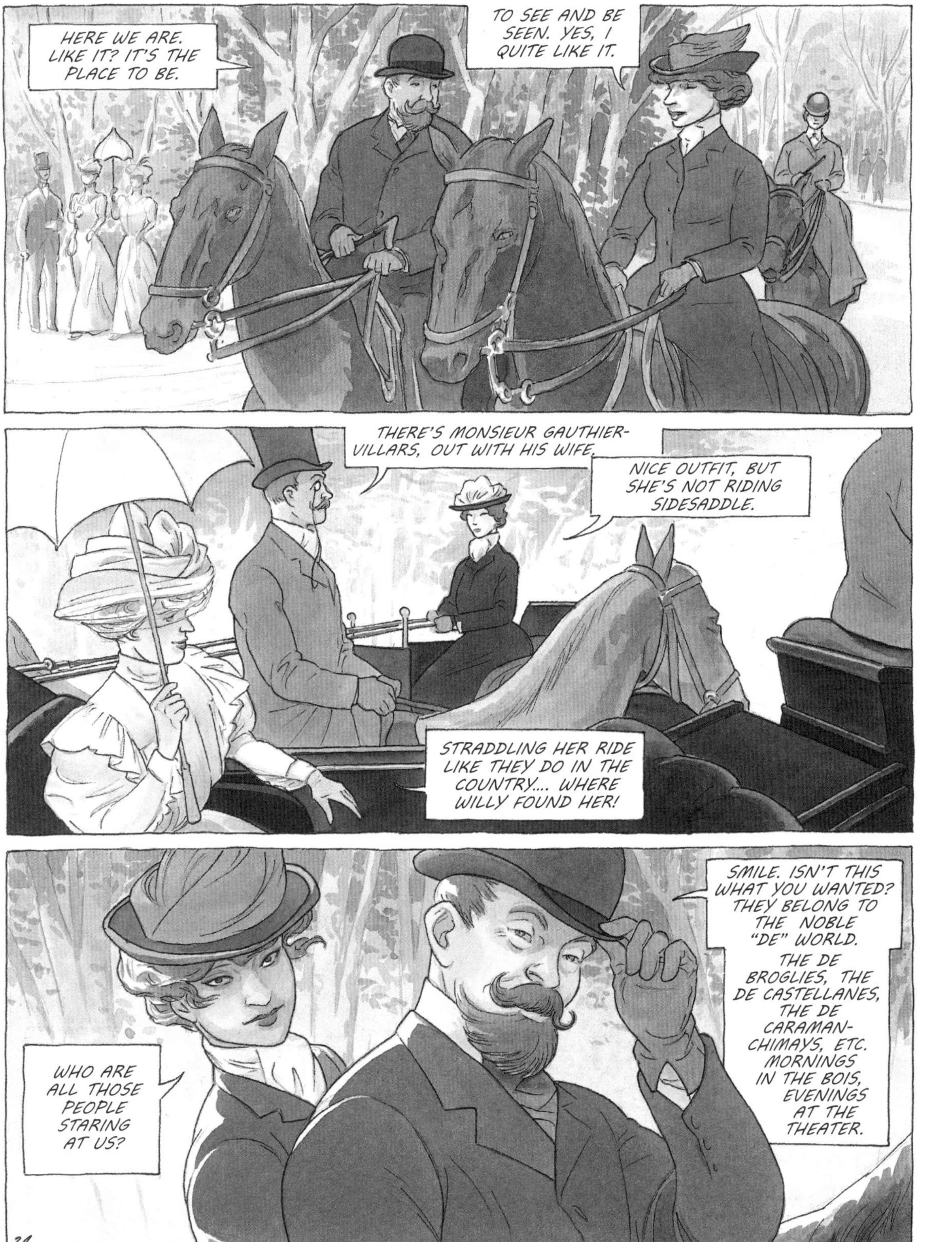
HERE WE ARE. LIKE IT? IT'S THE PLACE TO BE.
TO SEE AND BE SEEN. YES, I QUITE LIKE IT.
THERE'S MONSIEUR GAUTHIER-VILLARS, OUT WITH HIS WIFE.
NICE OUTFIT, BUT SHE'S NOT RIDING SIDESADDLE.
STRADDLING HER RIDE LIKE THEY DO IN THE COUNTRY.... WHERE WILLY FOUND HER!
SMILE. ISN'T THIS WHAT YOU WANTED? THEY BELONG TO THE NOBLE "DE" WORLD.
THE DE BROGLIES, THE DE CASTELLANES, THE DE CARAMAN-CHIMAYS, ETC. MORNINGS IN THE BOIS, EVENINGS AT THE THEATER.
WHO ARE ALL THOSE PEOPLE STARING AT US?
21

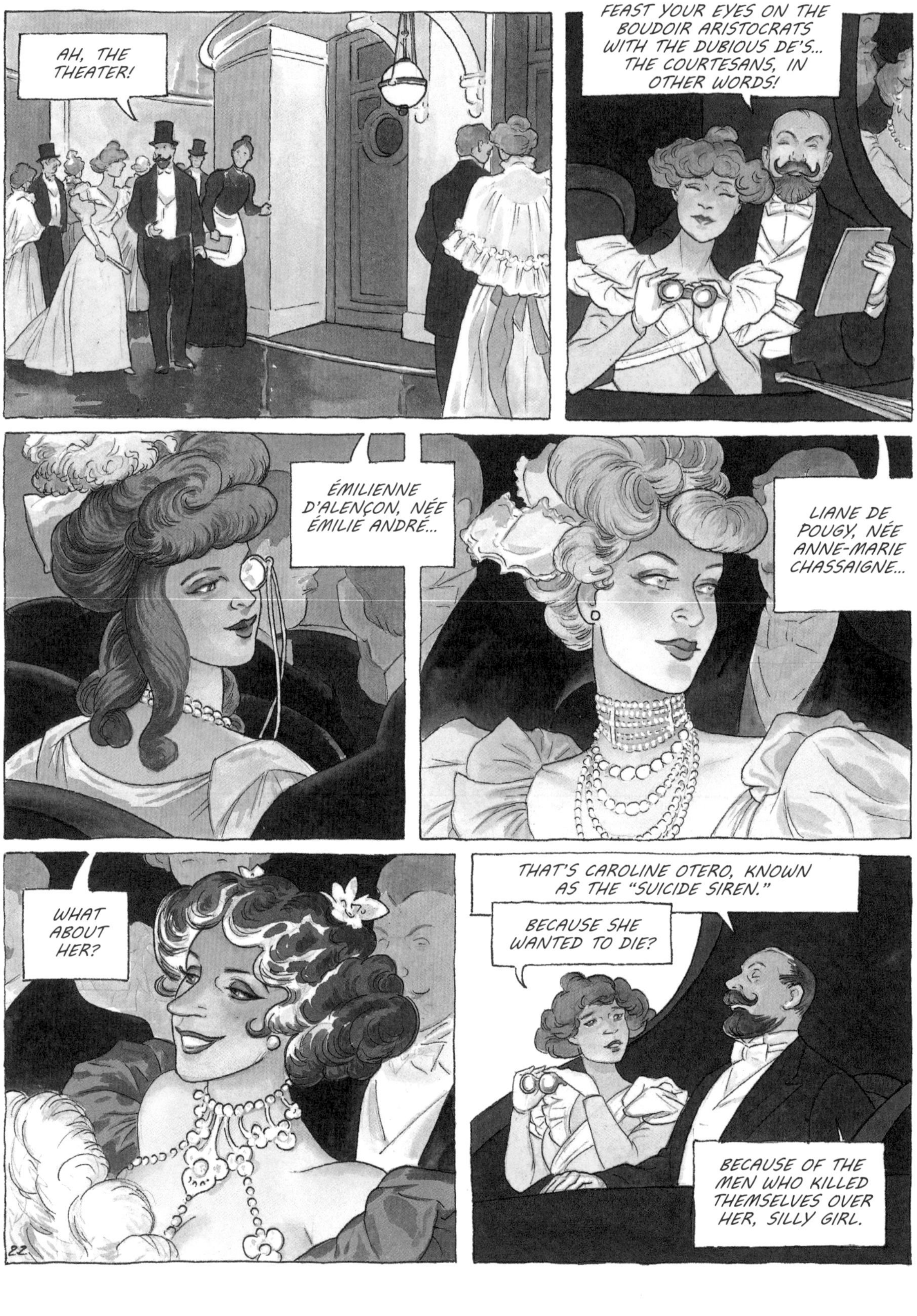
AH, THE THEATER!
FEAST YOUR EYES ON THE BOUDOIR ARISTOCRATS WITH THE DUBIOUS DE'S... THE COURTESANS, IN OTHER WORDS!
ÉMILIENNE D'ALENÇON, NÉE ÉMILIE ANDRÉ...
LIANE DE POUGY, NÉE ANNE-MARIE CHASSAIGNE...
WHAT ABOUT HER?
THAT'S CAROLINE OTERO, KNOWN AS THE "SUICIDE SIREN."
BECAUSE SHE WANTED TO DIE?
BECAUSE OF THE MEN WHO KILLED THEMSELVES OVER HER, SILLY GIRL.
22.

"Dear Mother,
The days go by so terribly fast...
Theater, morning outings, and concerts late at night. Next week, a dinner where shoulders must be bare. I do hate to display them in front of everyone."

HMM. SHE'S PLEASANT... A TRUE STORYTELLER.

WITH WICKED WIT, TOO! WILLY'S RUBBED OFF ON HER. HE TAMED HER IN NO TIME AT ALL.

DID HE SLIP OUT ALREADY?

HE'S GIVEN HER FREE REIN TONIGHT, AS HE HAS BUSINESS ELSEWHERE. MADAME GAUTHIER-VILLARS MAY BE HIS ONLY WIFE, BUT SHE ISN'T HIS LAST CONQUEST.

I CAN CONFIRM THAT HE STILL VISITS BROTHELS, AND NOT JUST--

AND SHE LETS HIM?

PERHAPS SHE DOESN'T KNOW?

OR MAYBE JUST NOT YET?

23

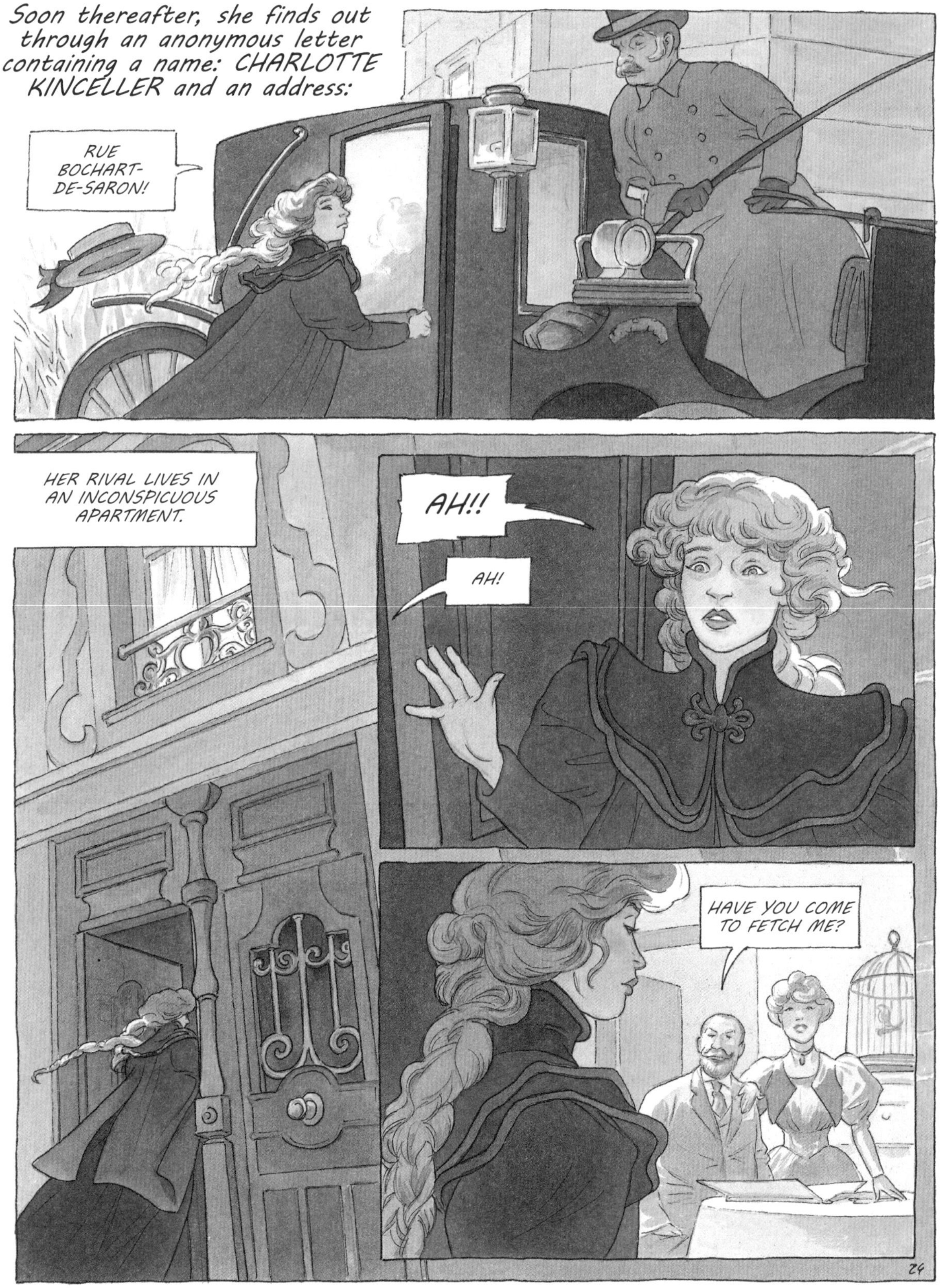
Soon thereafter, she finds out through an anonymous letter containing a name: CHARLOTTE KINCELLER and an address:
RUE BOCHART-DE-SARON!
HER RIVAL LIVES IN AN INCONSPICUOUS APARTMENT.
AH!!
AH!
HAVE YOU COME TO FETCH ME?

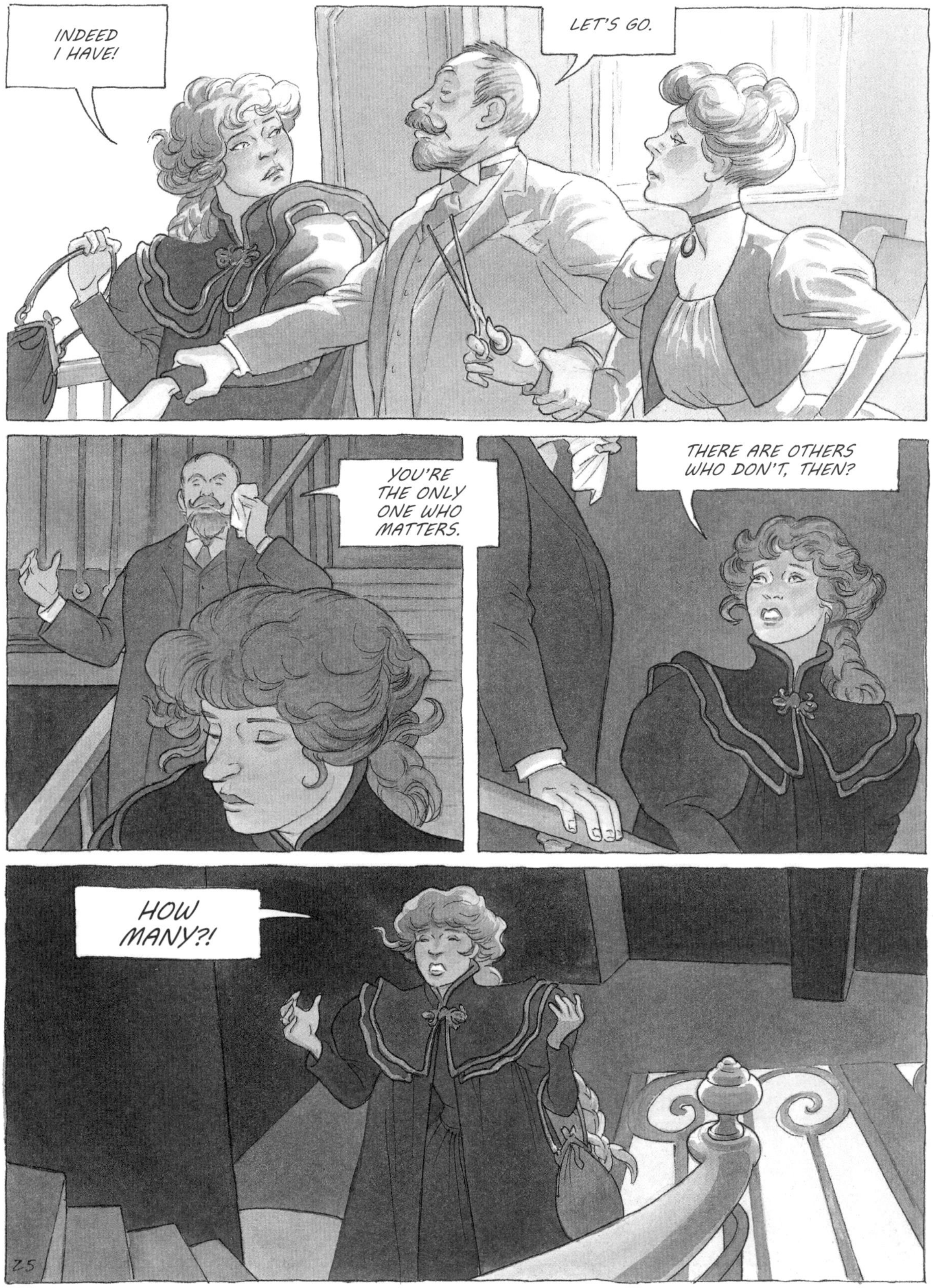
INDEED I HAVE!
LET'S GO.
YOU'RE THE ONLY ONE WHO MATTERS.
THERE ARE OTHERS WHO DON'T, THEN?
HOW MANY?!

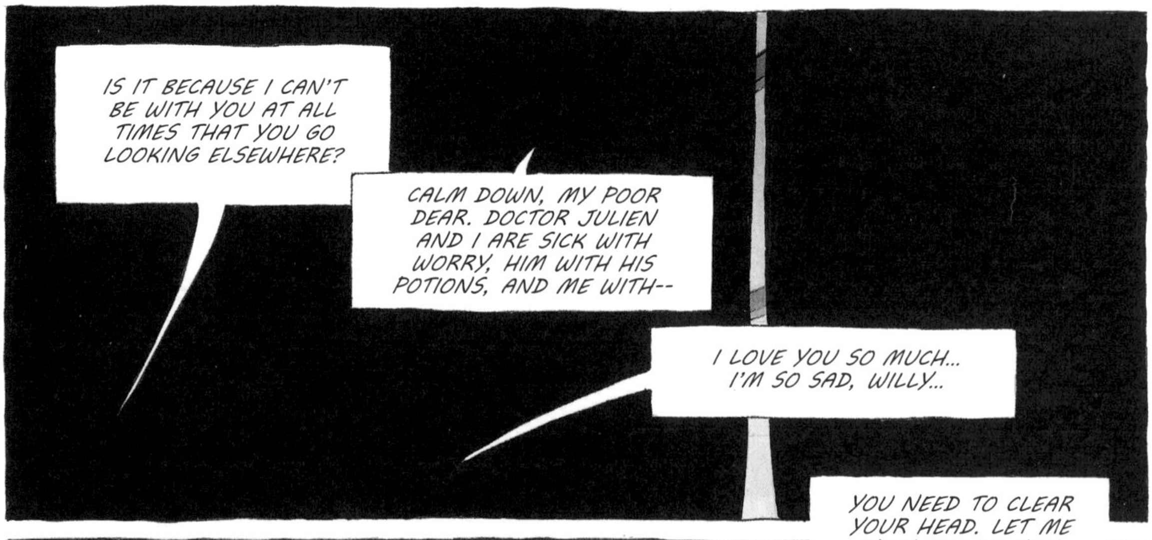
IS IT BECAUSE I CAN'T BE WITH YOU AT ALL TIMES THAT YOU GO LOOKING ELSEWHERE?
CALM DOWN, MY POOR DEAR. DOCTOR JULIEN AND I ARE SICK WITH WORRY, HIM WITH HIS POTIONS, AND ME WITH--
I LOVE YOU SO MUCH... I'M SO SAD, WILLY...

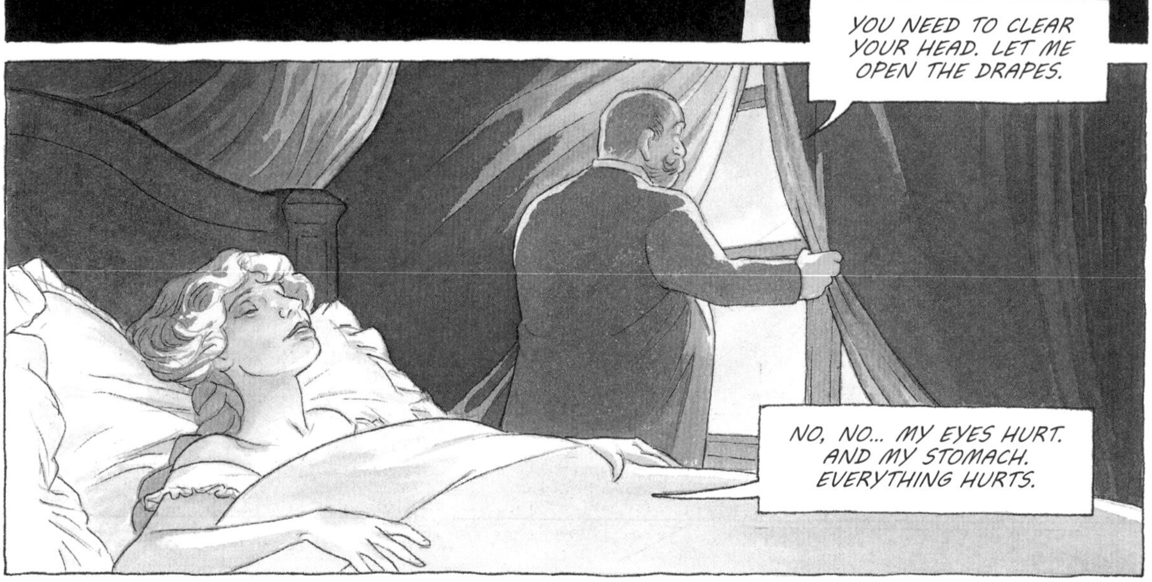
YOU NEED TO CLEAR YOUR HEAD. LET ME OPEN THE DRAPES.
NO, NO... MY EYES HURT. AND MY STOMACH. EVERYTHING HURTS.

Those, more than her depression, are the symptoms that worry Dr. JULIEN, as he also treats prostitutes with syphilis... "Get better, won't you! Help me! Don't let me labor alone to cure you!"

Believing she's doomed, he writes to her mother.

SIDO arrives at once.

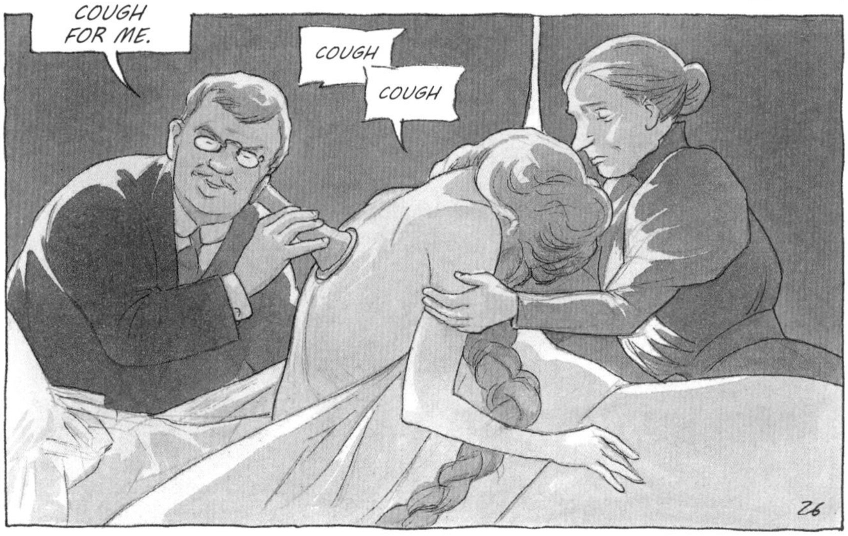
COUGH FOR ME.
COUGH
COUGH
26

"There comes a time in the life of all young people when dying seems just as normal and seductive to them as living does, and I hesitated.
Besides, how could I complain about an illness that returned SIDO to me?"

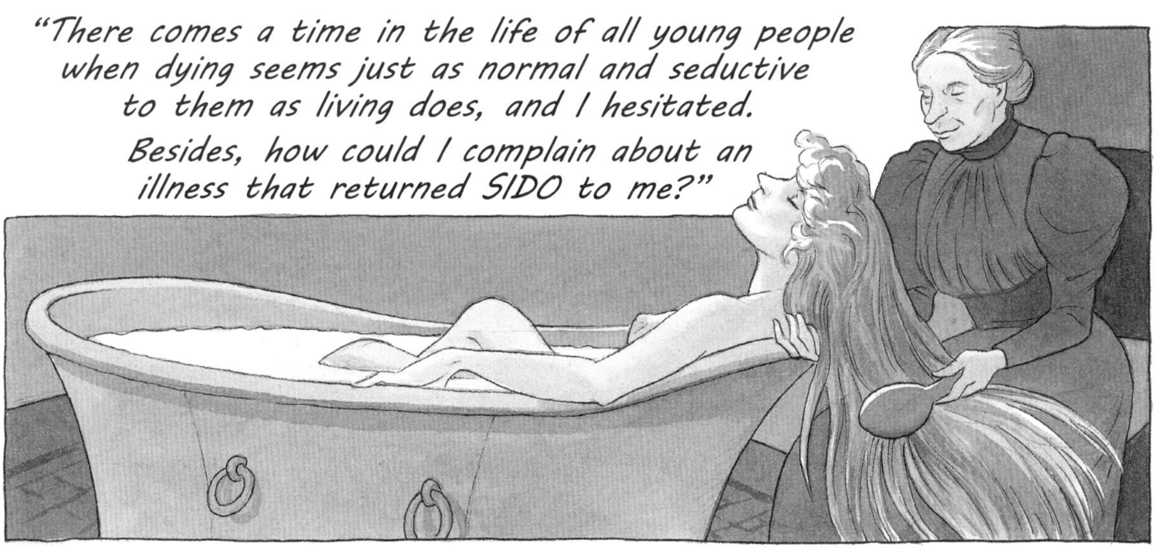

His wife may be thrilled, but WILLY grows impatient with his mother-in-law's extended stay and longs to see her go home. And so, as soon as COLETTE is feeling better and is up and walking again, he takes her to a seaside vacation in BRITTANY.

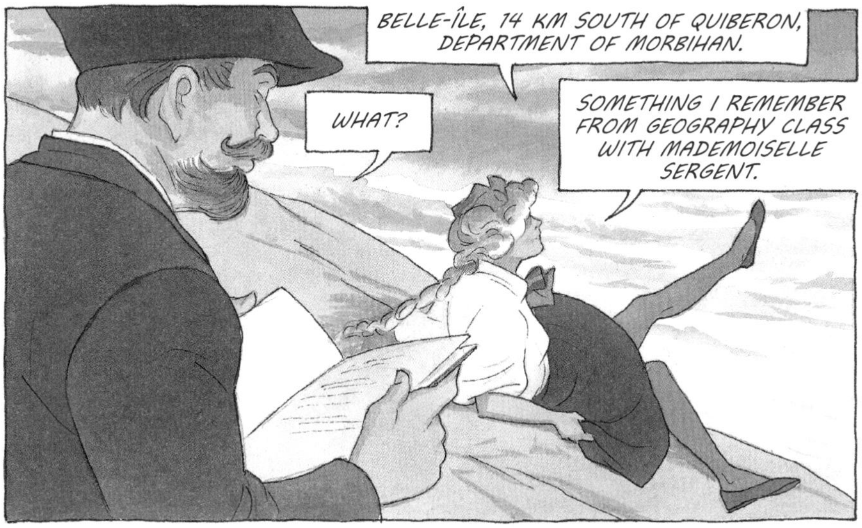
BELLE-ÎLE, 14 KM SOUTH OF QUIBERON, DEPARTMENT OF MORBIHAN.
WHAT?
SOMETHING I REMEMBER FROM GEOGRAPHY CLASS WITH MADEMOISELLE SERGENT.

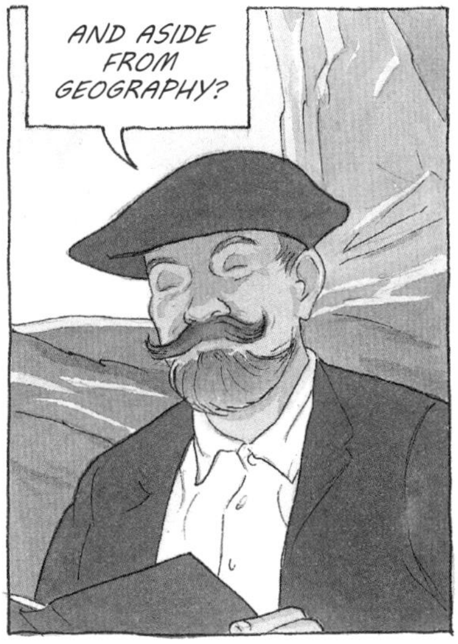
AND ASIDE FROM GEOGRAPHY?

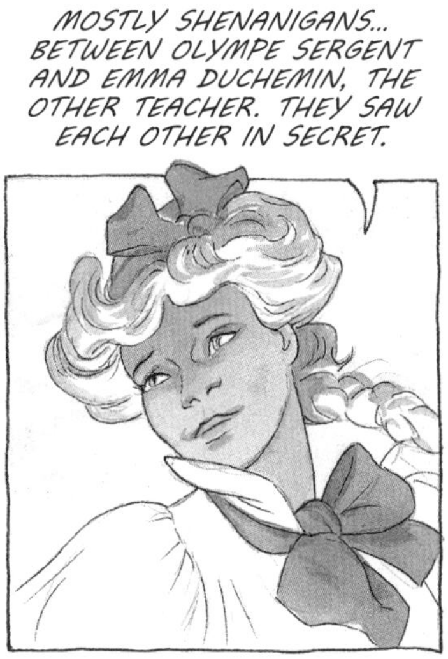
MOSTLY SHENANIGANS... BETWEEN OLYMPE SERGENT AND EMMA DUCHEMIN, THE OTHER TEACHER. THEY SAW EACH OTHER IN SECRET.

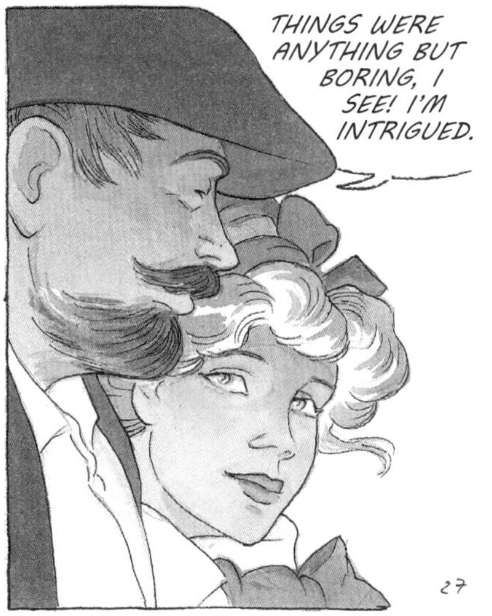
THINGS WERE ANYTHING BUT BORING, I SEE! I'M INTRIGUED.
27

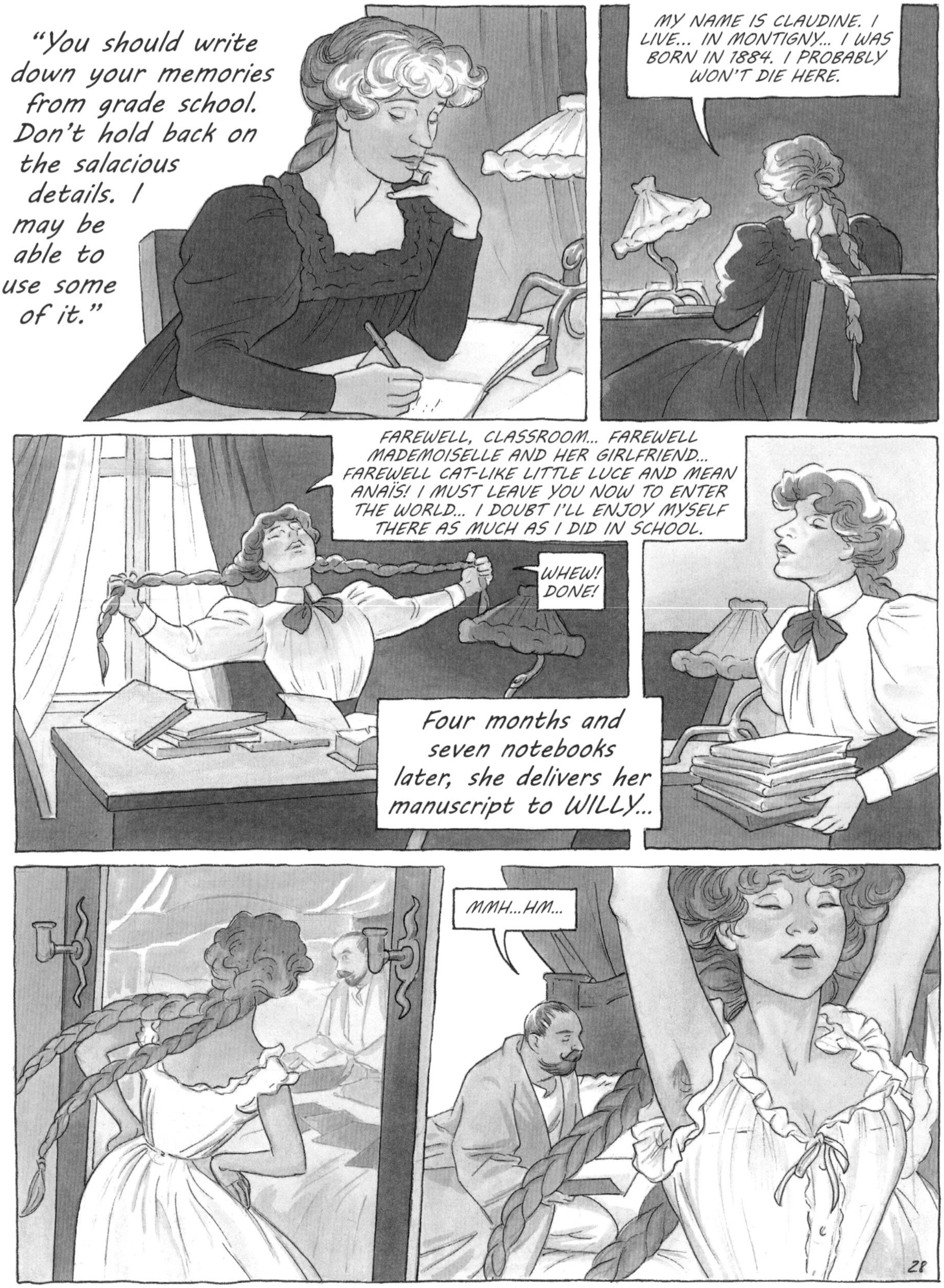
"You should write down your memories from grade school. Don't hold back on the salacious details. I may be able to use some of it."
MY NAME IS CLAUDINE. I LIVE... IN MONTIGNY... I WAS BORN IN 1884. I PROBABLY WON'T DIE HERE.
FAREWELL, CLASSROOM... FAREWELL MADEMOISELLE AND HER GIRLFRIEND... FAREWELL CAT-LIKE LITTLE LUCE AND MEAN ANAÏS! I MUST LEAVE YOU NOW TO ENTER THE WORLD... I DOUBT I'LL ENJOY MYSELF THERE AS MUCH AS I DID IN SCHOOL.
WHEW! DONE!
Four months and seven notebooks later, she delivers her manuscript to WILLY...
MMH...HM...
28

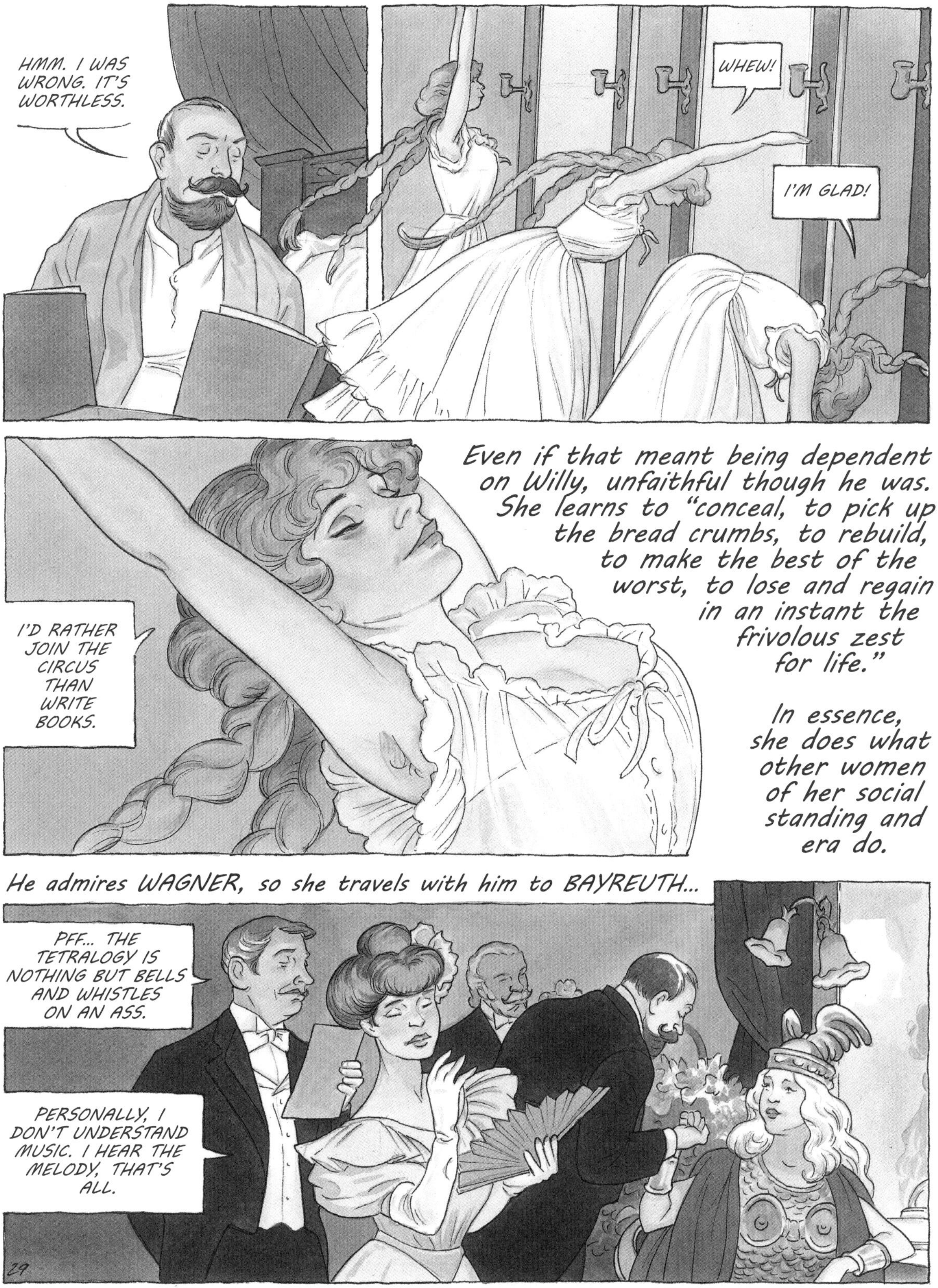
HMM. I WAS WRONG. IT'S WORTHLESS.
WHEW!
I'M GLAD!
Even if that meant being dependent on Willy, unfaithful though he was. She learns to "conceal, to pick up the bread crumbs, to rebuild, to make the best of the worst, to lose and regain in an instant the frivolous zest for life."
I'D RATHER JOIN THE CIRCUS THAN WRITE BOOKS.
In essence, she does what other women of her social standing and era do.
He admires WAGNER, so she travels with him to BAYREUTH...
PFF... THE TETRALOGY IS NOTHING BUT BELLS AND WHISTLES ON AN ASS.
PERSONALLY, I DON'T UNDERSTAND MUSIC. I HEAR THE MELODY, THAT'S ALL.
29

WILLY fights tooth and nail to defend the musicians he likes, jeering those he doesn't, including ERIK SATIE, his bête noire.

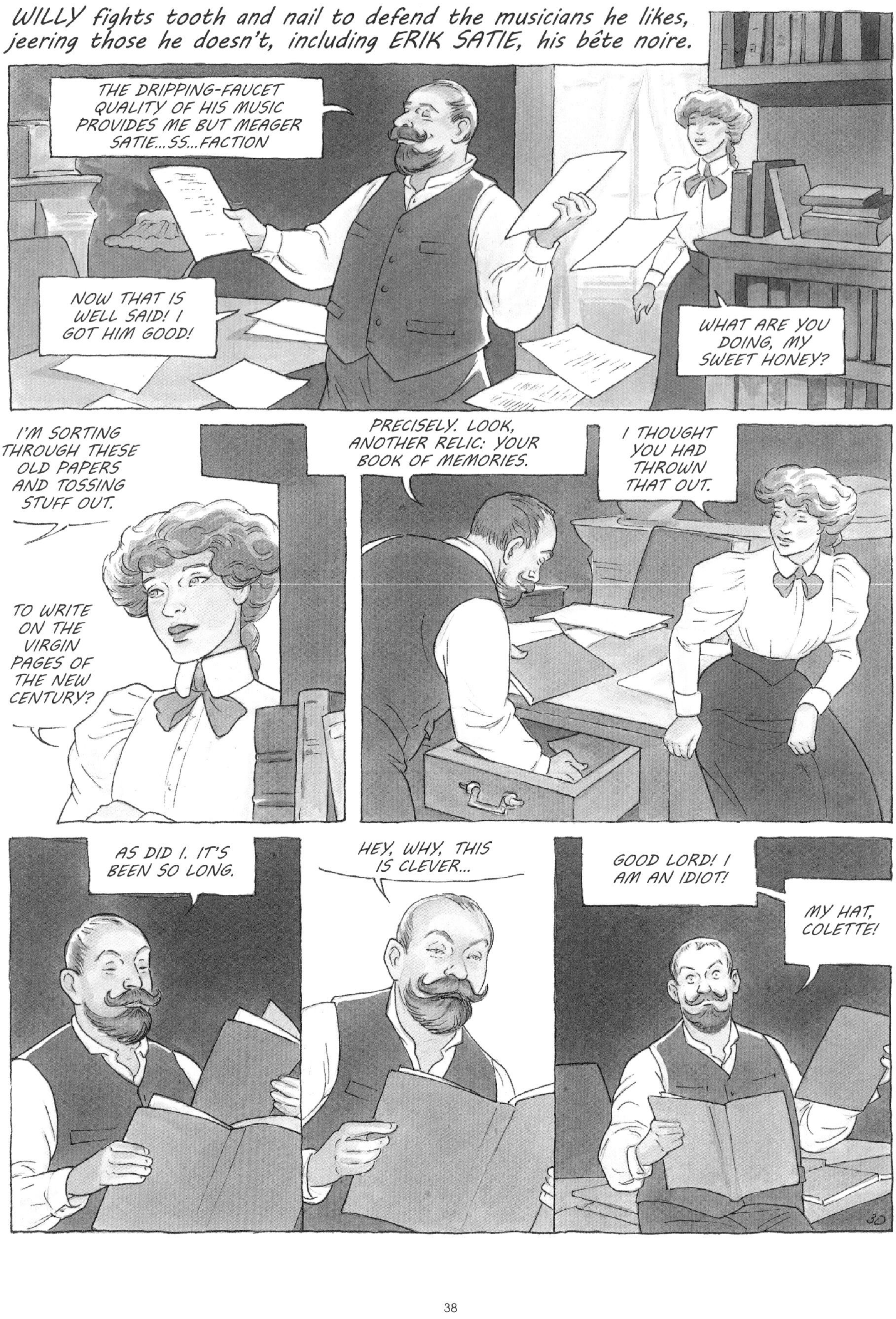
THE DRIPPING-FAUCET QUALITY OF HIS MUSIC PROVIDES ME BUT MEAGER SATIE...SS...FACTION
NOW THAT IS WELL SAID! I GOT HIM GOOD!
WHAT ARE YOU DOING, MY SWEET HONEY?
I'M SORTING THROUGH THESE OLD PAPERS AND TOSSING STUFF OUT.
TO WRITE ON THE VIRGIN PAGES OF THE NEW CENTURY?
PRECISELY. LOOK, ANOTHER RELIC: YOUR BOOK OF MEMORIES.
I THOUGHT YOU HAD THROWN THAT OUT.
AS DID I. IT'S BEEN SO LONG.
HEY, WHY, THIS IS CLEVER...
GOOD LORD! I AM AN IDIOT!
MY HAT, COLETTE!
30

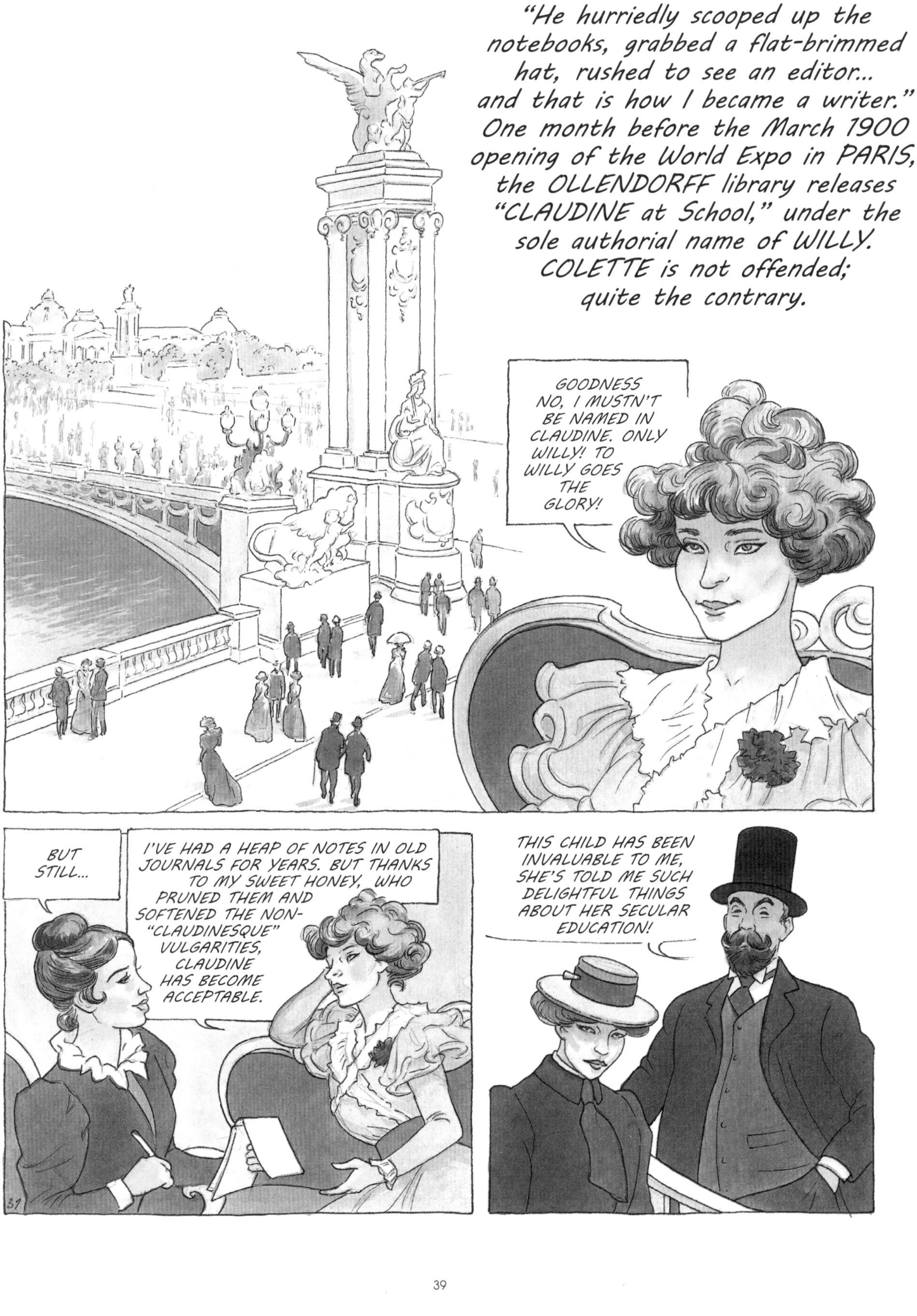
"He hurriedly scooped up the notebooks, grabbed a flat-brimmed hat, rushed to see an editor... and that is how I became a writer." One month before the March 1900 opening of the World Expo in PARIS, the OLLENDORFF library releases "CLAUDINE at School," under the sole authorial name of WILLY. COLETTE is not offended; quite the contrary.
GOODNESS NO, I MUSTN'T BE NAMED IN CLAUDINE. ONLY WILLY! TO WILLY GOES THE GLORY!
BUT STILL...
I'VE HAD A HEAP OF NOTES IN OLD JOURNALS FOR YEARS. BUT THANKS TO MY SWEET HONEY, WHO PRUNED THEM AND SOFTENED THE NON-"CLAUDINESQUE" VULGARITIES, CLAUDINE HAS BECOME ACCEPTABLE.
THIS CHILD HAS BEEN INVALUABLE TO ME, SHE'S TOLD ME SUCH DELIGHTFUL THINGS ABOUT HER SECULAR EDUCATION!

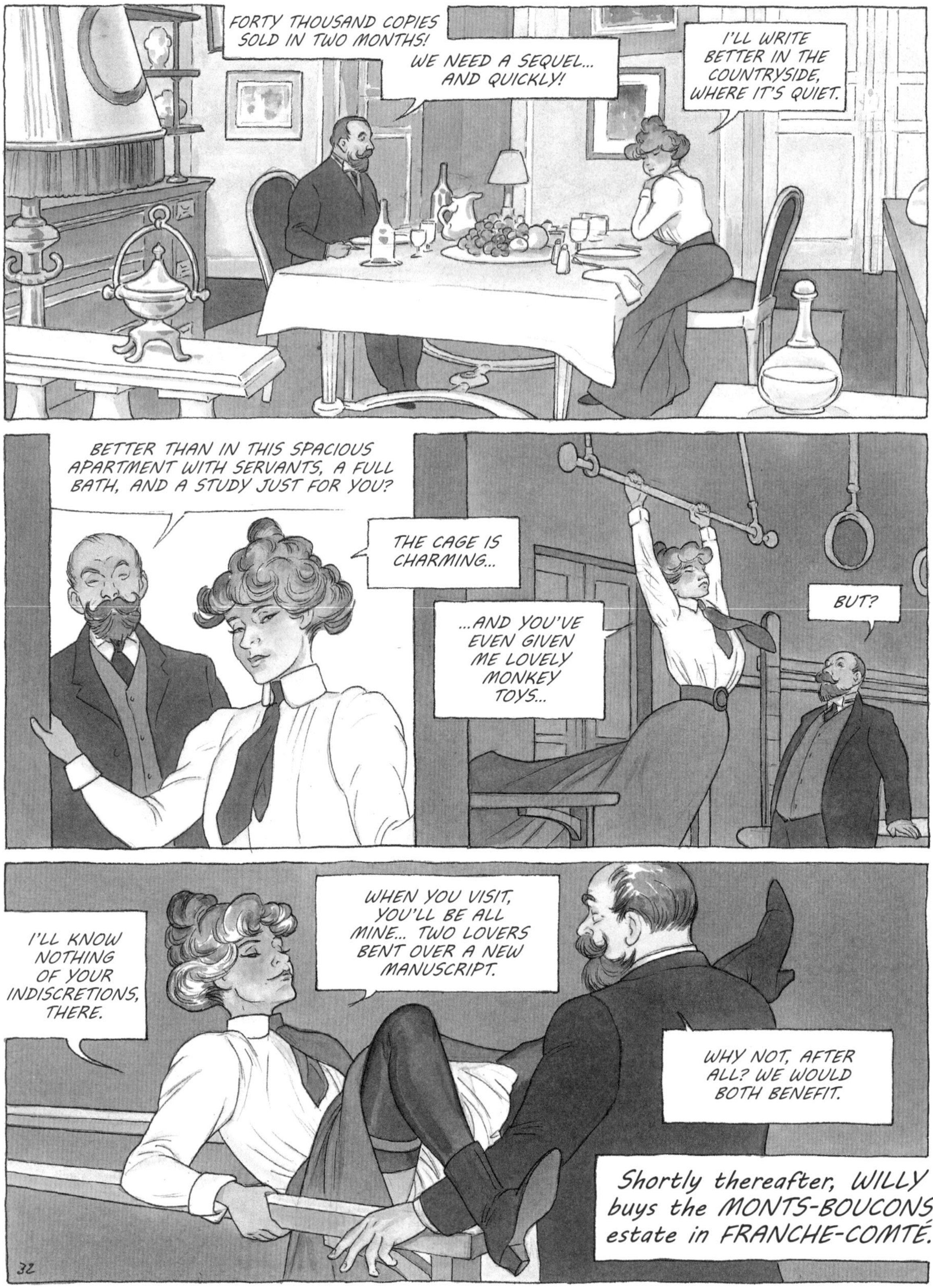
FORTY THOUSAND COPIES SOLD IN TWO MONTHS!
WE NEED A SEQUEL... AND QUICKLY!
I'LL WRITE BETTER IN THE COUNTRYSIDE, WHERE IT'S QUIET.
BETTER THAN IN THIS SPACIOUS APARTMENT WITH SERVANTS, A FULL BATH, AND A STUDY JUST FOR YOU?
THE CAGE IS CHARMING...
...AND YOU'VE EVEN GIVEN ME LOVELY MONKEY TOYS...
BUT?
I'LL KNOW NOTHING OF YOUR INDISCRETIONS, THERE.
WHEN YOU VISIT, YOU'LL BE ALL MINE... TWO LOVERS BENT OVER A NEW MANUSCRIPT.
WHY NOT, AFTER ALL? WE WOULD BOTH BENEFIT.
Shortly thereafter, WILLY buys the MONTS-BOUCONS estate in FRANCHE-COMTÉ.
32

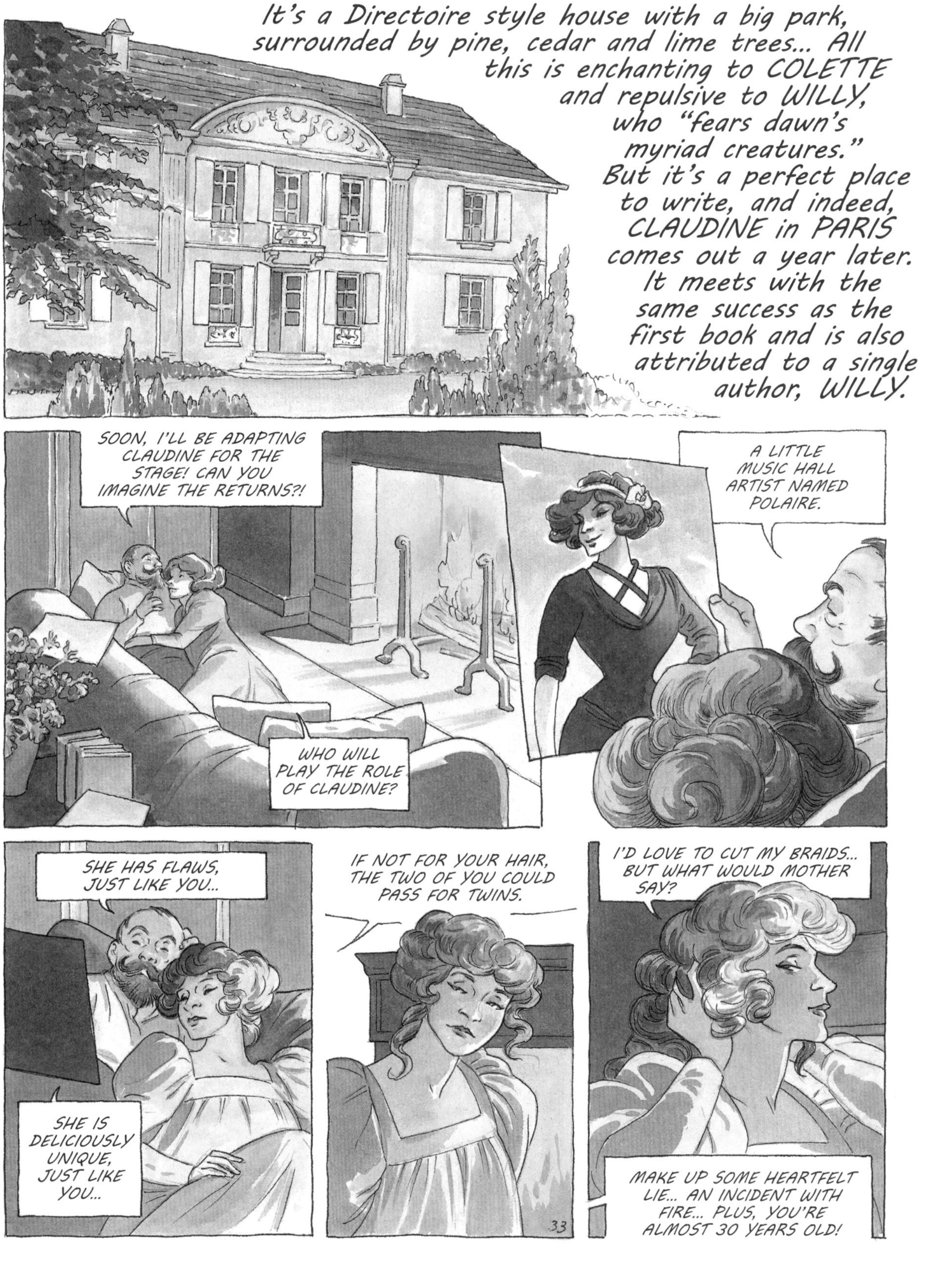
It's a Directoire style house with a big park, surrounded by pine, cedar and lime trees... All this is enchanting to COLETTE and repulsive to WILLY, who "fears dawn's myriad creatures." But it's a perfect place to write, and indeed, CLAUDINE in PARIS comes out a year later. It meets with the same success as the first book and is also attributed to a single author, WILLY.
SOON, I'LL BE ADAPTING CLAUDINE FOR THE STAGE! CAN YOU IMAGINE THE RETURNS?!
WHO WILL PLAY THE ROLE OF CLAUDINE?
A LITTLE MUSIC HALL ARTIST NAMED POLAIRE.
SHE HAS FLAWS, JUST LIKE YOU...
SHE IS DELICIOUSLY UNIQUE, JUST LIKE YOU...
IF NOT FOR YOUR HAIR, THE TWO OF YOU COULD PASS FOR TWINS.
I'D LOVE TO CUT MY BRAIDS... BUT WHAT WOULD MOTHER SAY?
MAKE UP SOME HEARTFELT LIE... AN INCIDENT WITH FIRE... PLUS, YOU'RE ALMOST 30 YEARS OLD!

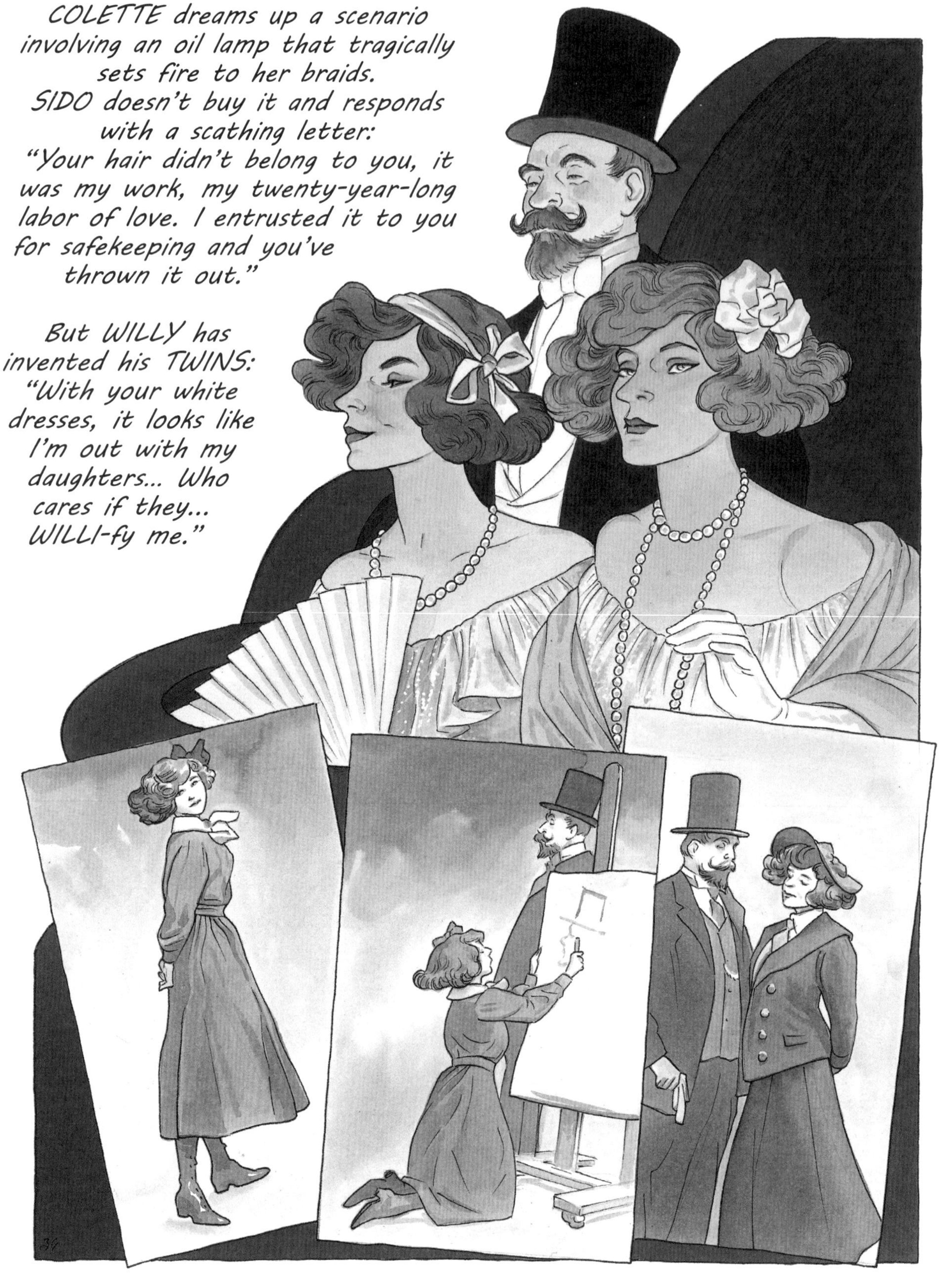
COLETTE dreams up a scenario involving an oil lamp that tragically sets fire to her braids.
SIDO doesn't buy it and responds with a scathing letter:
"Your hair didn't belong to you, it was my work, my twenty-year-long labor of love. I entrusted it to you for safekeeping and you've thrown it out."
But WILLY has invented his TWINS:
"With your white dresses, it looks like I'm out with my daughters... Who cares if they... WILLI-fy me."

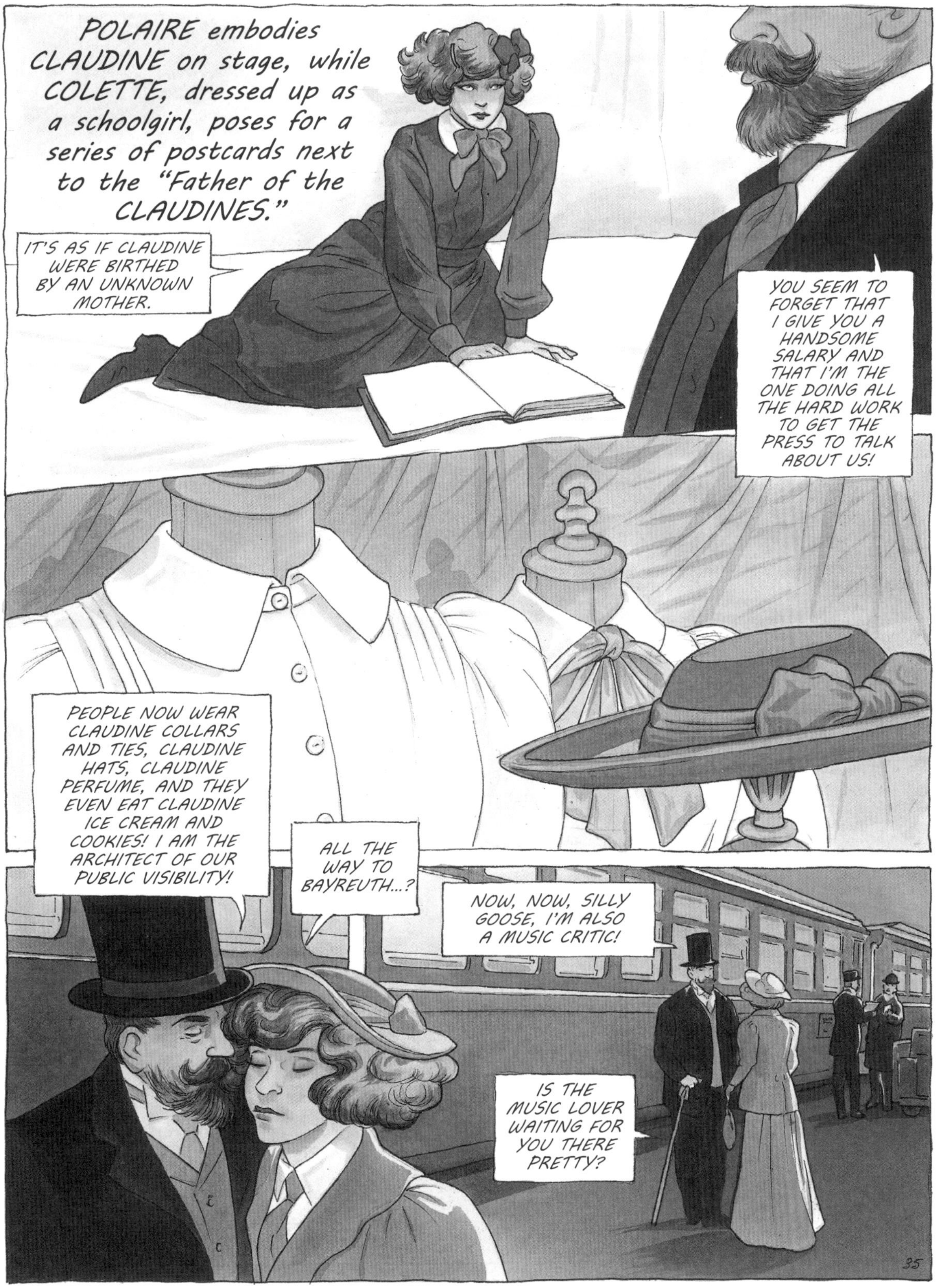
POLAIRE embodies CLAUDINE on stage, while COLETTE, dressed up as a schoolgirl, poses for a series of postcards next to the "Father of the CLAUDINES."
IT'S AS IF CLAUDINE WERE BIRTHED BY AN UNKNOWN MOTHER.
YOU SEEM TO FORGET THAT I GIVE YOU A HANDSOME SALARY AND THAT I'M THE ONE DOING ALL THE HARD WORK TO GET THE PRESS TO TALK ABOUT US!
PEOPLE NOW WEAR CLAUDINE COLLARS AND TIES, CLAUDINE HATS, CLAUDINE PERFUME, AND THEY EVEN EAT CLAUDINE ICE CREAM AND COOKIES! I AM THE ARCHITECT OF OUR PUBLIC VISIBILITY!
ALL THE WAY TO BAYREUTH...?
NOW, NOW, SILLY GOOSE, I'M ALSO A MUSIC CRITIC!
IS THE MUSIC LOVER WAITING FOR YOU THERE PRETTY?
35

"There is surely something in our relationship that's not working." Thus begins the third CLAUDINE book. WILLY no longer conceals his many conquests, while she has none. One could assume she was satisfied with the company of her friends, the cuddles from TOBY-DOG and KIKI-SWEETIE, the Angora cat, with writing in the beautiful MONTS-BOUCONS, and that "WILLY remained, as he had before, the best and the most handsome." And yet...

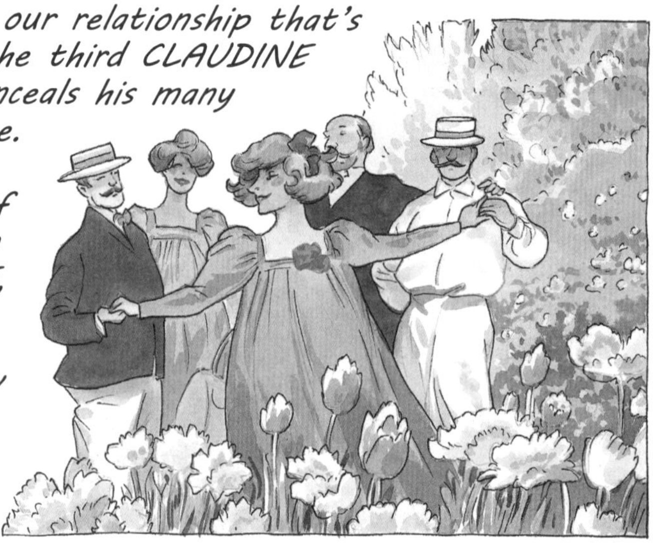

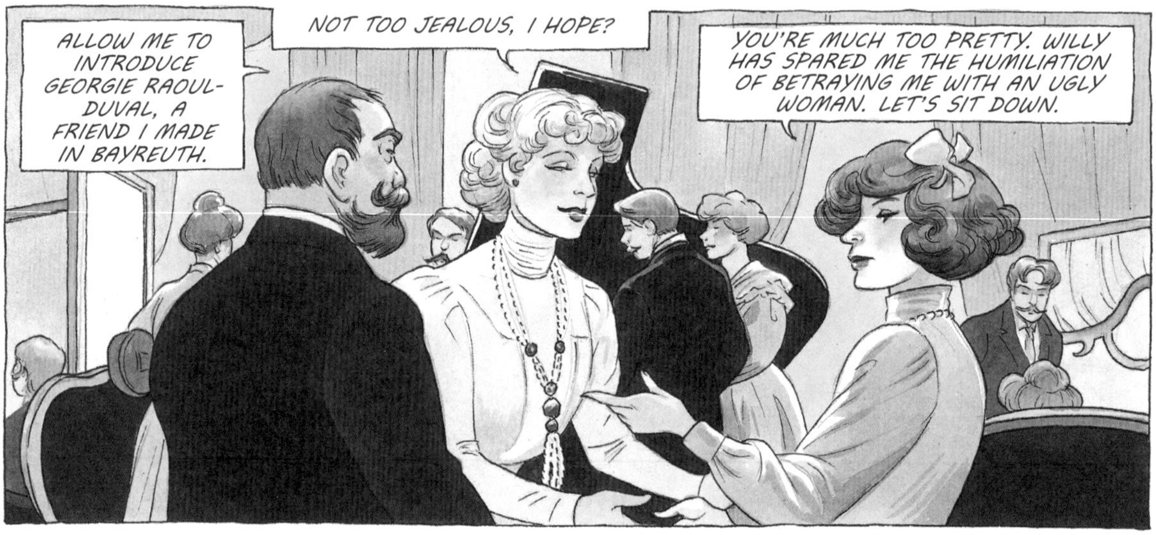

ALLOW ME TO INTRODUCE GEORGIE RAOUL-DUVAL, A FRIEND I MADE IN BAYREUTH.
NOT TOO JEALOUS, I HOPE?
YOU'RE MUCH TOO PRETTY. WILLY HAS SPARED ME THE HUMILIATION OF BETRAYING ME WITH AN UGLY WOMAN. LET'S SIT DOWN.

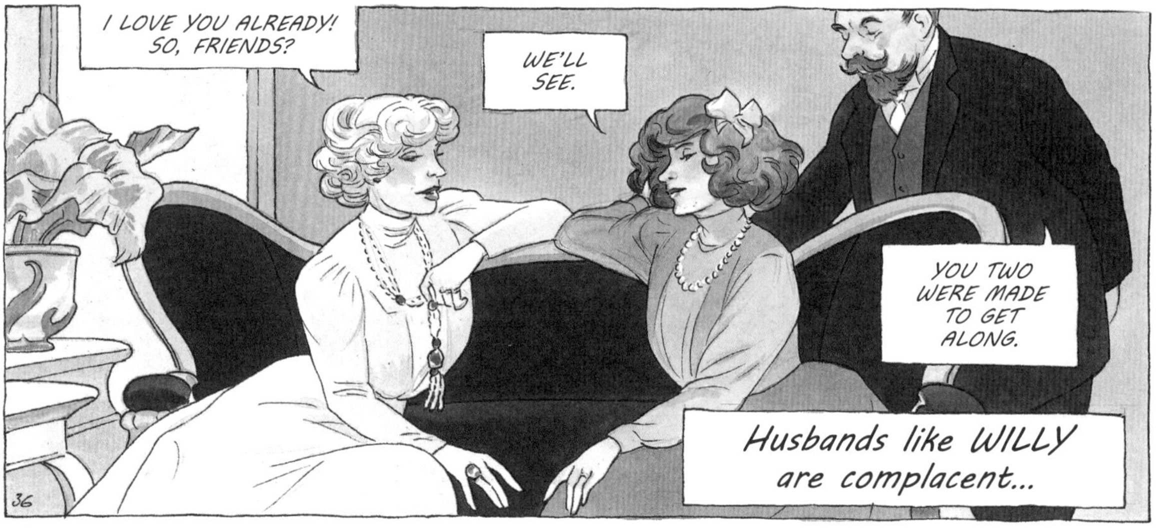

I LOVE YOU ALREADY! SO, FRIENDS?
WE'LL SEE.
YOU TWO WERE MADE TO GET ALONG.
Husbands like WILLY are complacent...
36

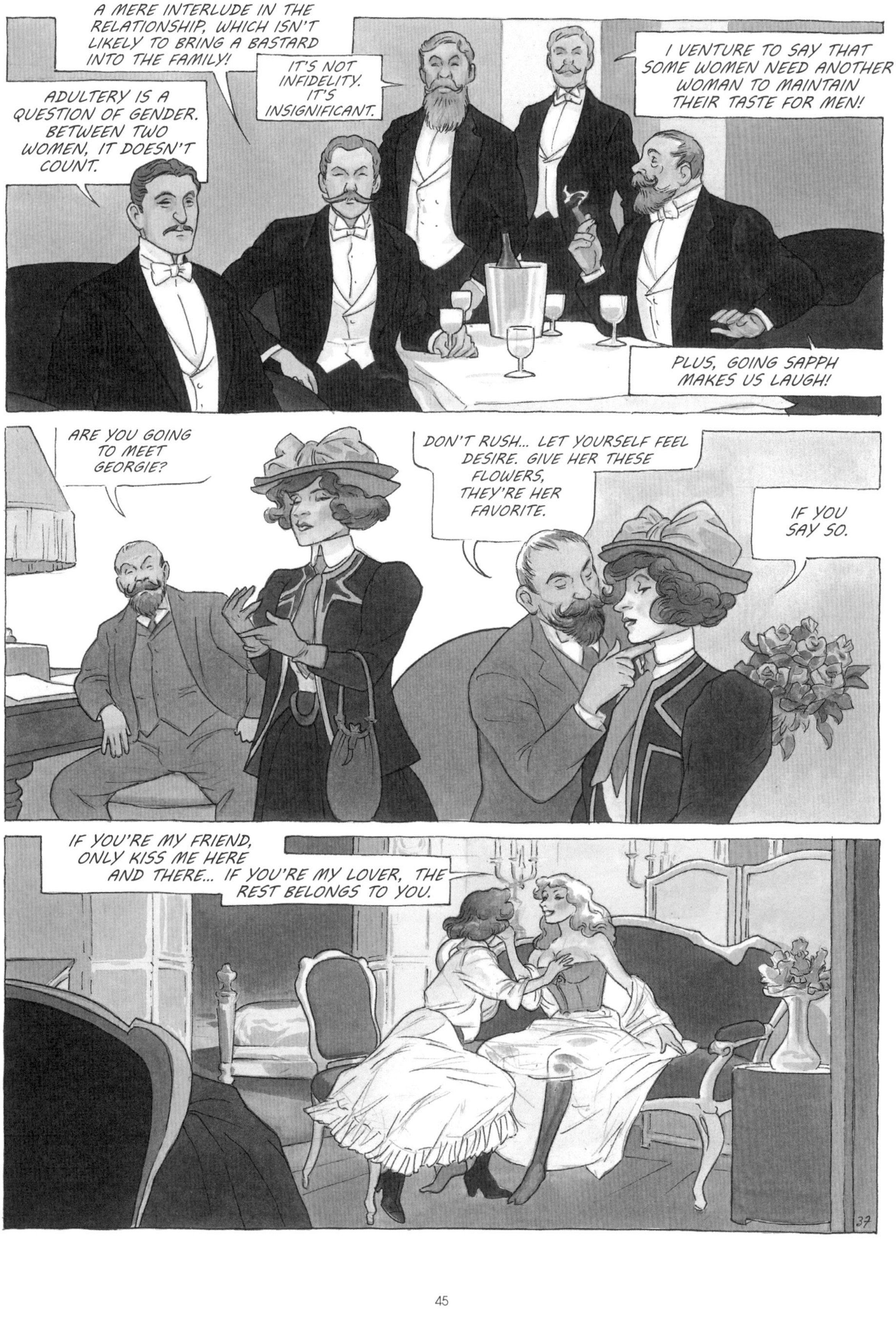
ADULTERY IS A QUESTION OF GENDER. BETWEEN TWO WOMEN, IT DOESN'T COUNT.
A MERE INTERLUDE IN THE RELATIONSHIP, WHICH ISN'T LIKELY TO BRING A BASTARD INTO THE FAMILY!
IT'S NOT INFIDELITY. IT'S INSIGNIFICANT.
I VENTURE TO SAY THAT SOME WOMEN NEED ANOTHER WOMAN TO MAINTAIN THEIR TASTE FOR MEN!
PLUS, GOING SAPPH MAKES US LAUGH!
ARE YOU GOING TO MEET GEORGIE?
DON'T RUSH... LET YOURSELF FEEL DESIRE. GIVE HER THESE FLOWERS, THEY'RE HER FAVORITE.
IF YOU SAY SO.
IF YOU'RE MY FRIEND, ONLY KISS ME HERE AND THERE... IF YOU'RE MY LOVER, THE REST BELONGS TO YOU.
37

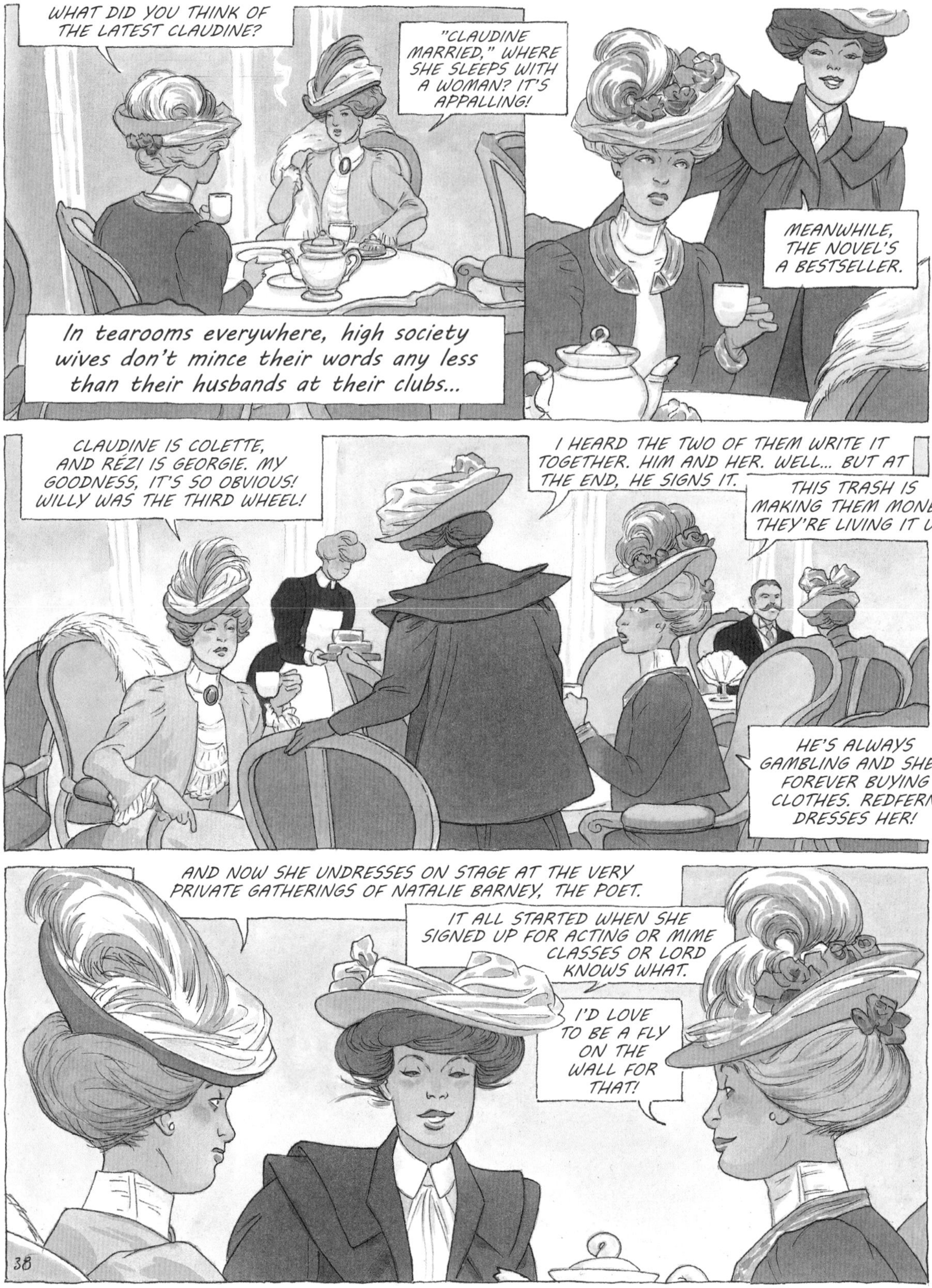
WHAT DID YOU THINK OF THE LATEST CLAUDINE?
"CLAUDINE MARRIED," WHERE SHE SLEEPS WITH A WOMAN? IT'S APPALLING!
In tearooms everywhere, high society wives don't mince their words any less than their husbands at their clubs...
MEANWHILE, THE NOVEL'S A BESTSELLER.
CLAUDINE IS COLETTE, AND RÉZI IS GEORGIE. MY GOODNESS, IT'S SO OBVIOUS! WILLY WAS THE THIRD WHEEL!
I HEARD THE TWO OF THEM WRITE IT TOGETHER. HIM AND HER. WELL... BUT AT THE END, HE SIGNS IT.
THIS TRASH IS MAKING THEM MONEY. THEY'RE LIVING IT UP.
HE'S ALWAYS GAMBLING AND SHE'S FOREVER BUYING CLOTHES. REDFERN DRESSES HER!
AND NOW SHE UNDRESSES ON STAGE AT THE VERY PRIVATE GATHERINGS OF NATALIE BARNEY, THE POET.
IT ALL STARTED WHEN SHE SIGNED UP FOR ACTING OR MIME CLASSES OR LORD KNOWS WHAT.
I'D LOVE TO BE A FLY ON THE WALL FOR THAT!
38

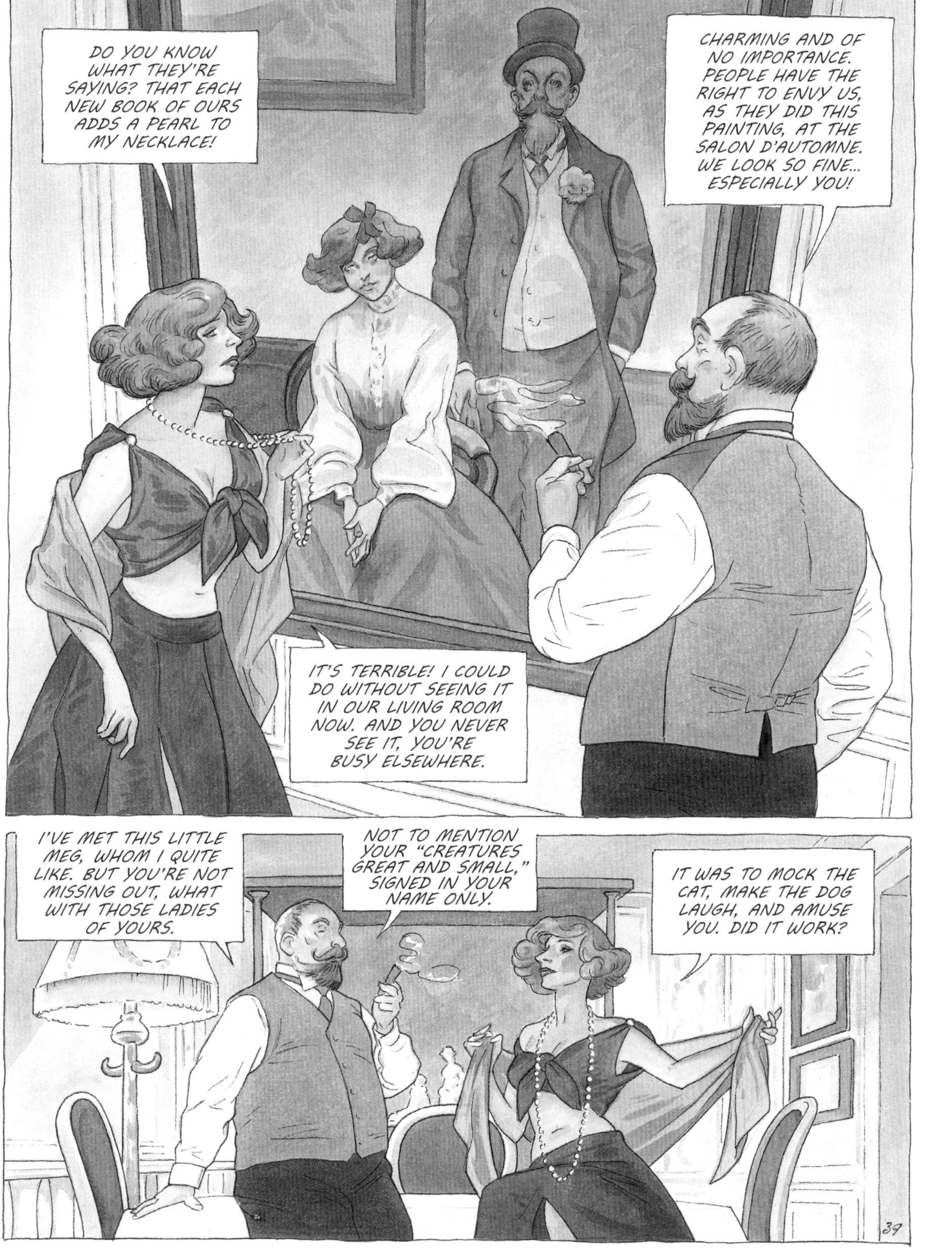
DO YOU KNOW WHAT THEY'RE SAYING? THAT EACH NEW BOOK OF OURS ADDS A PEARL TO MY NECKLACE!
CHARMING AND OF NO IMPORTANCE. PEOPLE HAVE THE RIGHT TO ENVY US, AS THEY DID THIS PAINTING, AT THE SALON D'AUTOMNE. WE LOOK SO FINE... ESPECIALLY YOU!
IT'S TERRIBLE! I COULD DO WITHOUT SEEING IT IN OUR LIVING ROOM NOW. AND YOU NEVER SEE IT, YOU'RE BUSY ELSEWHERE.
I'VE MET THIS LITTLE MEG, WHOM I QUITE LIKE. BUT YOU'RE NOT MISSING OUT, WHAT WITH THOSE LADIES OF YOURS.
NOT TO MENTION YOUR "CREATURES GREAT AND SMALL," SIGNED IN YOUR NAME ONLY.
IT WAS TO MOCK THE CAT, MAKE THE DOG LAUGH, AND AMUSE YOU. DID IT WORK?
39

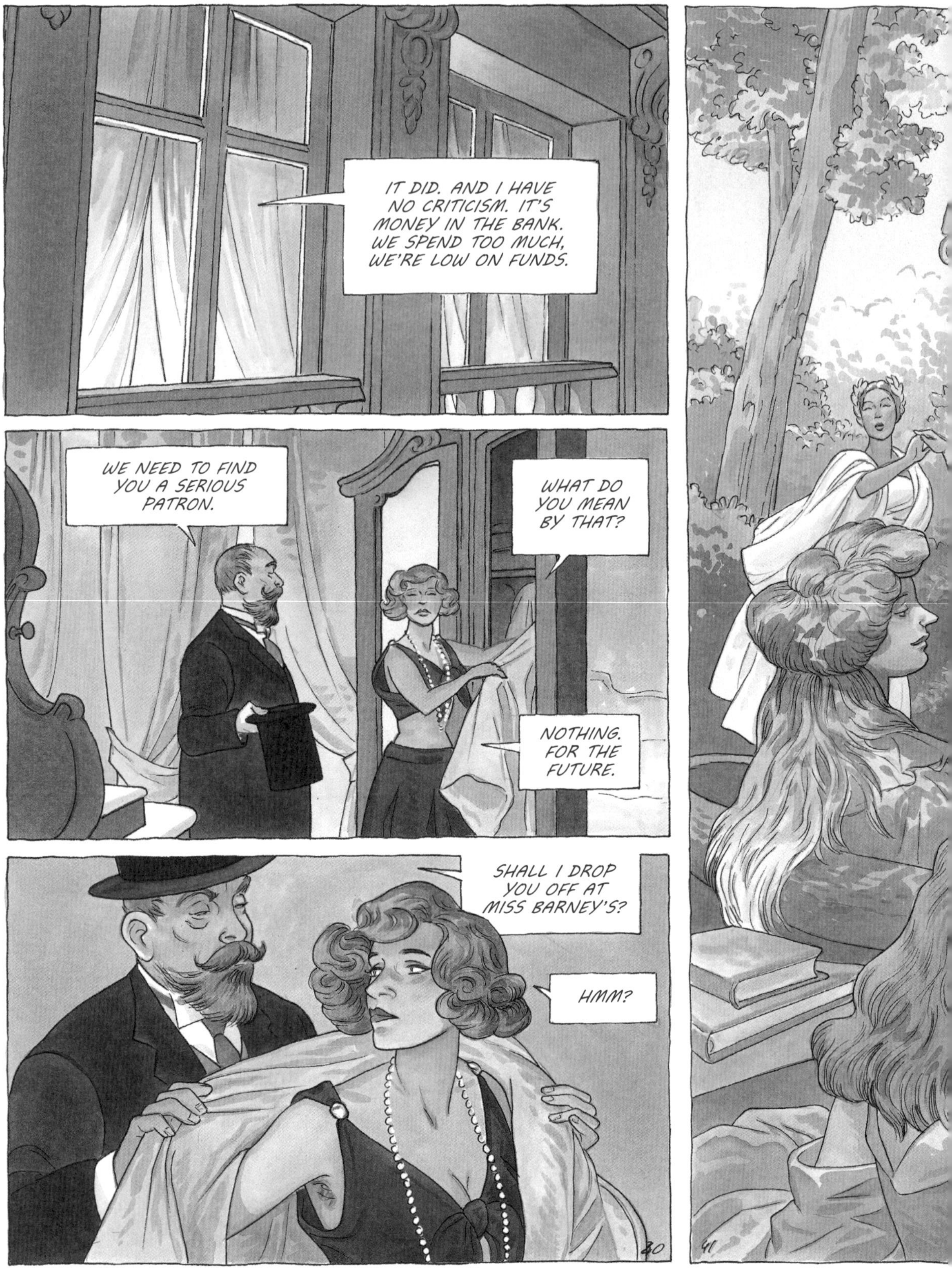
IT DID. AND I HAVE NO CRITICISM. IT'S MONEY IN THE BANK. WE SPEND TOO MUCH, WE'RE LOW ON FUNDS.
WE NEED TO FIND YOU A SERIOUS PATRON.
WHAT DO YOU MEAN BY THAT?
NOTHING. FOR THE FUTURE.
SHALL I DROP YOU OFF AT MISS BARNEY'S?
HMM?

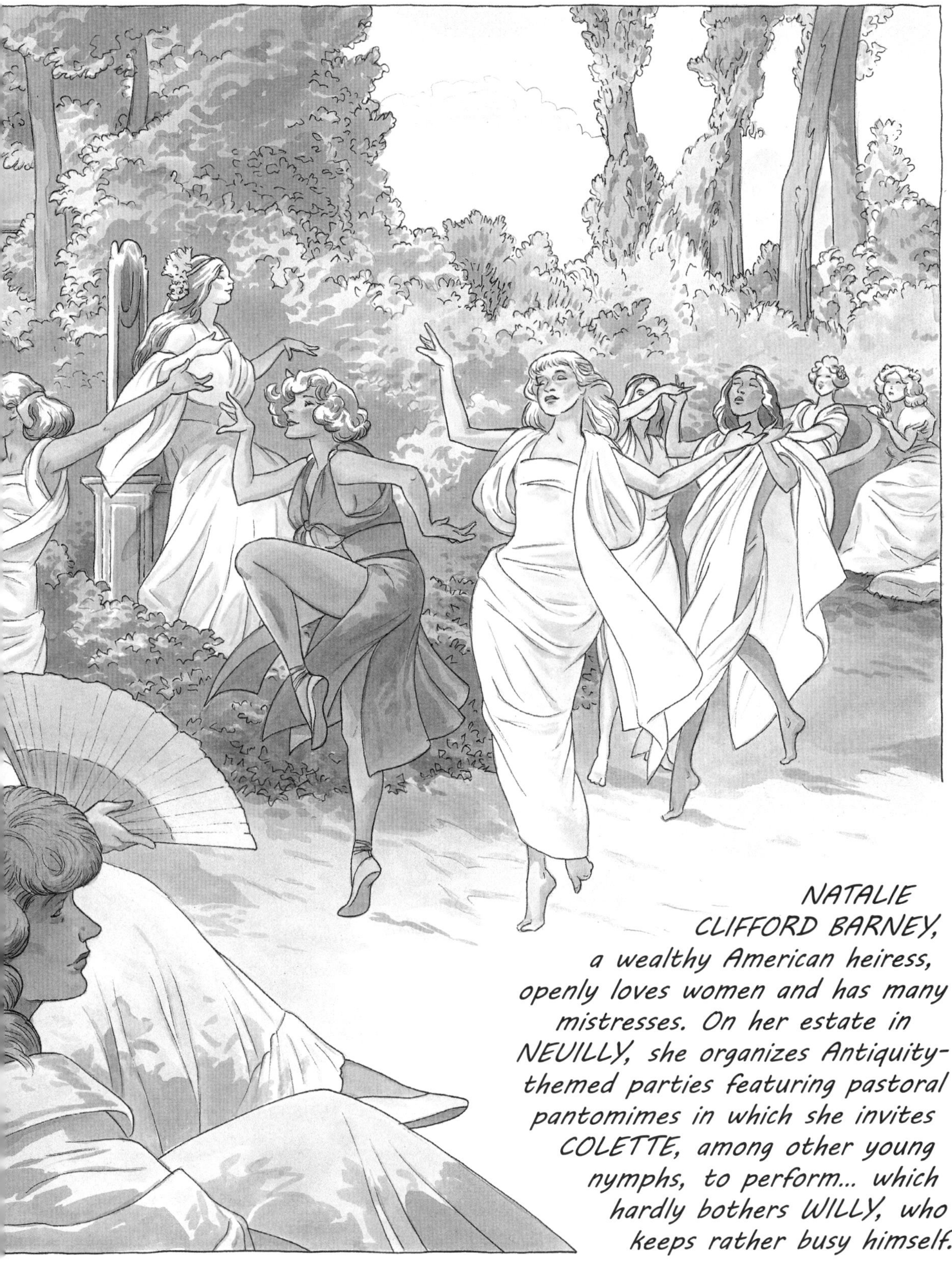
NATALIE CLIFFORD BARNEY, a wealthy American heiress, openly loves women and has many mistresses. On her estate in NEUILLY, she organizes Antiquity-themed parties featuring pastoral pantomimes in which she invites COLETTE, among other young nymphs, to perform... which hardly bothers WILLY, who keeps rather busy himself.

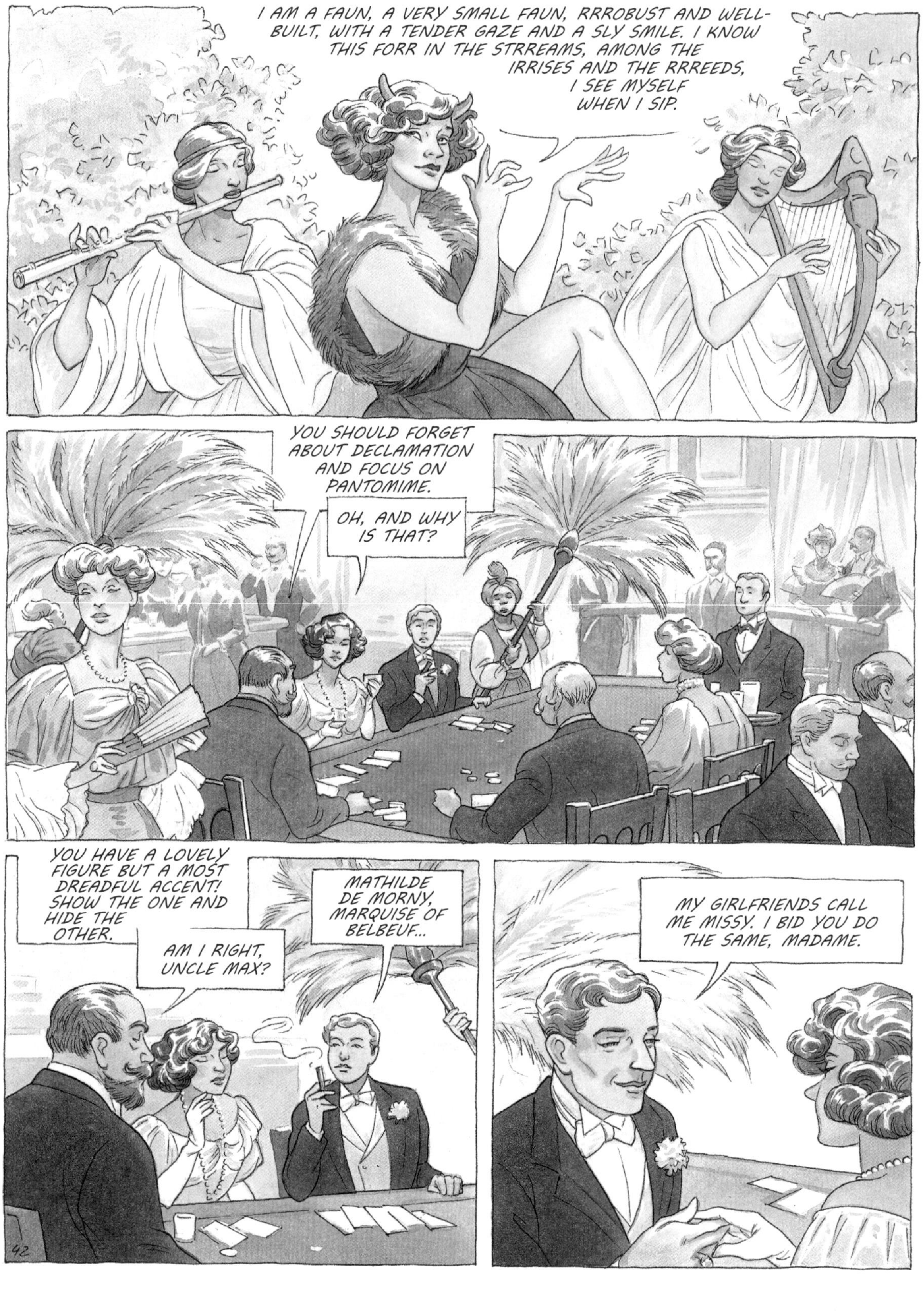
I AM A FAUN, A VERY SMALL FAUN, RRROBUST AND WELL-BUILT, WITH A TENDER GAZE AND A SLY SMILE. I KNOW THIS FORR IN THE STRREAMS, AMONG THE IRRISES AND THE RRREEDS, I SEE MYSELF WHEN I SIP.
YOU SHOULD FORGET ABOUT DECLAMATION AND FOCUS ON PANTOMIME.
OH, AND WHY IS THAT?
YOU HAVE A LOVELY FIGURE BUT A MOST DREADFUL ACCENT! SHOW THE ONE AND HIDE THE OTHER.
AM I RIGHT, UNCLE MAX?
MATHILDE DE MORNY, MARQUISE OF BELBEUF...
42
MY GIRLFRIENDS CALL ME MISSY. I BID YOU DO THE SAME, MADAME.

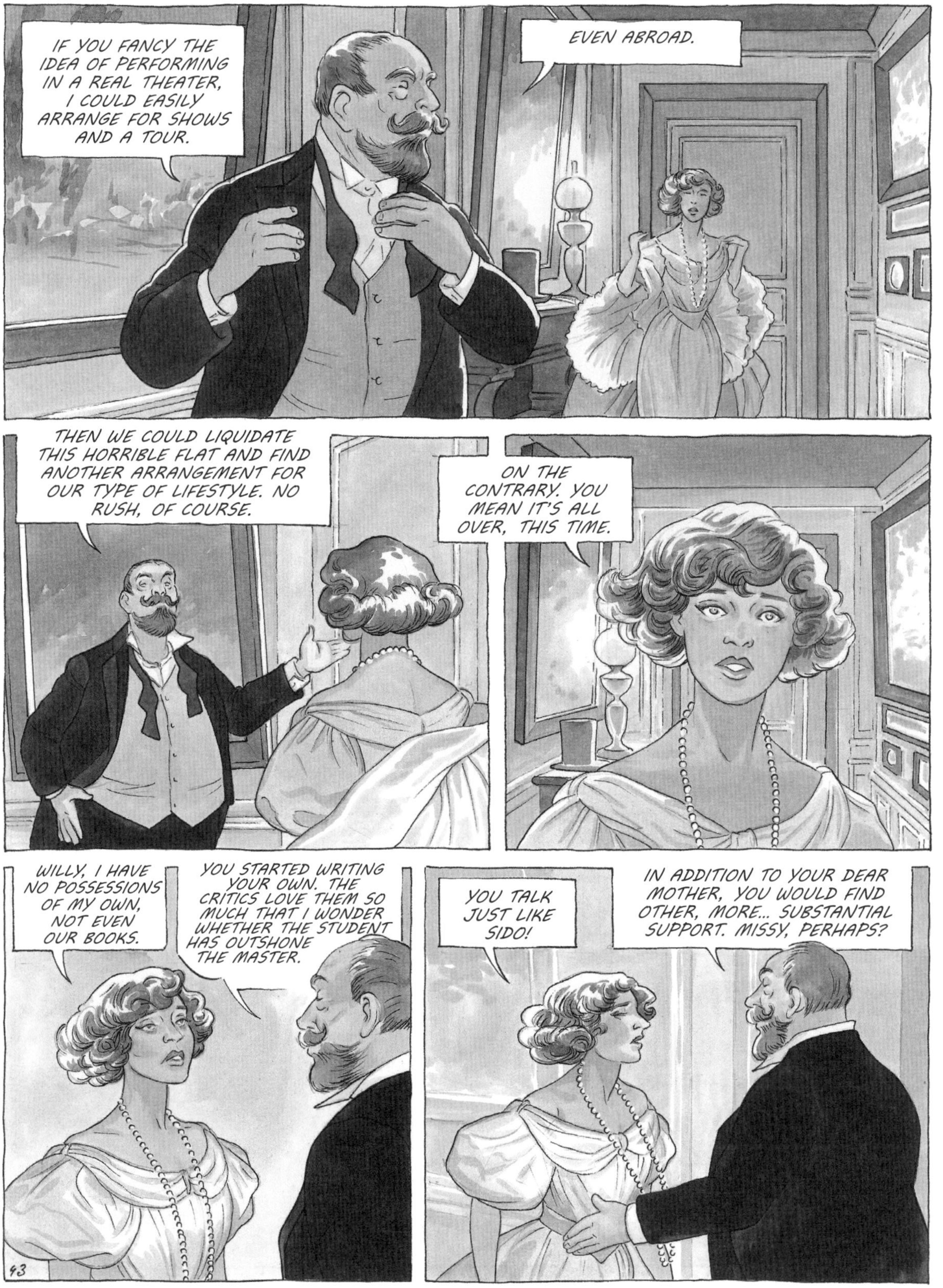
IF YOU FANCY THE IDEA OF PERFORMING IN A REAL THEATER, I COULD EASILY ARRANGE FOR SHOWS AND A TOUR.
EVEN ABROAD.
THEN WE COULD LIQUIDATE THIS HORRIBLE FLAT AND FIND ANOTHER ARRANGEMENT FOR OUR TYPE OF LIFESTYLE. NO RUSH, OF COURSE.
ON THE CONTRARY. YOU MEAN IT'S ALL OVER, THIS TIME.
WILLY, I HAVE NO POSSESSIONS OF MY OWN, NOT EVEN OUR BOOKS.
YOU STARTED WRITING YOUR OWN. THE CRITICS LOVE THEM SO MUCH THAT I WONDER WHETHER THE STUDENT HAS OUTSHONE THE MASTER.
43
YOU TALK JUST LIKE SIDO!
IN ADDITION TO YOUR DEAR MOTHER, YOU WOULD FIND OTHER, MORE... SUBSTANTIAL SUPPORT. MISSY, PERHAPS?

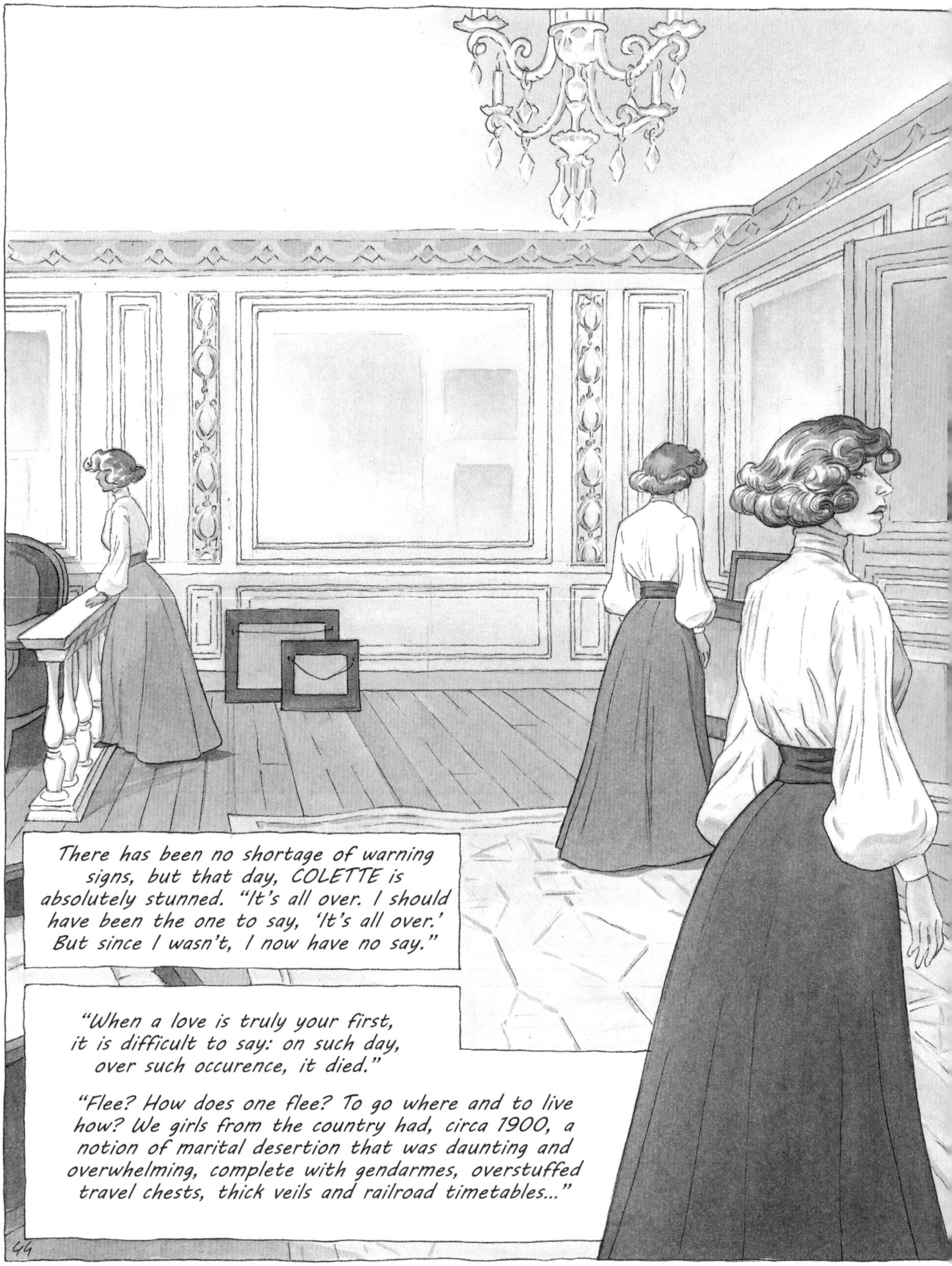
There has been no shortage of warning signs, but that day, COLETTE is absolutely stunned. "It's all over. I should have been the one to say, 'It's all over.' But since I wasn't, I now have no say."
"When a love is truly your first, it is difficult to say: on such day, over such occurence, it died."
"Flee? How does one flee? To go where and to live how? We girls from the country had, circa 1900, a notion of marital desertion that was daunting and overwhelming, complete with gendarmes, overstuffed travel chests, thick veils and railroad timetables..."
44

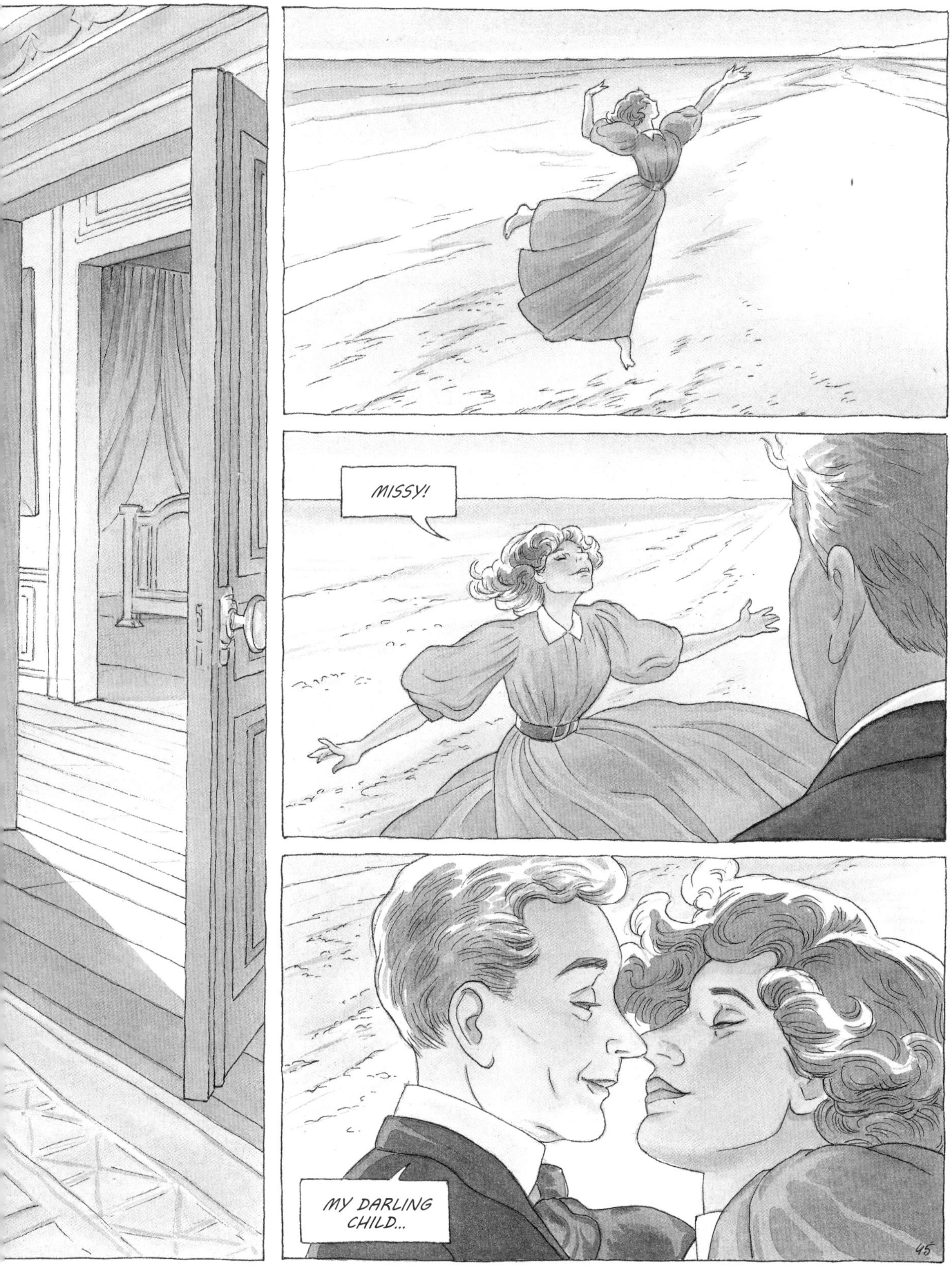
MISSY!
MY DARLING CHILD...

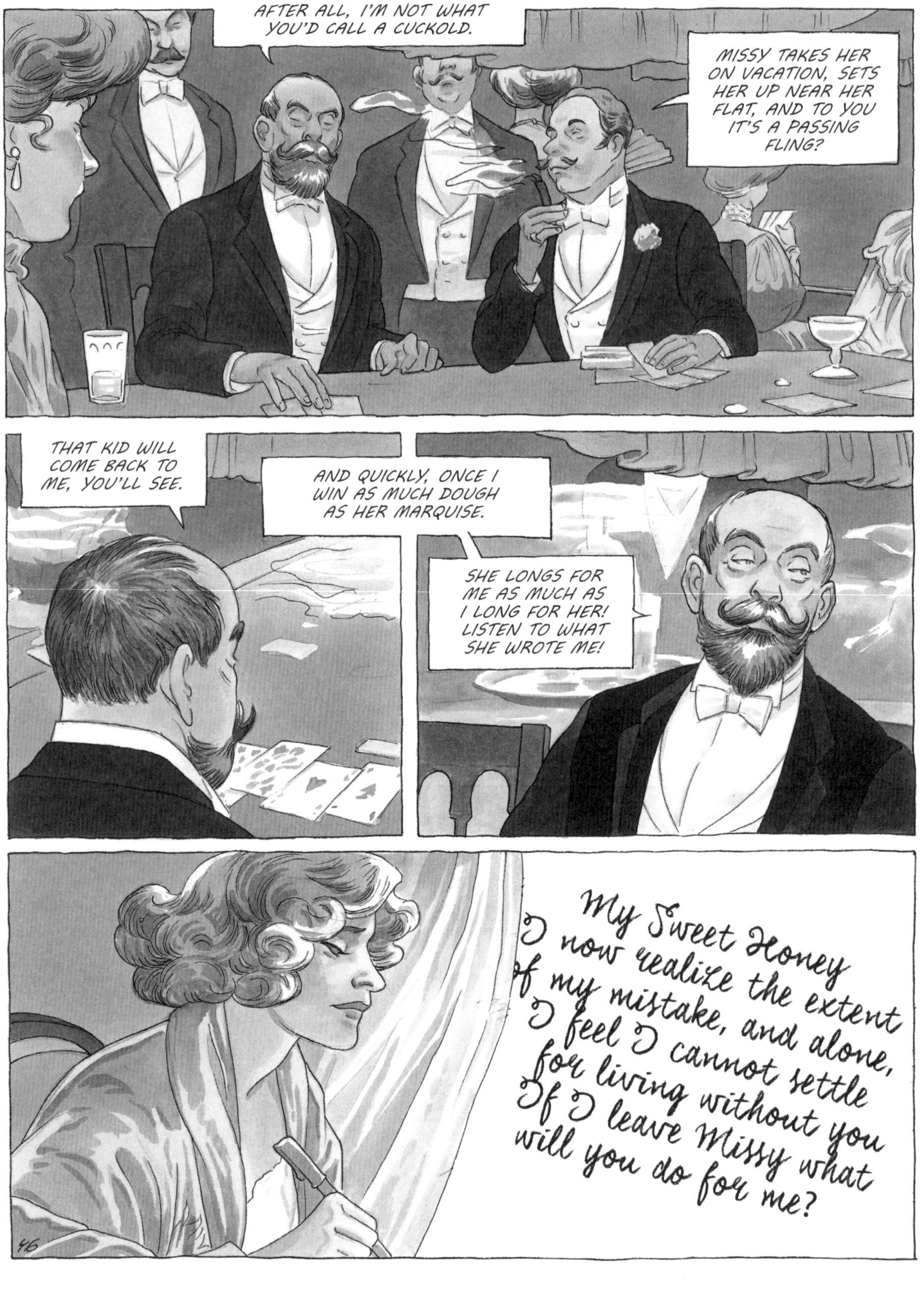
AFTER ALL, I'M NOT WHAT YOU'D CALL A CUCKOLD.
MISSY TAKES HER ON VACATION, SETS HER UP NEAR HER FLAT, AND TO YOU IT'S A PASSING FLING?
THAT KID WILL COME BACK TO ME, YOU'LL SEE.
AND QUICKLY, ONCE I WIN AS MUCH DOUGH AS HER MARQUISE.
SHE LONGS FOR ME AS MUCH AS I LONG FOR HER! LISTEN TO WHAT SHE WROTE ME!
My Sweet Honey
I now realize the extent
of my mistake, and alone,
I feel I cannot settle
for living without you
If I leave Missy what
will you do for me?
46

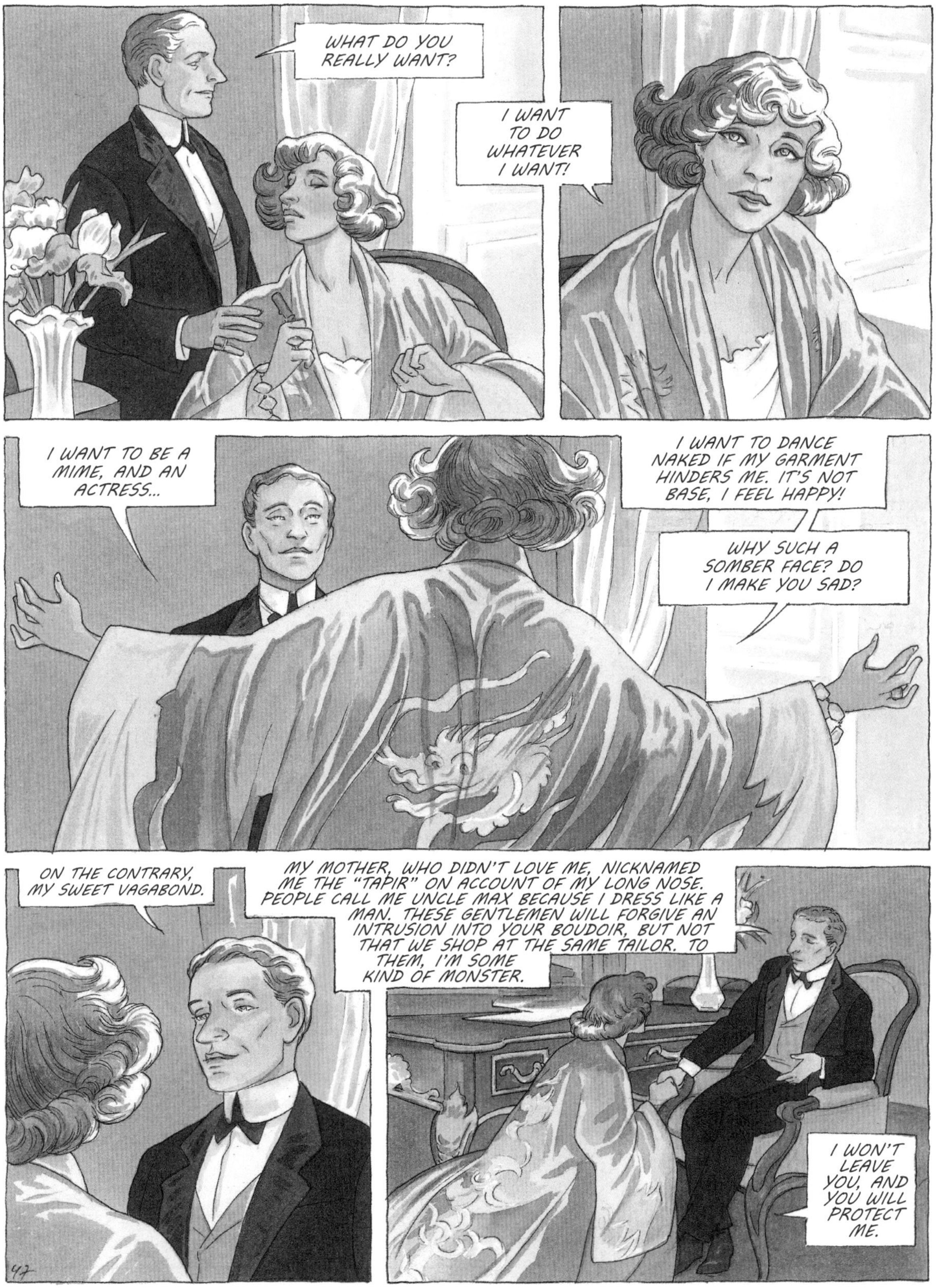
WHAT DO YOU REALLY WANT?
I WANT TO DO WHATEVER I WANT!
I WANT TO BE A MIME, AND AN ACTRESS...
I WANT TO DANCE NAKED IF MY GARMENT HINDERS ME. IT'S NOT BASE, I FEEL HAPPY!
WHY SUCH A SOMBER FACE? DO I MAKE YOU SAD?
ON THE CONTRARY, MY SWEET VAGABOND.
MY MOTHER, WHO DIDN'T LOVE ME, NICKNAMED ME THE "TAPIR" ON ACCOUNT OF MY LONG NOSE. PEOPLE CALL ME UNCLE MAX BECAUSE I DRESS LIKE A MAN. THESE GENTLEMEN WILL FORGIVE AN INTRUSION INTO YOUR BOUDOIR, BUT NOT THAT WE SHOP AT THE SAME TAILOR. TO THEM, I'M SOME KIND OF MONSTER.
I WON'T LEAVE YOU, AND YOU WILL PROTECT ME.

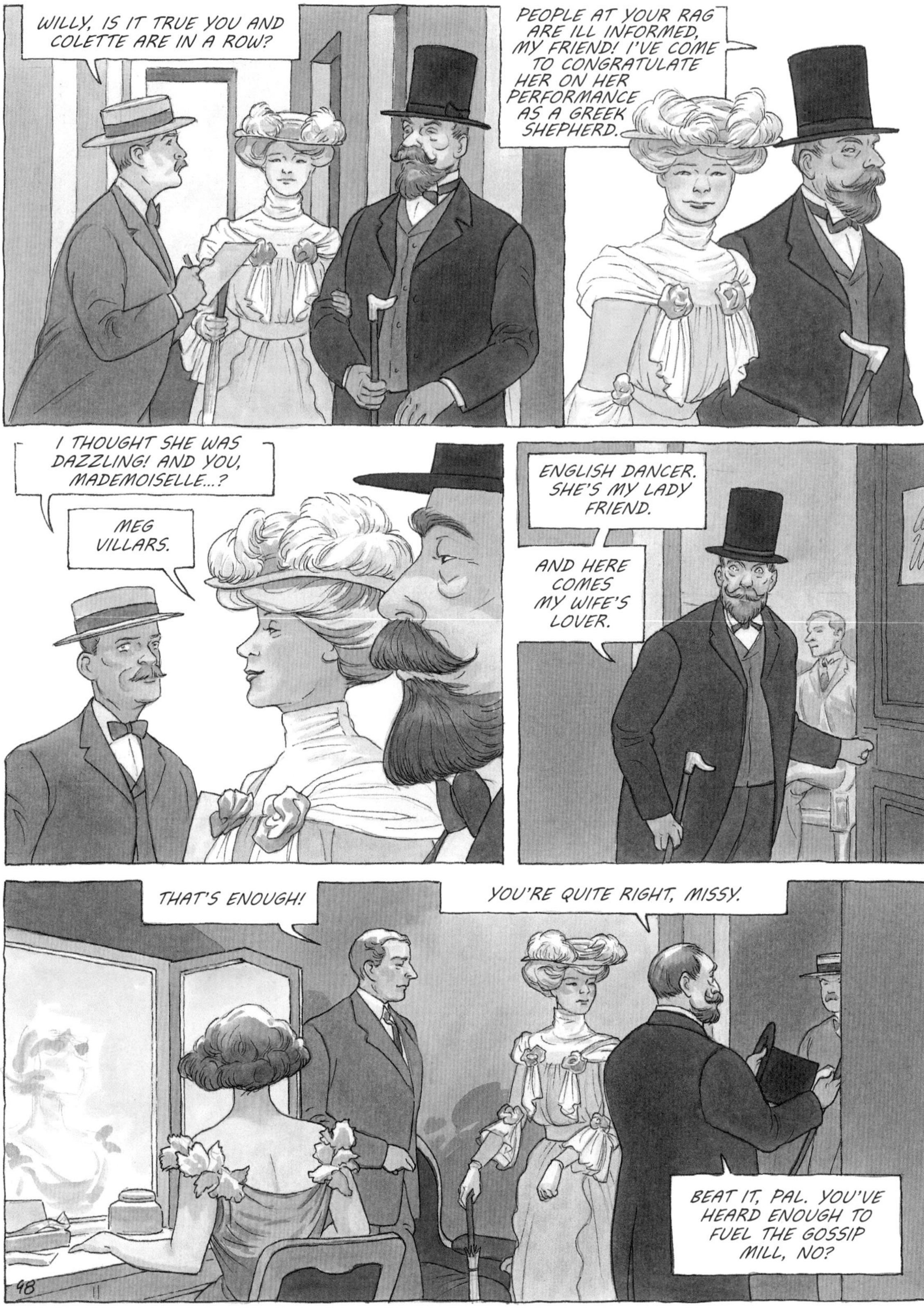

WILLY, IS IT TRUE YOU AND COLETTE ARE IN A ROW?
PEOPLE AT YOUR RAG ARE ILL INFORMED, MY FRIEND! I'VE COME TO CONGRATULATE HER ON HER PERFORMANCE AS A GREEK SHEPHERD.
I THOUGHT SHE WAS DAZZLING! AND YOU, MADEMOISELLE...?
MEG VILLARS.
ENGLISH DANCER. SHE'S MY LADY FRIEND.
AND HERE COMES MY WIFE'S LOVER.
THAT'S ENOUGH!
YOU'RE QUITE RIGHT, MISSY.
BEAT IT, PAL. YOU'VE HEARD ENOUGH TO FUEL THE GOSSIP MILL, NO?
48

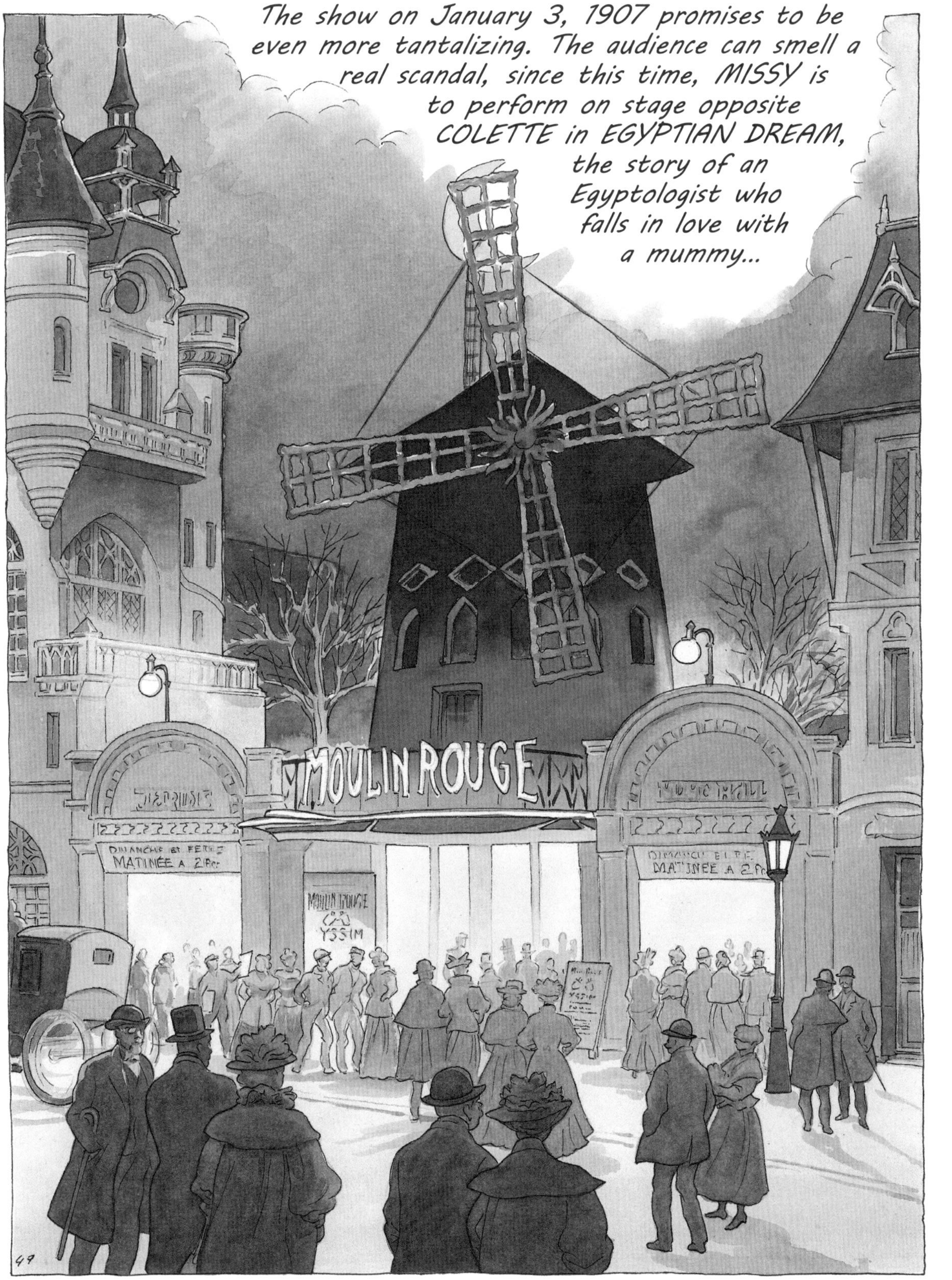
The show on January 3, 1907 promises to be even more tantalizing. The audience can smell a real scandal, since this time, MISSY is to perform on stage opposite COLETTE in EGYPTIAN DREAM, the story of an Egyptologist who falls in love with a mummy...
MOULIN ROUGE
MOULIN ROUGE
YSSIM

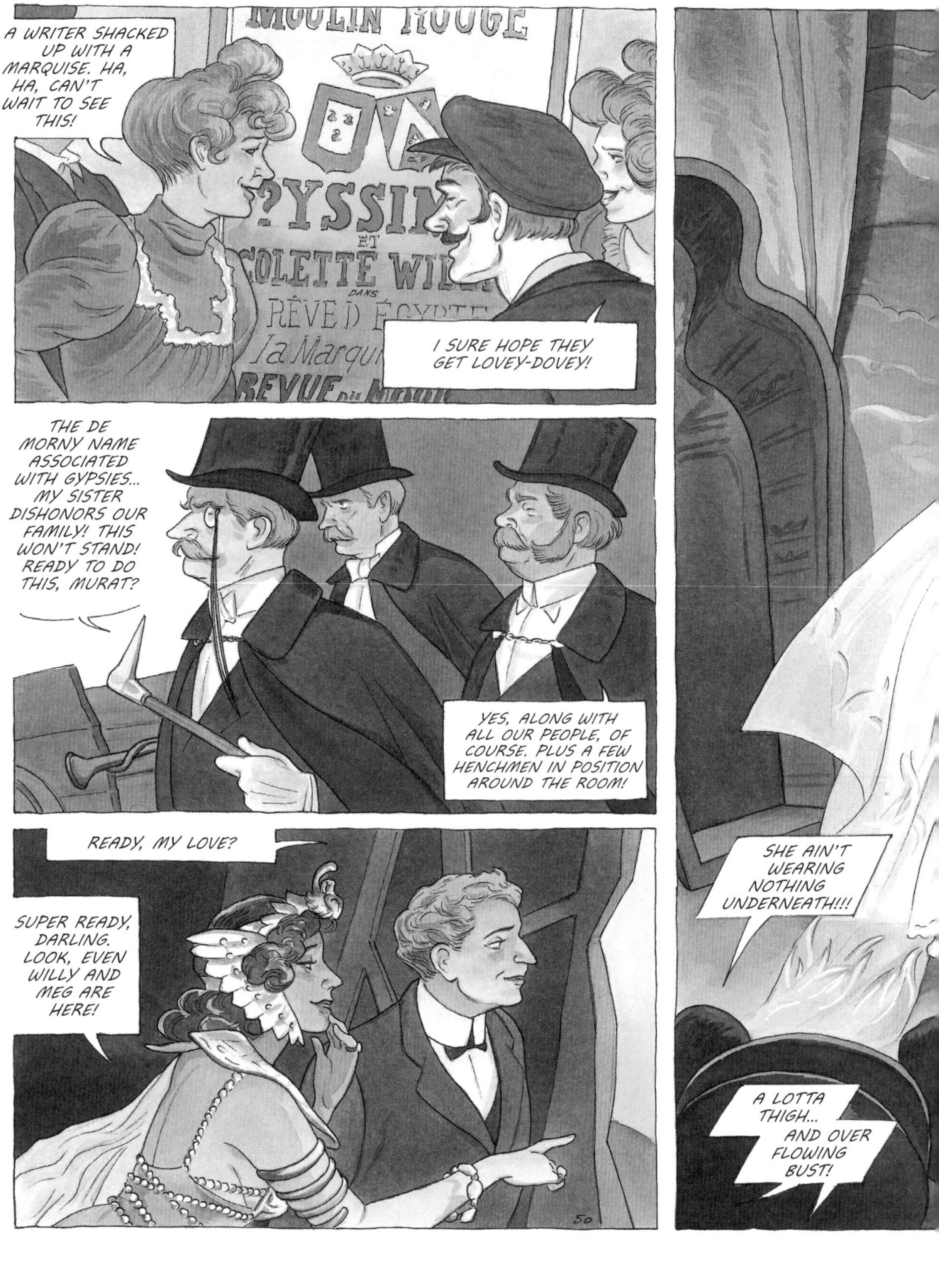
A WRITER SHACKED UP WITH A MARQUISE. HA, HA, CAN'T WAIT TO SEE THIS!
I SURE HOPE THEY GET LOVEY-DOVEY!
THE DE MORNY NAME ASSOCIATED WITH GYPSIES... MY SISTER DISHONORS OUR FAMILY! THIS WON'T STAND! READY TO DO THIS, MURAT?
YES, ALONG WITH ALL OUR PEOPLE, OF COURSE. PLUS A FEW HENCHMEN IN POSITION AROUND THE ROOM!
READY, MY LOVE?
SUPER READY, DARLING. LOOK, EVEN WILLY AND MEG ARE HERE!
SHE AIN'T WEARING NOTHING UNDERNEATH!!!
A LOTTA THIGH... AND OVER FLOWING BUST!

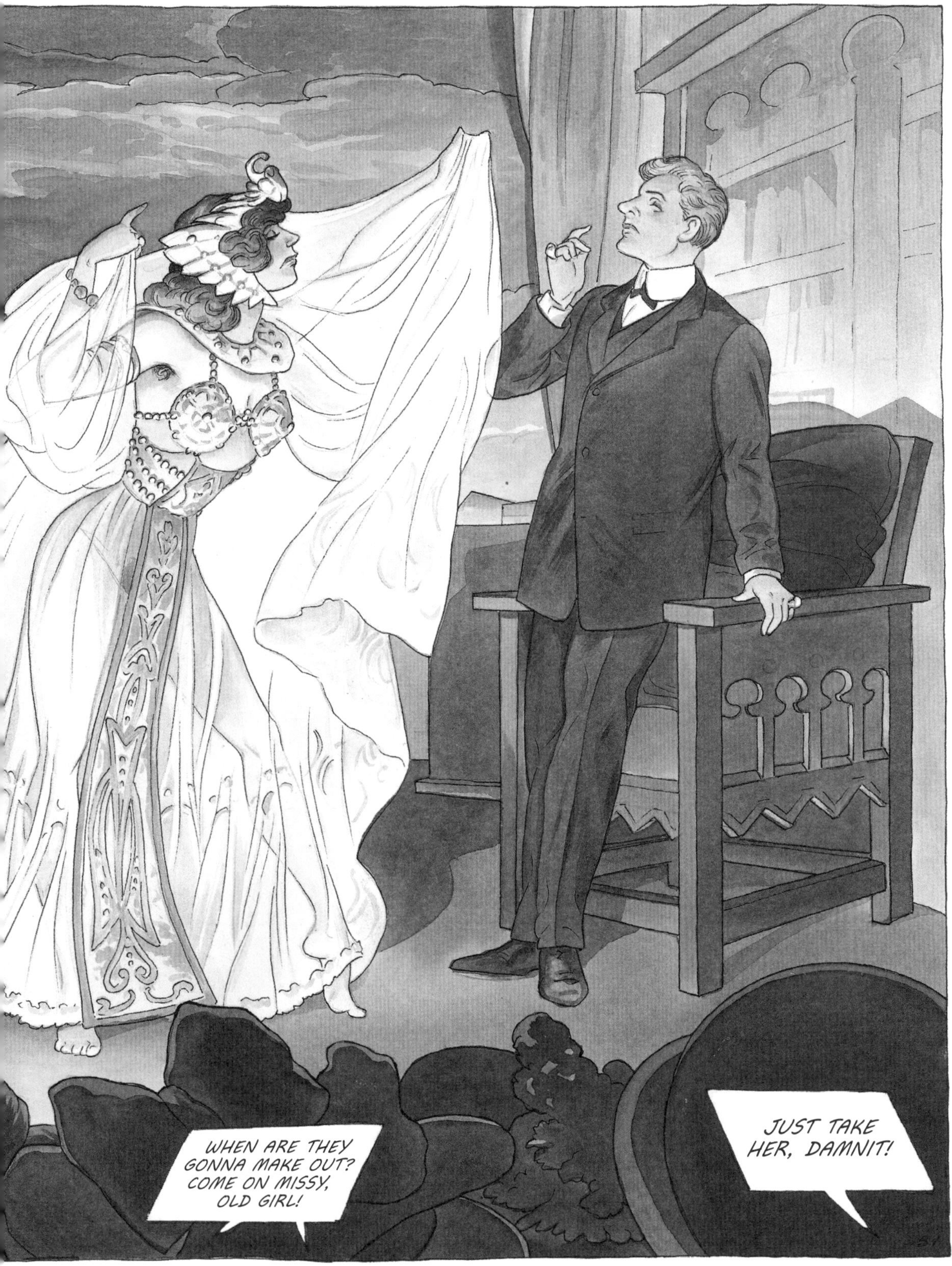
WHEN ARE THEY GONNA MAKE OUT? COME ON MISSY, OLD GIRL!
JUST TAKE HER, DAMNIT!

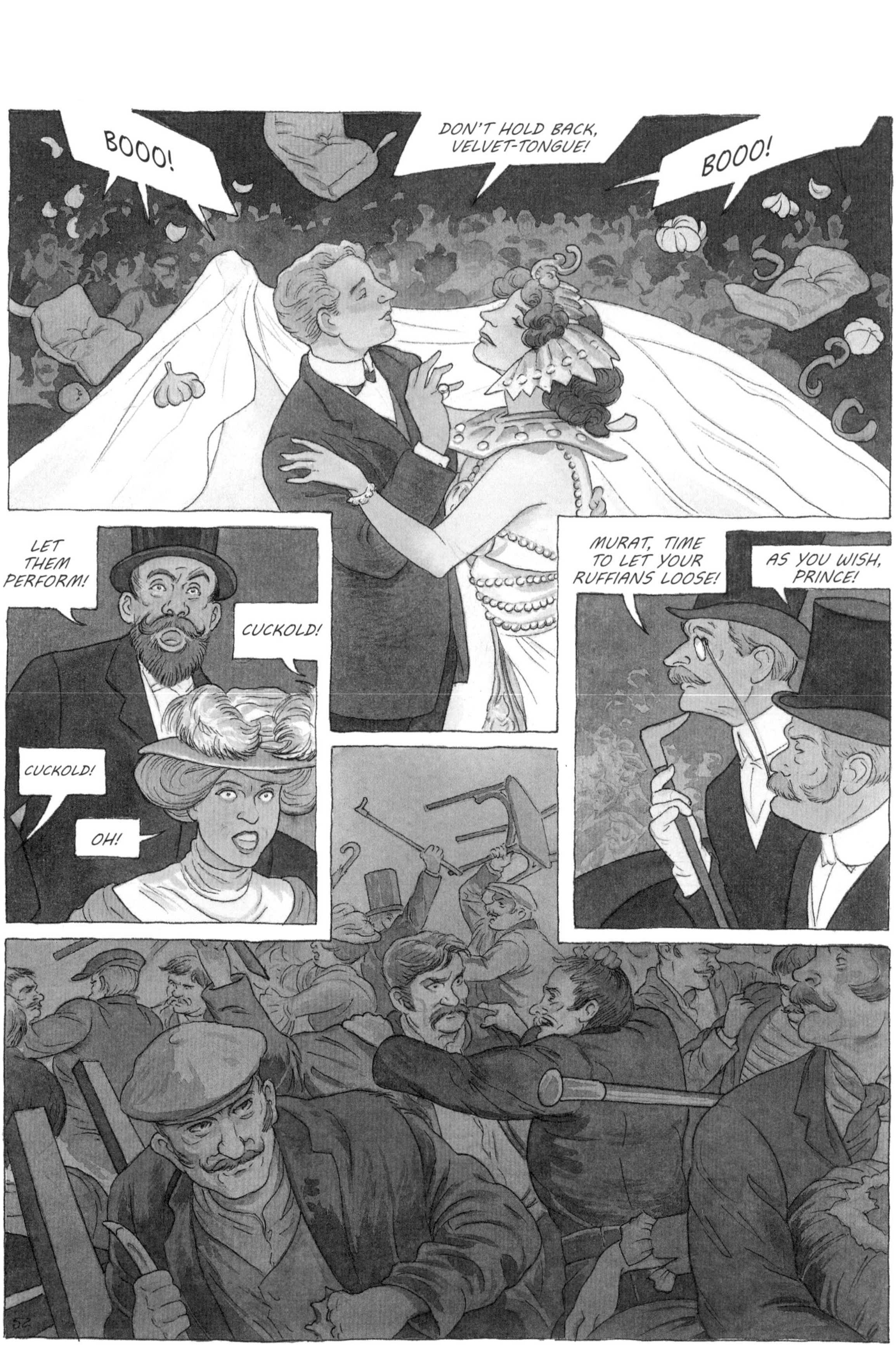
BOOO!
DON'T HOLD BACK, VELVET-TONGUE!
BOOO!
LET THEM PERFORM!
CUCKOLD!
CUCKOLD!
OH!
MURAT, TIME TO LET YOUR RUFFIANS LOOSE!
AS YOU WISH, PRINCE!

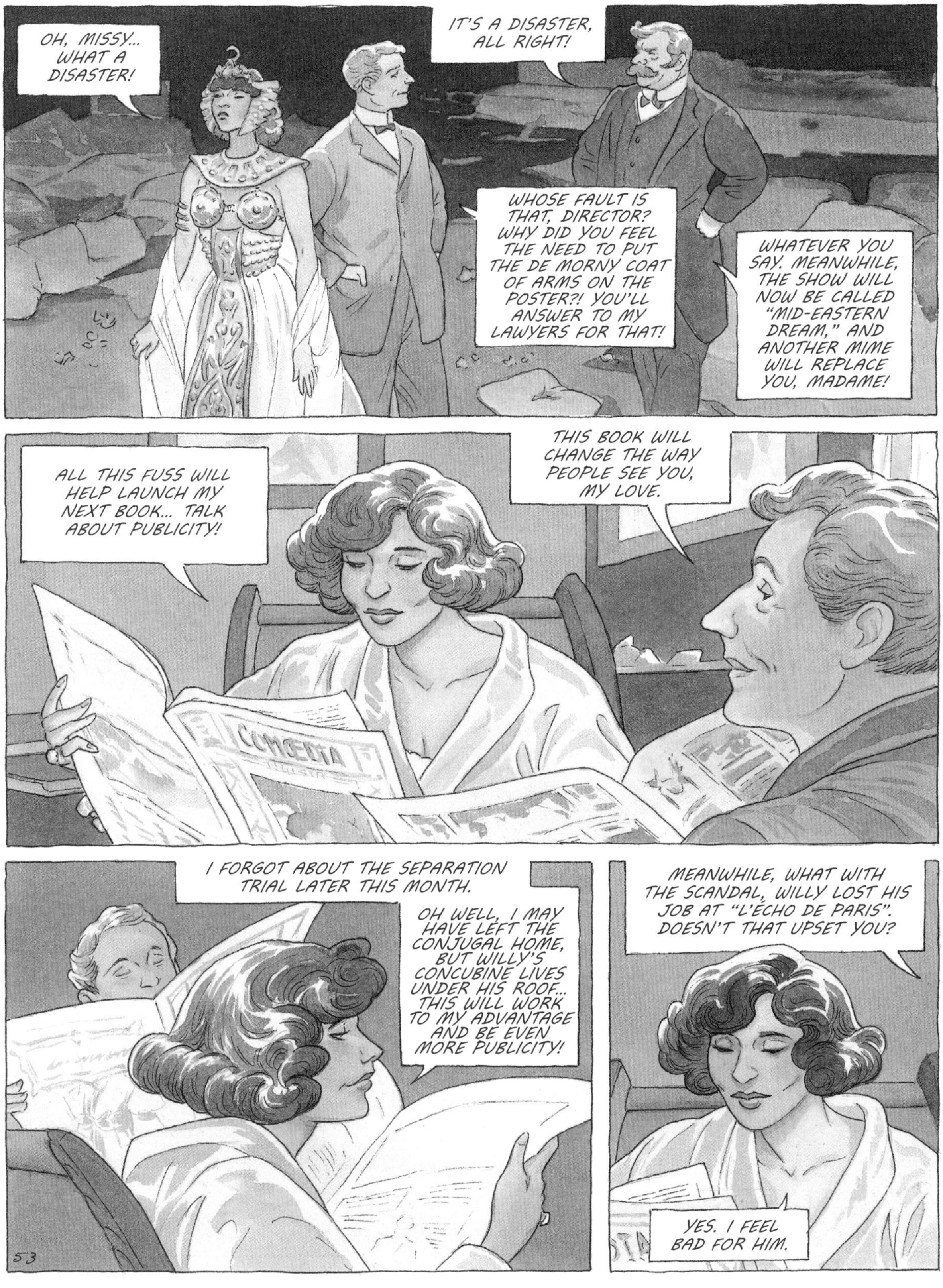
OH, MISSY... WHAT A DISASTER!
IT'S A DISASTER, ALL RIGHT!
WHOSE FAULT IS THAT, DIRECTOR? WHY DID YOU FEEL THE NEED TO PUT THE DE MORNY COAT OF ARMS ON THE POSTER?! YOU'LL ANSWER TO MY LAWYERS FOR THAT!
WHATEVER YOU SAY. MEANWHILE, THE SHOW WILL NOW BE CALLED "MID-EASTERN DREAM," AND ANOTHER MIME WILL REPLACE YOU, MADAME!
ALL THIS FUSS WILL HELP LAUNCH MY NEXT BOOK... TALK ABOUT PUBLICITY!
THIS BOOK WILL CHANGE THE WAY PEOPLE SEE YOU, MY LOVE.
COMŒDIA
I FORGOT ABOUT THE SEPARATION TRIAL LATER THIS MONTH.
OH WELL, I MAY HAVE LEFT THE CONJUGAL HOME, BUT WILLY'S CONCUBINE LIVES UNDER HIS ROOF... THIS WILL WORK TO MY ADVANTAGE AND BE EVEN MORE PUBLICITY!
MEANWHILE, WHAT WITH THE SCANDAL, WILLY LOST HIS JOB AT "L'ÉCHO DE PARIS". DOESN'T THAT UPSET YOU?
YES. I FEEL BAD FOR HIM.
53

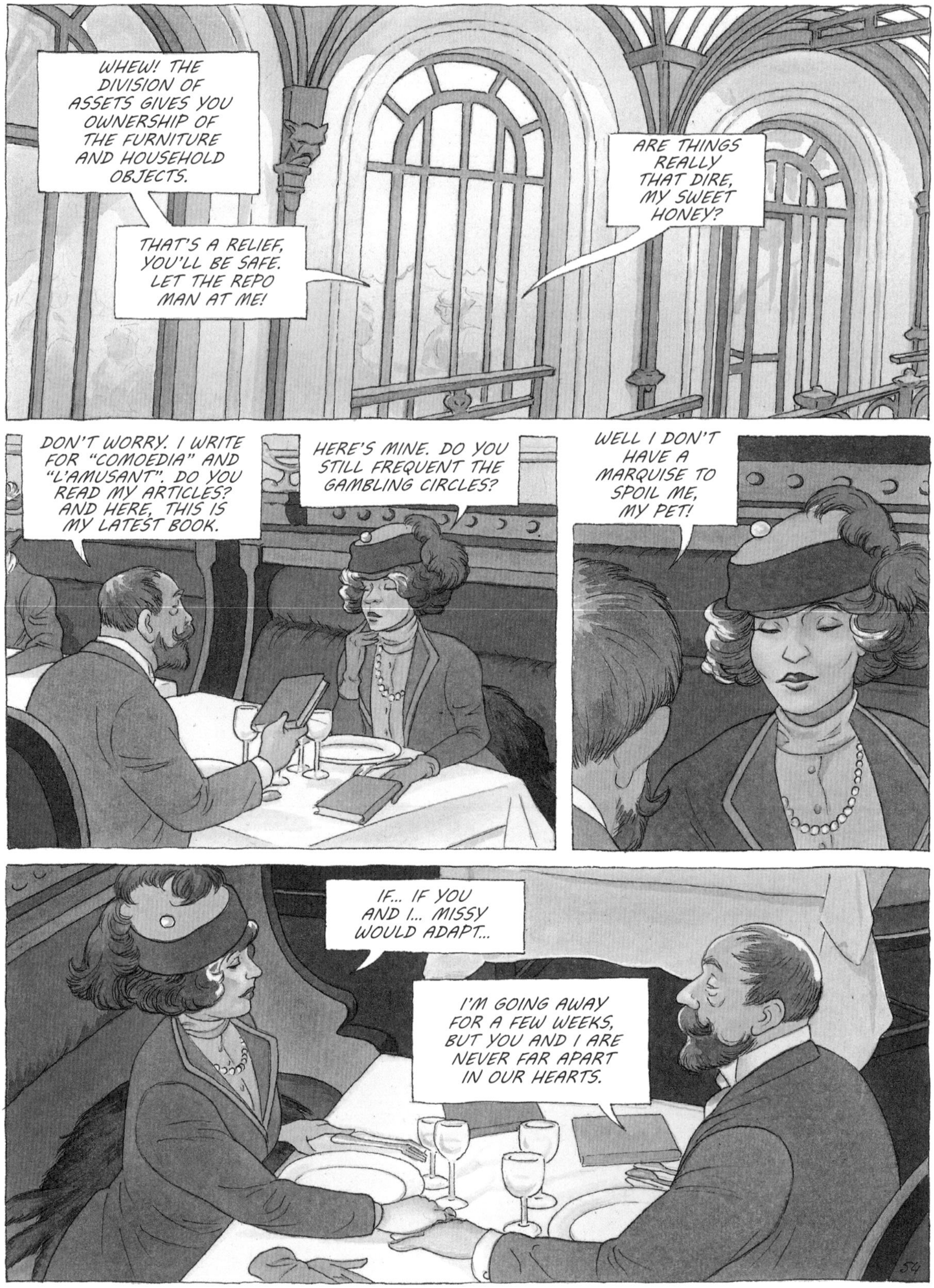
WHEW! THE DIVISION OF ASSETS GIVES YOU OWNERSHIP OF THE FURNITURE AND HOUSEHOLD OBJECTS.
THAT'S A RELIEF, YOU'LL BE SAFE. LET THE REPO MAN AT ME!
ARE THINGS REALLY THAT DIRE, MY SWEET HONEY?
DON'T WORRY. I WRITE FOR "COMOEDIA" AND "L'AMUSANT". DO YOU READ MY ARTICLES? AND HERE, THIS IS MY LATEST BOOK.
HERE'S MINE. DO YOU STILL FREQUENT THE GAMBLING CIRCLES?
WELL I DON'T HAVE A MARQUISE TO SPOIL ME, MY PET!
IF... IF YOU AND I... MISSY WOULD ADAPT...
I'M GOING AWAY FOR A FEW WEEKS, BUT YOU AND I ARE NEVER FAR APART IN OUR HEARTS.
54

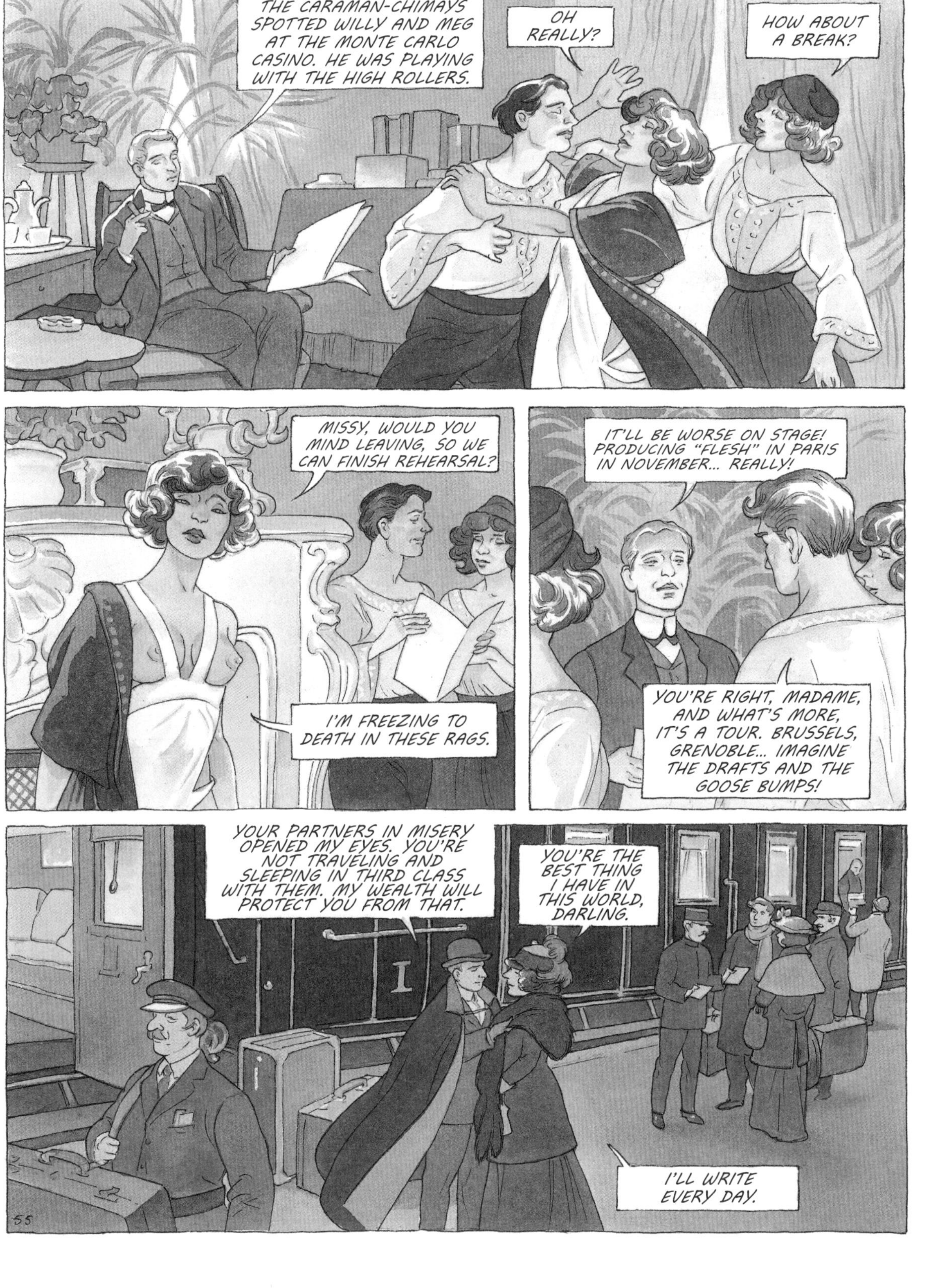
THE CARAMAN-CHIMAYS SPOTTED WILLY AND MEG AT THE MONTE CARLO CASINO. HE WAS PLAYING WITH THE HIGH ROLLERS.
OH REALLY?
HOW ABOUT A BREAK?
MISSY, WOULD YOU MIND LEAVING, SO WE CAN FINISH REHEARSAL?
I'M FREEZING TO DEATH IN THESE RAGS.
IT'LL BE WORSE ON STAGE! PRODUCING "FLESH" IN PARIS IN NOVEMBER... REALLY!
YOU'RE RIGHT, MADAME, AND WHAT'S MORE, IT'S A TOUR. BRUSSELS, GRENOBLE... IMAGINE THE DRAFTS AND THE GOOSE BUMPS!
YOUR PARTNERS IN MISERY OPENED MY EYES. YOU'RE NOT TRAVELING AND SLEEPING IN THIRD CLASS WITH THEM. MY WEALTH WILL PROTECT YOU FROM THAT.
YOU'RE THE BEST THING I HAVE IN THIS WORLD, DARLING.
I'LL WRITE EVERY DAY.
55

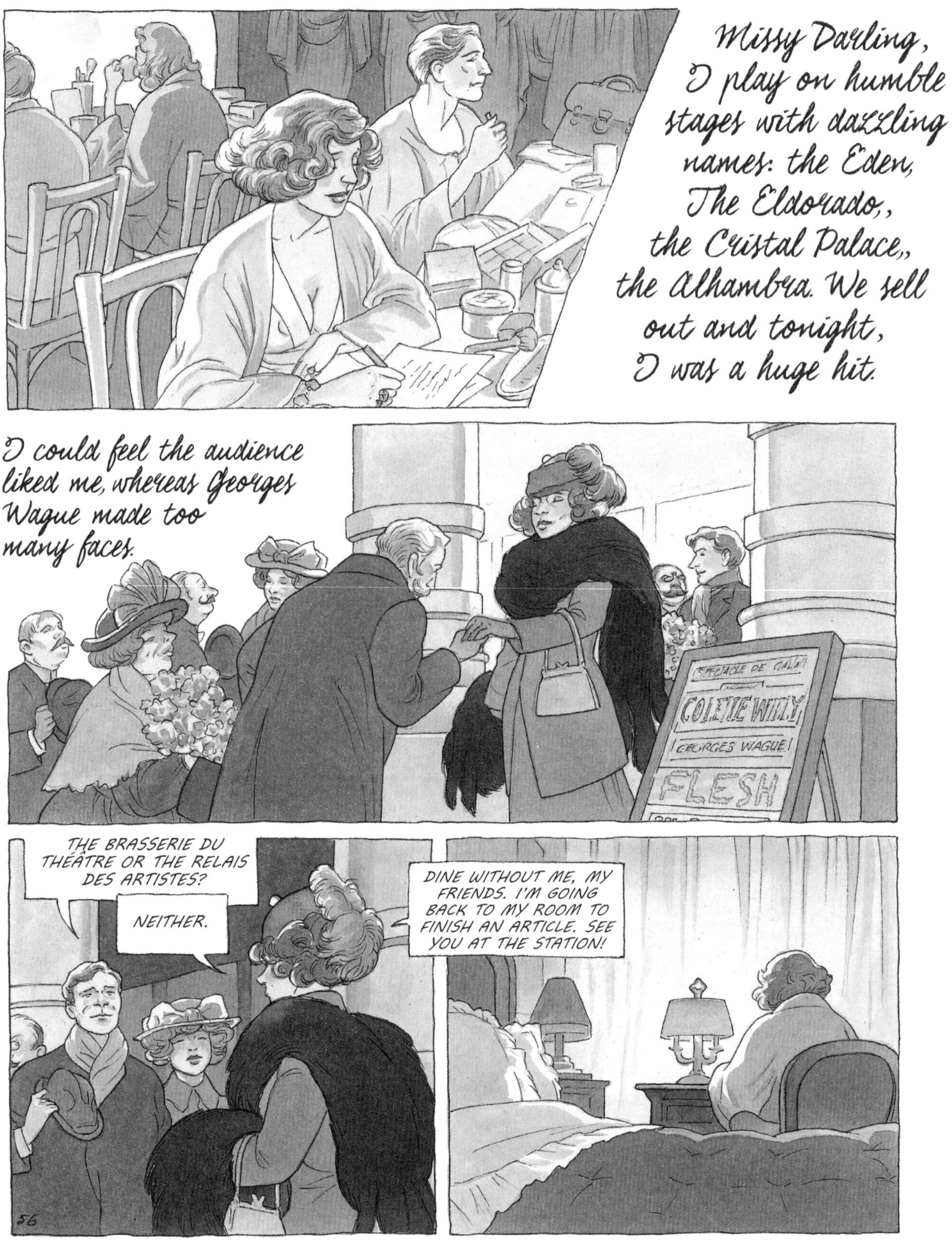
Missy Darling, I play on humble stages with dazzling names: the Eden, The Eldorado,, the Cristal Palace,, the Alhambra. We sell out and tonight, I was a huge hit.
I could feel the audience liked me, whereas Georges Wague made too many faces.
SPECTACLE DE GALA
COLETTE WILLY
GEORGES WAGUE
FLESH
THE BRASSERIE DU THÉÂTRE OR THE RELAIS DES ARTISTES?
NEITHER.
DINE WITHOUT ME, MY FRIENDS. I'M GOING BACK TO MY ROOM TO FINISH AN ARTICLE. SEE YOU AT THE STATION!

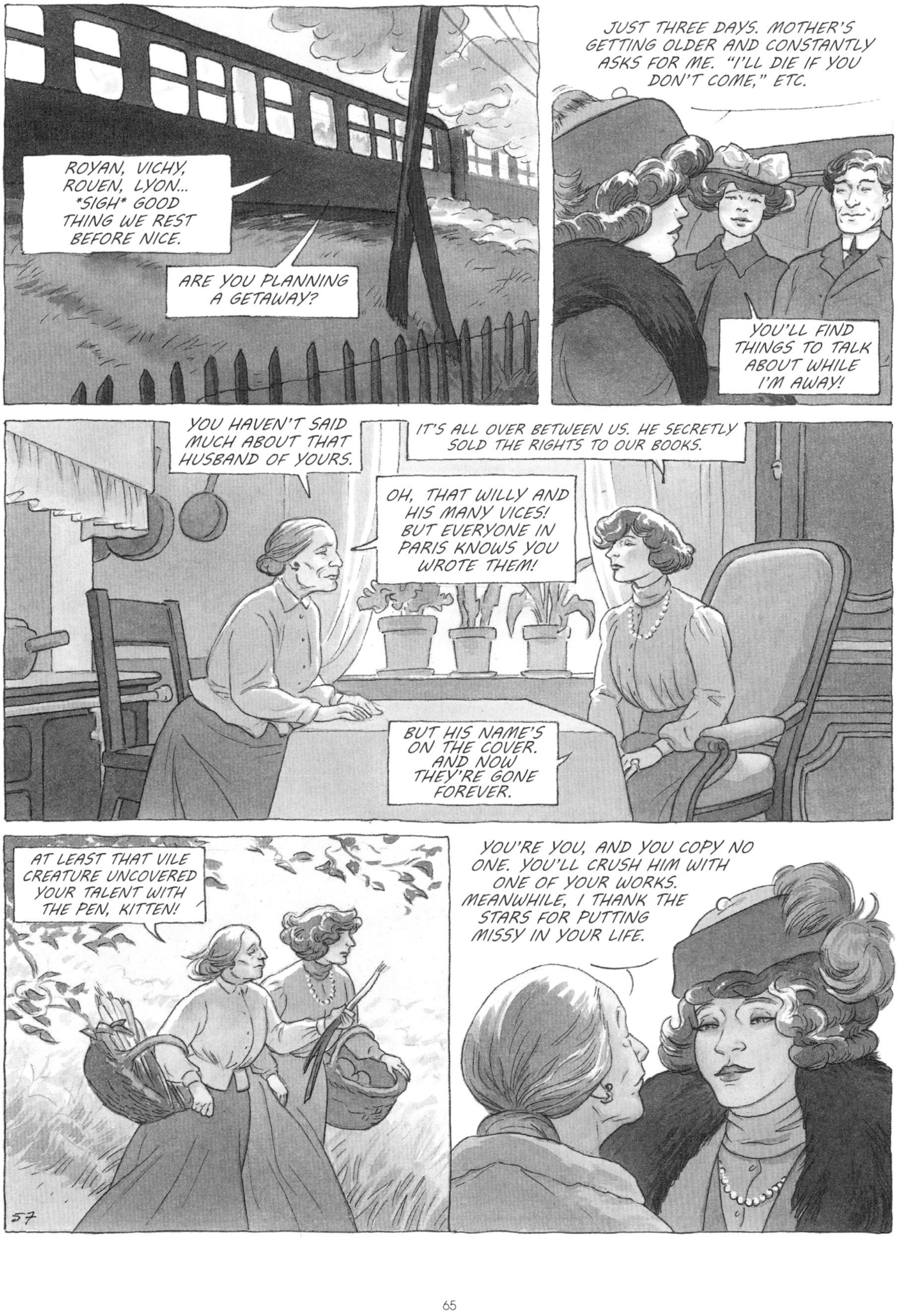
ROYAN, VICHY, ROUEN, LYON... *SIGH* GOOD THING WE REST BEFORE NICE.
ARE YOU PLANNING A GETAWAY?
JUST THREE DAYS. MOTHER'S GETTING OLDER AND CONSTANTLY ASKS FOR ME. "I'LL DIE IF YOU DON'T COME," ETC.
YOU'LL FIND THINGS TO TALK ABOUT WHILE I'M AWAY!
YOU HAVEN'T SAID MUCH ABOUT THAT HUSBAND OF YOURS.
IT'S ALL OVER BETWEEN US. HE SECRETLY SOLD THE RIGHTS TO OUR BOOKS.
OH, THAT WILLY AND HIS MANY VICES! BUT EVERYONE IN PARIS KNOWS YOU WROTE THEM!
BUT HIS NAME'S ON THE COVER. AND NOW THEY'RE GONE FOREVER.
AT LEAST THAT VILE CREATURE UNCOVERED YOUR TALENT WITH THE PEN, KITTEN!
YOU'RE YOU, AND YOU COPY NO ONE. YOU'LL CRUSH HIM WITH ONE OF YOUR WORKS. MEANWHILE, I THANK THE STARS FOR PUTTING MISSY IN YOUR LIFE.
57

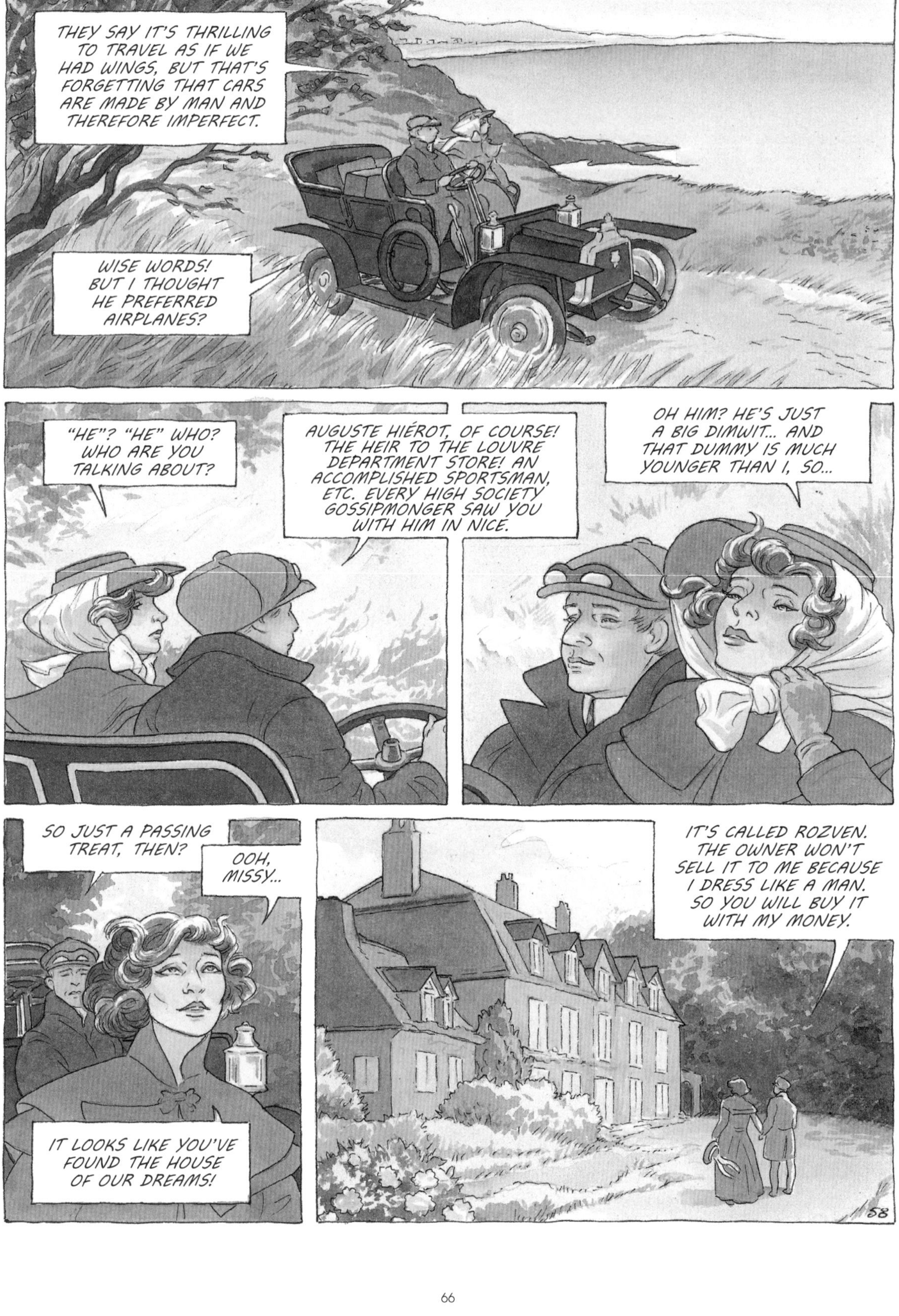
THEY SAY IT'S THRILLING TO TRAVEL AS IF WE HAD WINGS, BUT THAT'S FORGETTING THAT CARS ARE MADE BY MAN AND THEREFORE IMPERFECT.
WISE WORDS! BUT I THOUGHT HE PREFERRED AIRPLANES?
"HE"? "HE" WHO? WHO ARE YOU TALKING ABOUT?
AUGUSTE HIÉROT, OF COURSE! THE HEIR TO THE LOUVRE DEPARTMENT STORE! AN ACCOMPLISHED SPORTSMAN, ETC. EVERY HIGH SOCIETY GOSSIPMONGER SAW YOU WITH HIM IN NICE.
OH HIM? HE'S JUST A BIG DIMWIT... AND THAT DUMMY IS MUCH YOUNGER THAN I, SO...
SO JUST A PASSING TREAT, THEN?
OOH, MISSY...
IT LOOKS LIKE YOU'VE FOUND THE HOUSE OF OUR DREAMS!
IT'S CALLED ROZVEN. THE OWNER WON'T SELL IT TO ME BECAUSE I DRESS LIKE A MAN. SO YOU WILL BUY IT WITH MY MONEY.
58

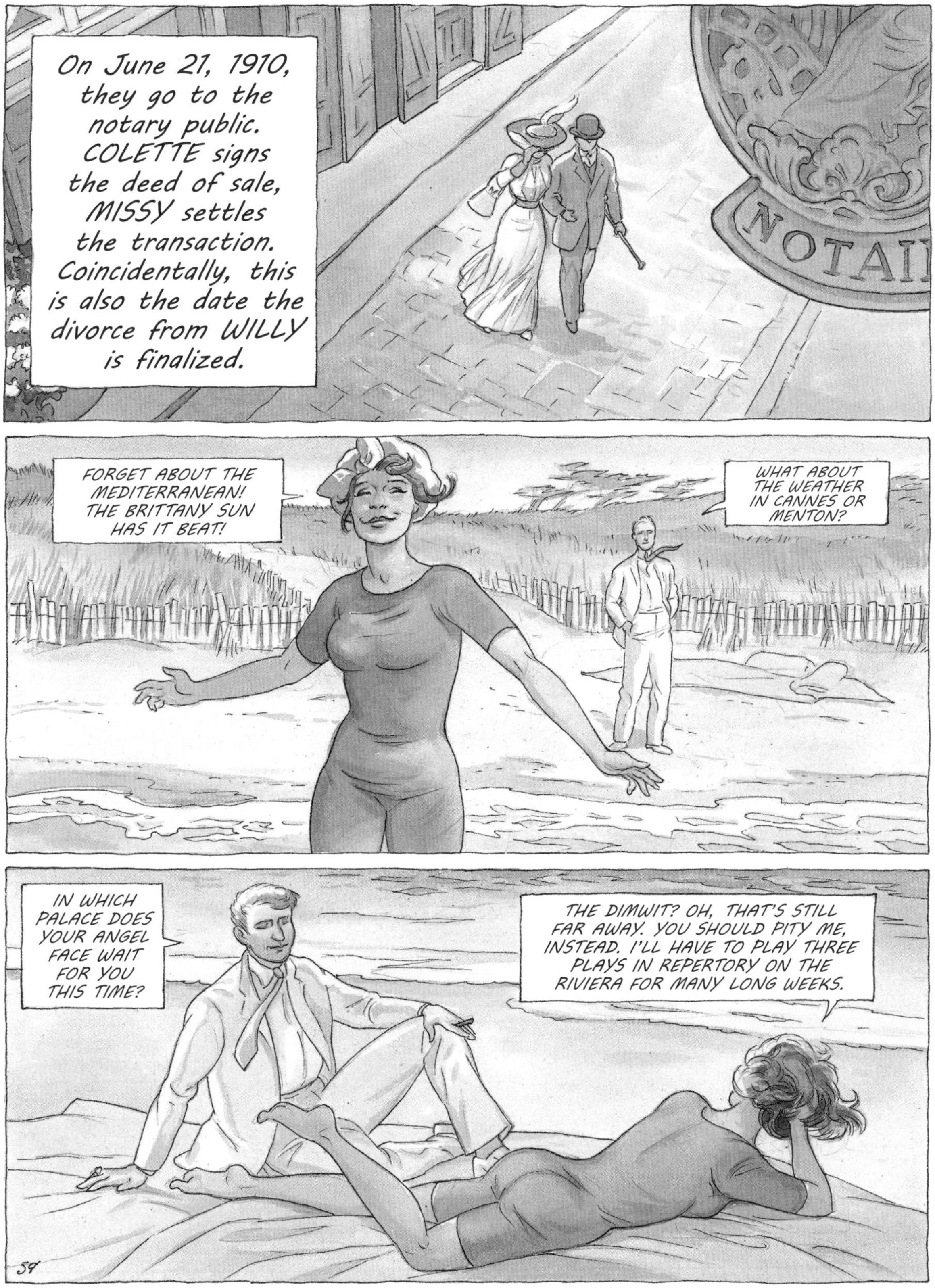
On June 21, 1910, they go to the notary public. COLETTE signs the deed of sale, MISSY settles the transaction. Coincidentally, this is also the date the divorce from WILLY is finalized.
NOTAI
FORGET ABOUT THE MEDITERRANEAN! THE BRITTANY SUN HAS IT BEAT!
WHAT ABOUT THE WEATHER IN CANNES OR MENTON?
IN WHICH PALACE DOES YOUR ANGEL FACE WAIT FOR YOU THIS TIME?
THE DIMWIT? OH, THAT'S STILL FAR AWAY. YOU SHOULD PITY ME, INSTEAD. I'LL HAVE TO PLAY THREE PLAYS IN REPERTORY ON THE RIVIERA FOR MANY LONG WEEKS.

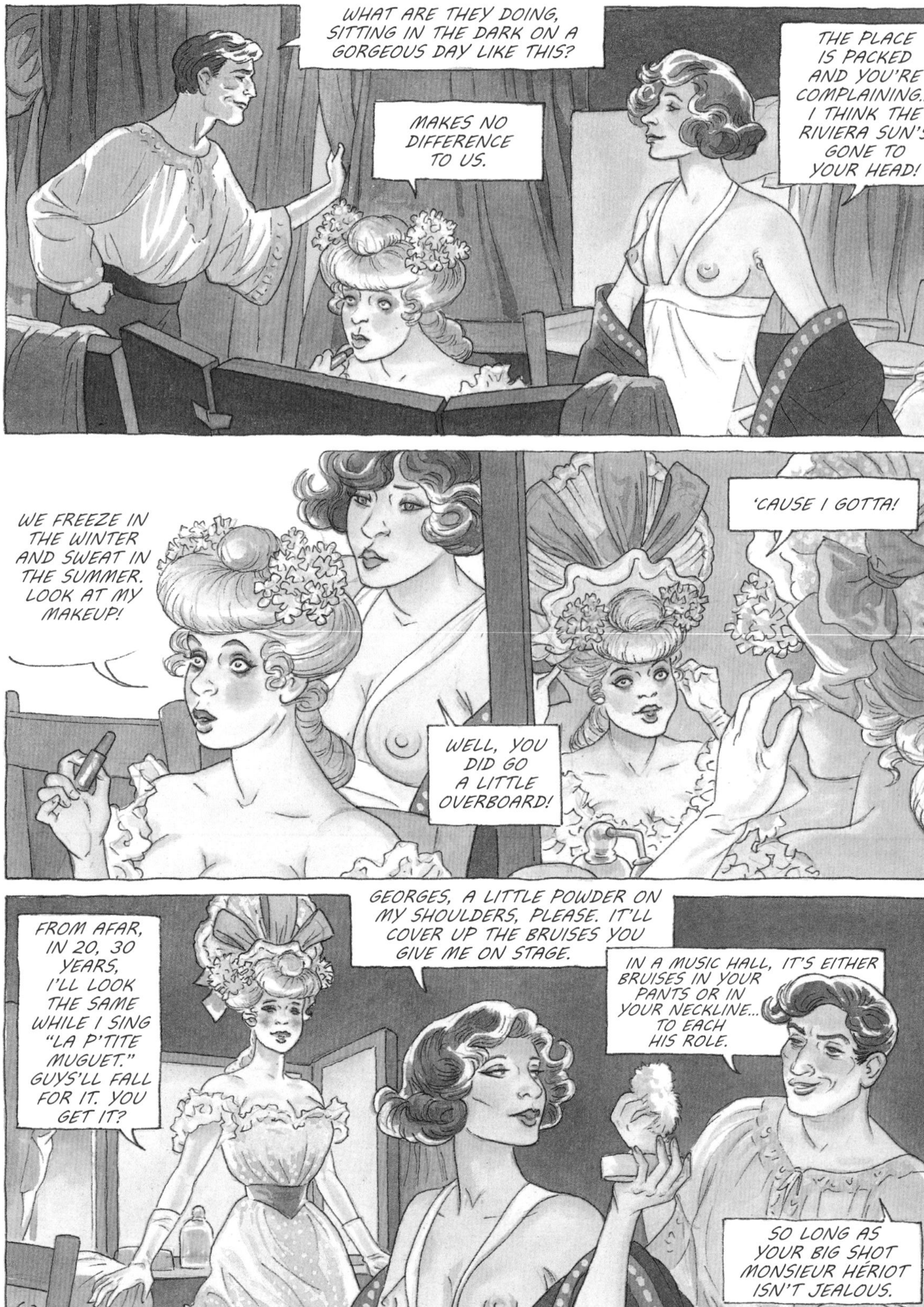
WHAT ARE THEY DOING, SITTING IN THE DARK ON A GORGEOUS DAY LIKE THIS?
MAKES NO DIFFERENCE TO US.
THE PLACE IS PACKED AND YOU'RE COMPLAINING... I THINK THE RIVIERA SUN'S GONE TO YOUR HEAD!
WE FREEZE IN THE WINTER AND SWEAT IN THE SUMMER. LOOK AT MY MAKEUP!
WELL, YOU DID GO A LITTLE OVERBOARD!
'CAUSE I GOTTA!
FROM AFAR, IN 20, 30 YEARS, I'LL LOOK THE SAME WHILE I SING "LA P'TITE MUGUET." GUYS'LL FALL FOR IT. YOU GET IT?
GEORGES, A LITTLE POWDER ON MY SHOULDERS, PLEASE. IT'LL COVER UP THE BRUISES YOU GIVE ME ON STAGE.
IN A MUSIC HALL, IT'S EITHER BRUISES IN YOUR PANTS OR IN YOUR NECKLINE... TO EACH HIS ROLE.
SO LONG AS YOUR BIG SHOT MONSIEUR HÉRIOT ISN'T JEALOUS.
60

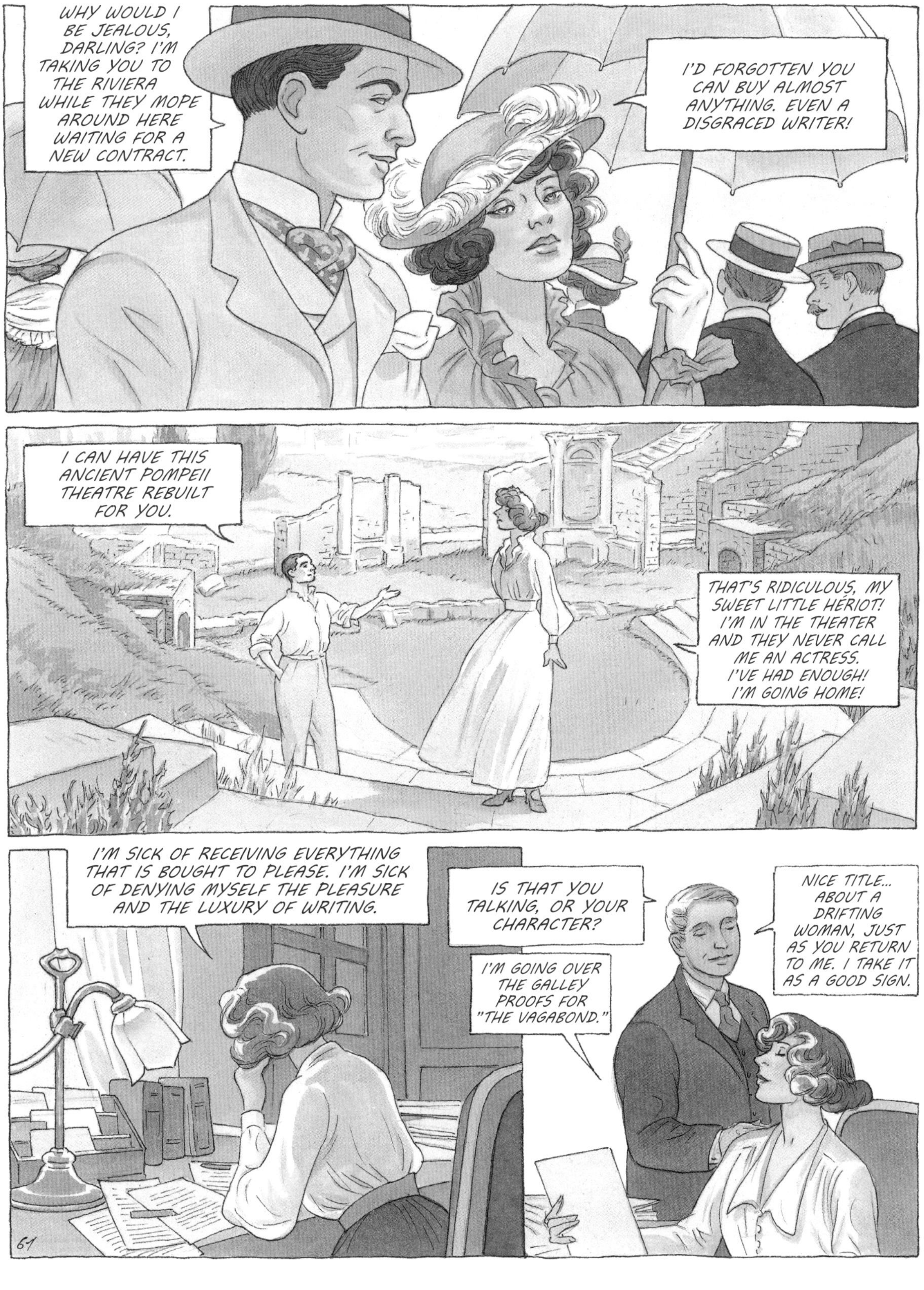
WHY WOULD I BE JEALOUS, DARLING? I'M TAKING YOU TO THE RIVIERA WHILE THEY MOPE AROUND HERE WAITING FOR A NEW CONTRACT.
I'D FORGOTTEN YOU CAN BUY ALMOST ANYTHING. EVEN A DISGRACED WRITER!
I CAN HAVE THIS ANCIENT POMPEII THEATRE REBUILT FOR YOU.
THAT'S RIDICULOUS, MY SWEET LITTLE HÉRIOT! I'M IN THE THEATER AND THEY NEVER CALL ME AN ACTRESS. I'VE HAD ENOUGH! I'M GOING HOME!
I'M SICK OF RECEIVING EVERYTHING THAT IS BOUGHT TO PLEASE. I'M SICK OF DENYING MYSELF THE PLEASURE AND THE LUXURY OF WRITING.
IS THAT YOU TALKING, OR YOUR CHARACTER?
I'M GOING OVER THE GALLEY PROOFS FOR "THE VAGABOND."
NICE TITLE... ABOUT A DRIFTING WOMAN, JUST AS YOU RETURN TO ME. I TAKE IT AS A GOOD SIGN.

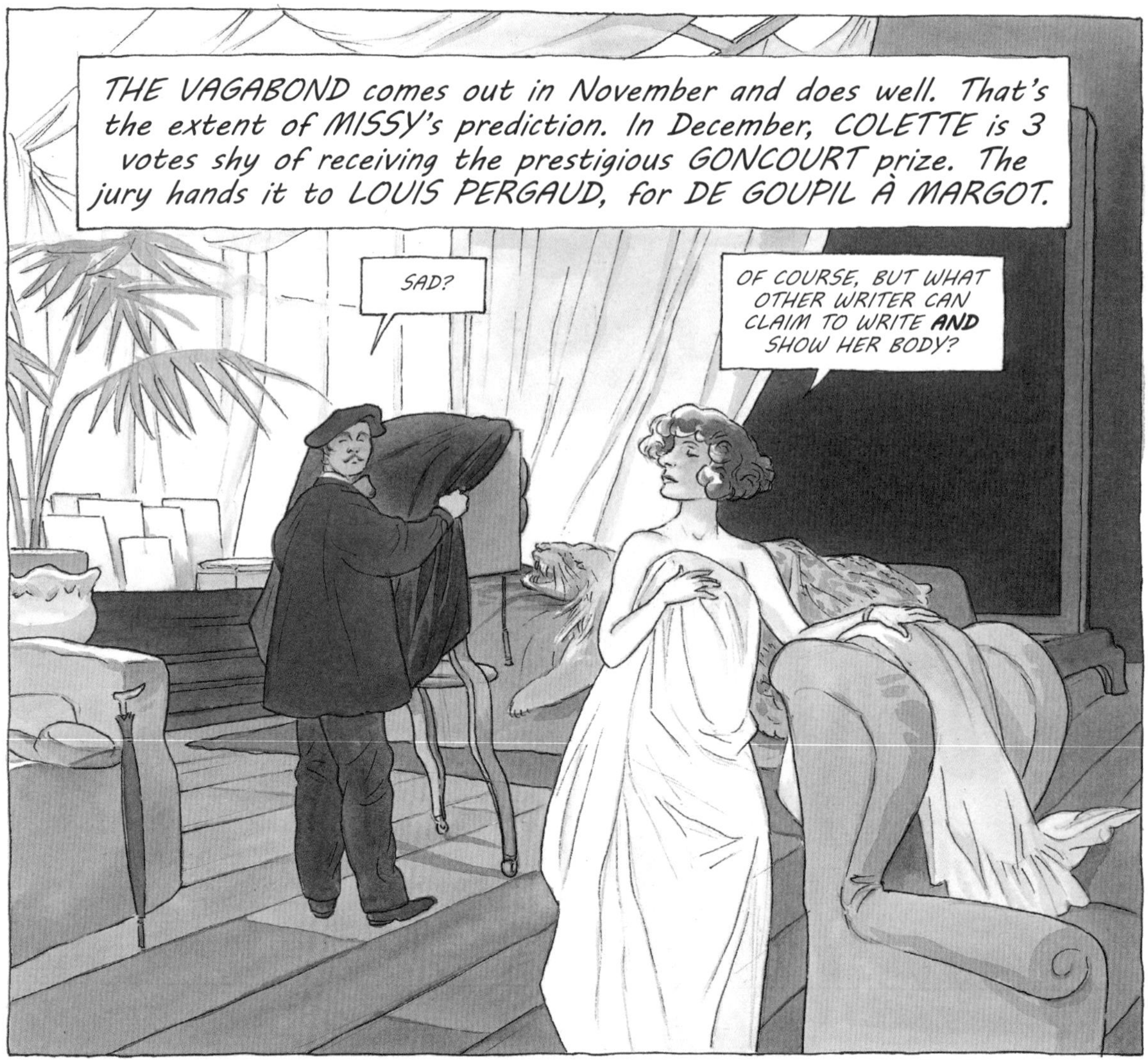
THE VAGABOND comes out in November and does well. That's the extent of MISSY's prediction. In December, COLETTE is 3 votes shy of receiving the prestigious GONCOURT prize. The jury hands it to LOUIS PERGAUD, for DE GOUPIL À MARGOT.
SAD?
OF COURSE, BUT WHAT OTHER WRITER CAN CLAIM TO WRITE **AND** SHOW HER BODY?

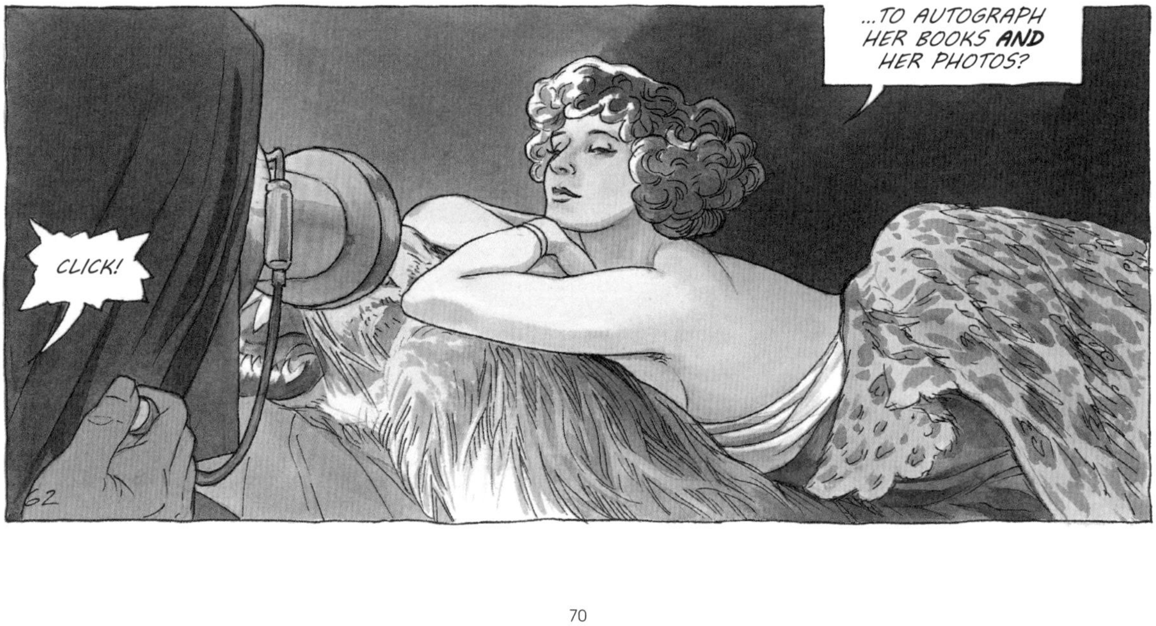
...TO AUTOGRAPH HER BOOKS **AND** HER PHOTOS?
CLICK!

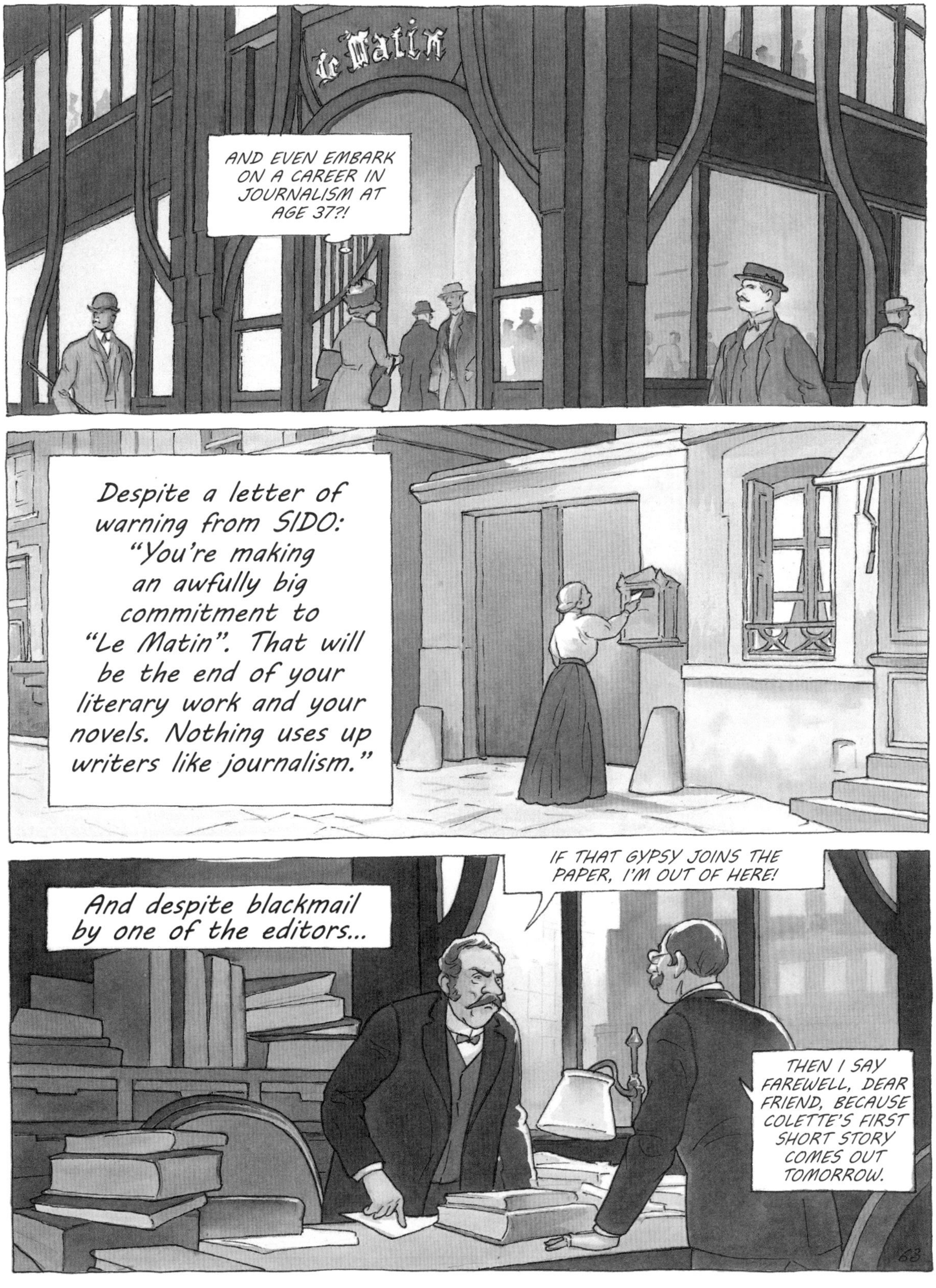
Le Matin
AND EVEN EMBARK ON A CAREER IN JOURNALISM AT AGE 37?!
Despite a letter of warning from SIDO: "You're making an awfully big commitment to "Le Matin". That will be the end of your literary work and your novels. Nothing uses up writers like journalism."
And despite blackmail by one of the editors...
IF THAT GYPSY JOINS THE PAPER, I'M OUT OF HERE!
THEN I SAY FAREWELL, DEAR FRIEND, BECAUSE COLETTE'S FIRST SHORT STORY COMES OUT TOMORROW.
63

But another LE MATIN editor is going to turn COLETTE's life upside down: Baron HENRY de JOUVENEL des URSINS. He's known to have given up politics for journalism and to have a bit of money. And....

...he has two sons BERTRAND, from a brief marriage to CLAIRE BOAS, and RENAUD, from his mistress, ISABELLE DE COMMINGES. Regardless, it's love at first sight.

64

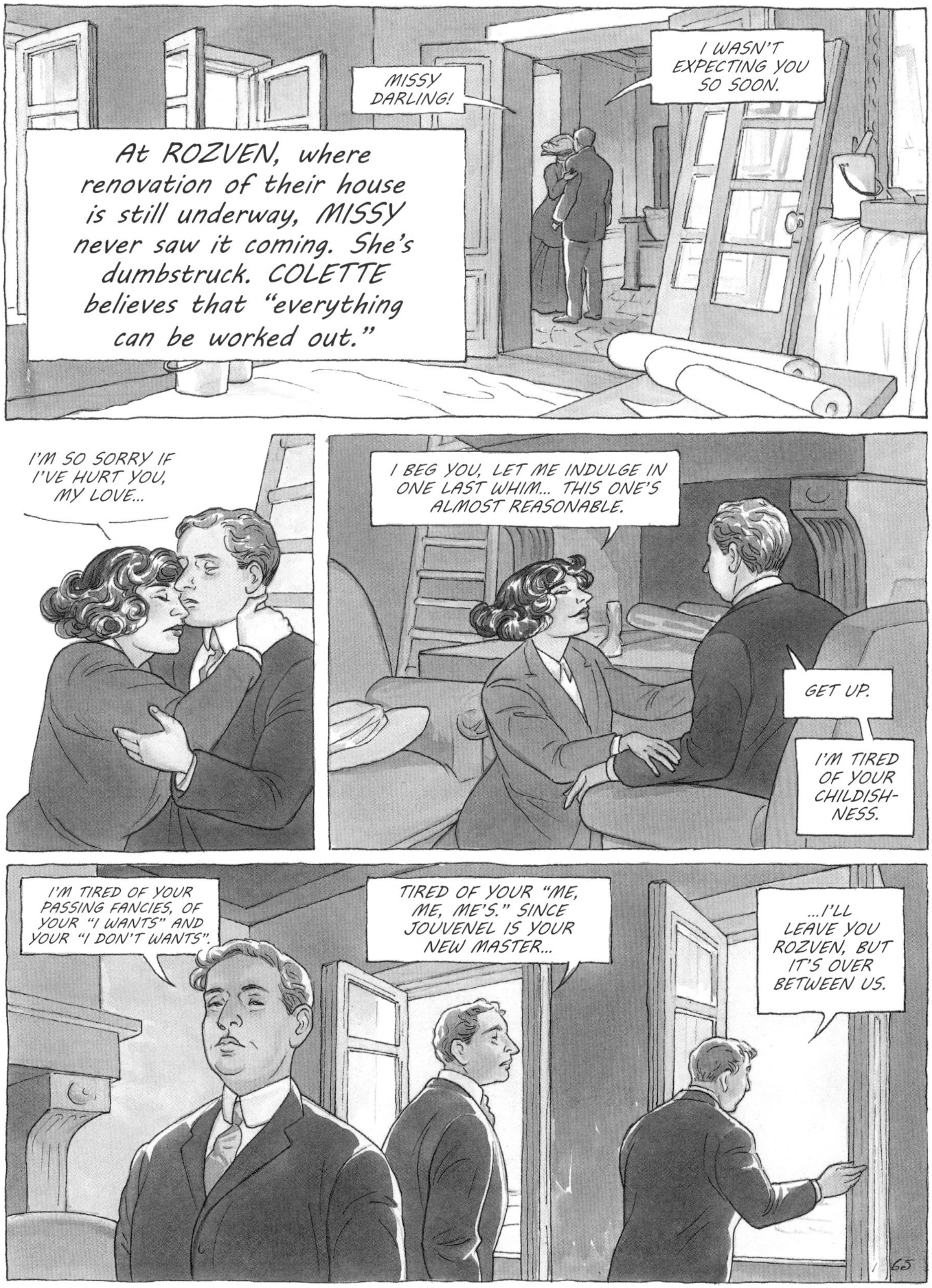
At ROZVEN, where renovation of their house is still underway, MISSY never saw it coming. She's dumbstruck. COLETTE believes that "everything can be worked out."
MISSY DARLING!
I WASN'T EXPECTING YOU SO SOON.
I'M SO SORRY IF I'VE HURT YOU, MY LOVE...
I BEG YOU, LET ME INDULGE IN ONE LAST WHIM... THIS ONE'S ALMOST REASONABLE.
GET UP.
I'M TIRED OF YOUR CHILDISH-NESS.
I'M TIRED OF YOUR PASSING FANCIES, OF YOUR "I WANTS" AND YOUR "I DON'T WANTS".
TIRED OF YOUR "ME, ME, ME'S." SINCE JOUVENEL IS YOUR NEW MASTER...
...I'LL LEAVE YOU ROZVEN, BUT IT'S OVER BETWEEN US.
65

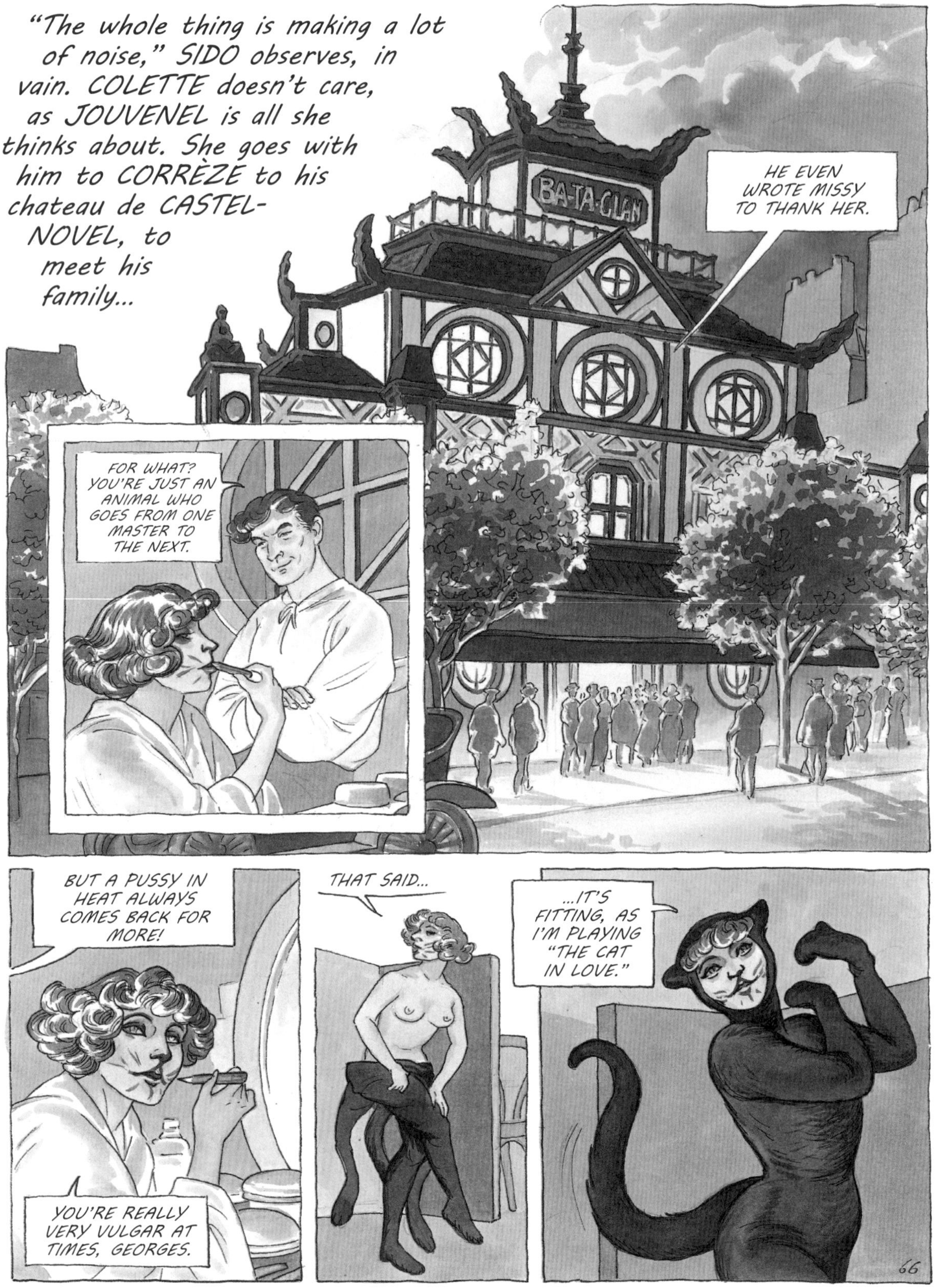
"The whole thing is making a lot of noise," SIDO observes, in vain. COLETTE doesn't care, as JOUVENEL is all she thinks about. She goes with him to CORRÈZE to his chateau de CASTEL-NOVEL, to meet his family...
BA-TA-CLAN
HE EVEN WROTE MISSY TO THANK HER.
FOR WHAT? YOU'RE JUST AN ANIMAL WHO GOES FROM ONE MASTER TO THE NEXT.
BUT A PUSSY IN HEAT ALWAYS COMES BACK FOR MORE!
YOU'RE REALLY VERY VULGAR AT TIMES, GEORGES.
THAT SAID...
...IT'S FITTING, AS I'M PLAYING "THE CAT IN LOVE."
66

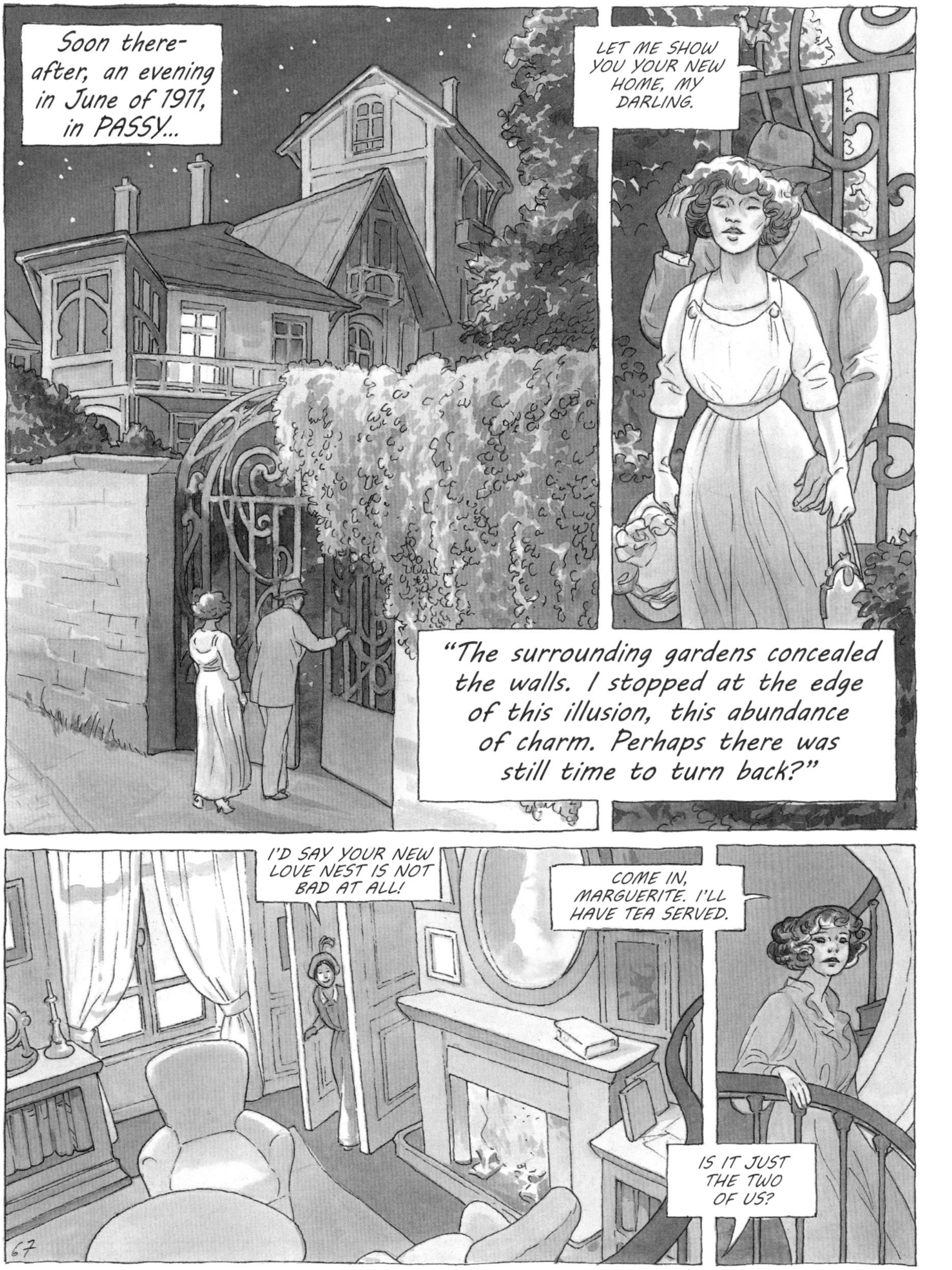

Soon there-after, an evening in June of 1911, in PASSY...
LET ME SHOW YOU YOUR NEW HOME, MY DARLING.
"The surrounding gardens concealed the walls. I stopped at the edge of this illusion, this abundance of charm. Perhaps there was still time to turn back?"
I'D SAY YOUR NEW LOVE NEST IS NOT BAD AT ALL!
COME IN, MARGUERITE. I'LL HAVE TEA SERVED.
IS IT JUST THE TWO OF US?
67

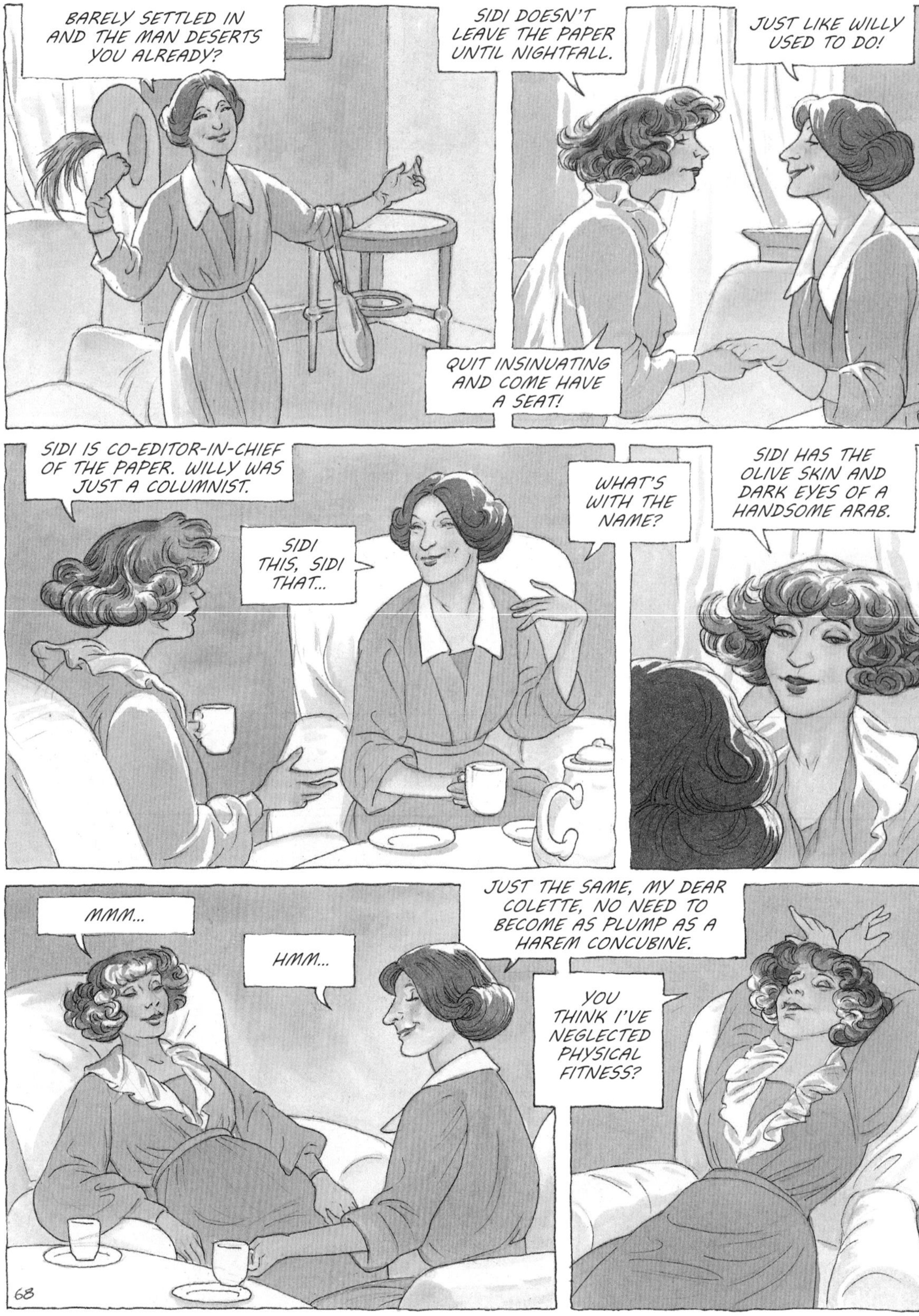
BARELY SETTLED IN AND THE MAN DESERTS YOU ALREADY?
SIDI DOESN'T LEAVE THE PAPER UNTIL NIGHTFALL.
JUST LIKE WILLY USED TO DO!
QUIT INSINUATING AND COME HAVE A SEAT!
SIDI IS CO-EDITOR-IN-CHIEF OF THE PAPER. WILLY WAS JUST A COLUMNIST.
SIDI THIS, SIDI THAT...
WHAT'S WITH THE NAME?
SIDI HAS THE OLIVE SKIN AND DARK EYES OF A HANDSOME ARAB.
MMM...
HMM...
JUST THE SAME, MY DEAR COLETTE, NO NEED TO BECOME AS PLUMP AS A HAREM CONCUBINE.
YOU THINK I'VE NEGLECTED PHYSICAL FITNESS?
68

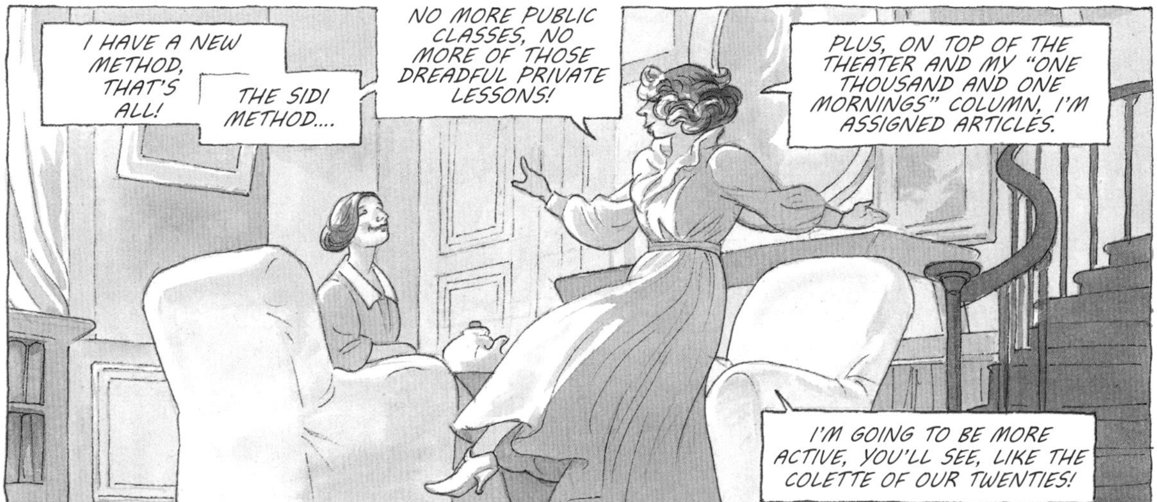
I HAVE A NEW METHOD, THAT'S ALL!
THE SIDI METHOD....
NO MORE PUBLIC CLASSES, NO MORE OF THOSE DREADFUL PRIVATE LESSONS!
PLUS, ON TOP OF THE THEATER AND MY "ONE THOUSAND AND ONE MORNINGS" COLUMN, I'M ASSIGNED ARTICLES.
I'M GOING TO BE MORE ACTIVE, YOU'LL SEE, LIKE THE COLETTE OF OUR TWENTIES!

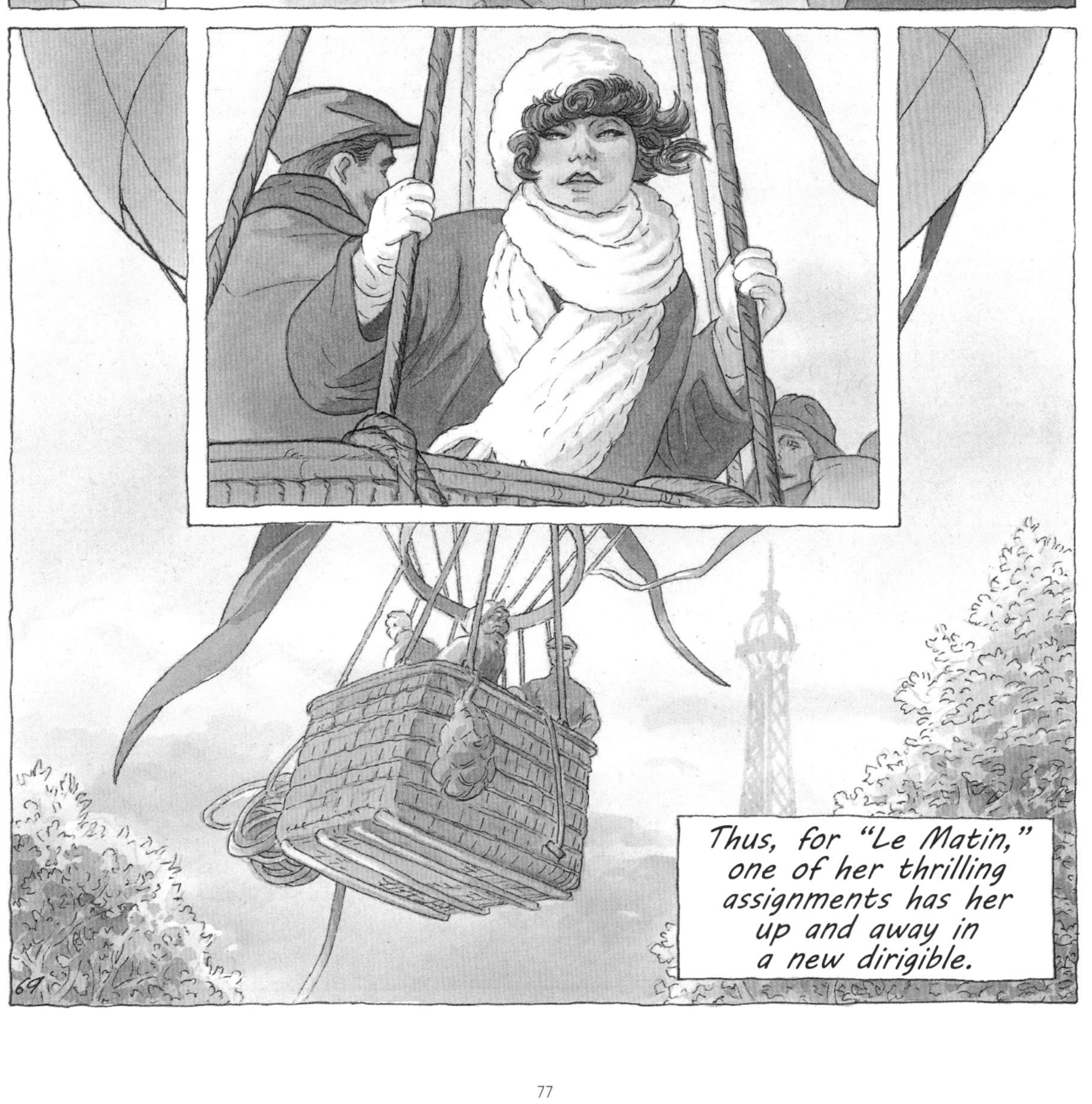
Thus, for "Le Matin," one of her thrilling assignments has her up and away in a new dirigible.
69

In May, the BONNOT gang is captured at their lair in CHOISY-LE-ROI.

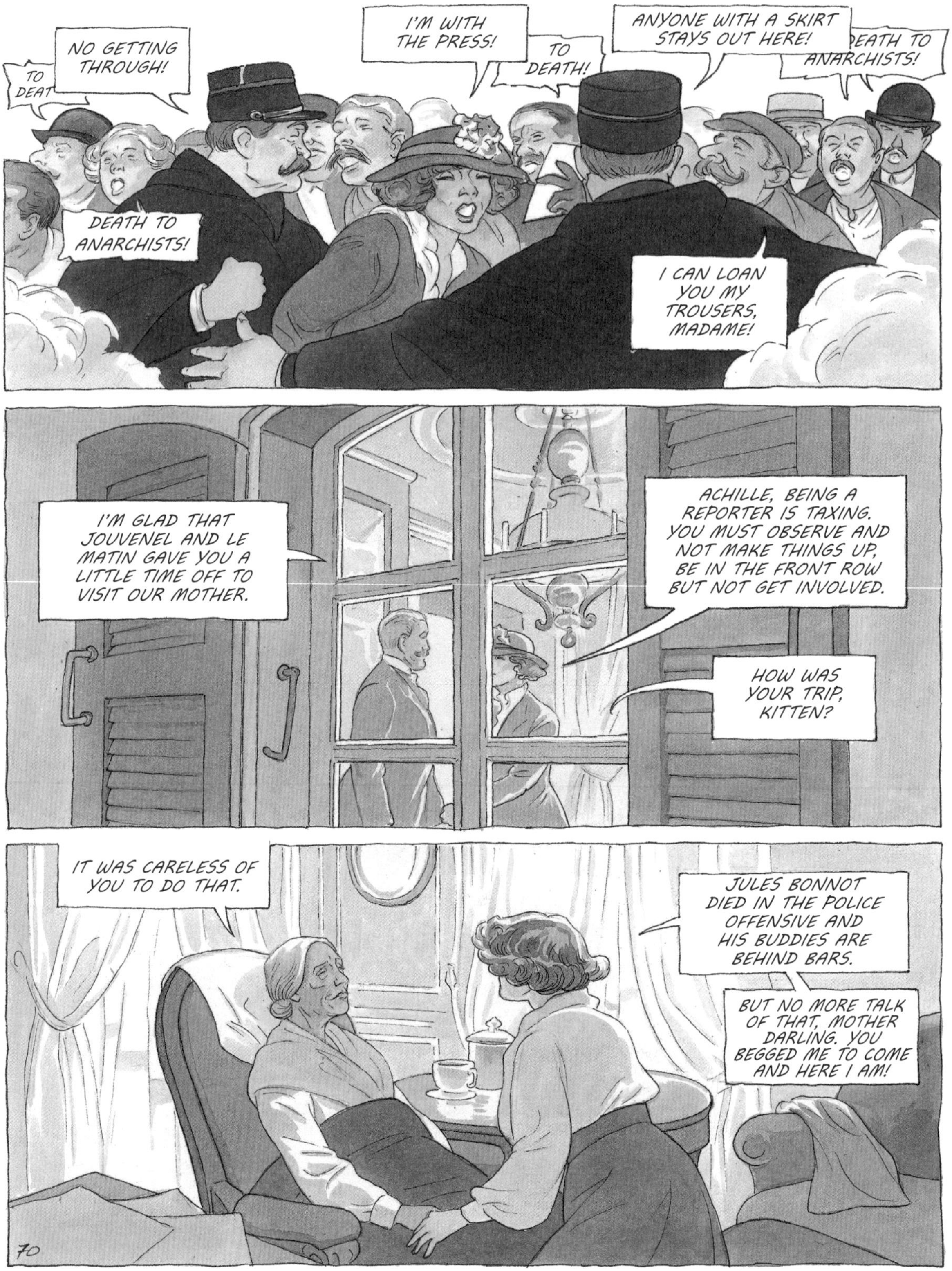
TO DEAT
NO GETTING THROUGH!
I'M WITH THE PRESS!
TO DEATH!
ANYONE WITH A SKIRT STAYS OUT HERE!
EATH TO ANARCHISTS!
DEATH TO ANARCHISTS!
I CAN LOAN YOU MY TROUSERS, MADAME!
I'M GLAD THAT JOUVENEL AND LE MATIN GAVE YOU A LITTLE TIME OFF TO VISIT OUR MOTHER.
ACHILLE, BEING A REPORTER IS TAXING. YOU MUST OBSERVE AND NOT MAKE THINGS UP, BE IN THE FRONT ROW BUT NOT GET INVOLVED.
HOW WAS YOUR TRIP, KITTEN?
IT WAS CARELESS OF YOU TO DO THAT.
JULES BONNOT DIED IN THE POLICE OFFENSIVE AND HIS BUDDIES ARE BEHIND BARS.
BUT NO MORE TALK OF THAT, MOTHER DARLING. YOU BEGGED ME TO COME AND HERE I AM!
70

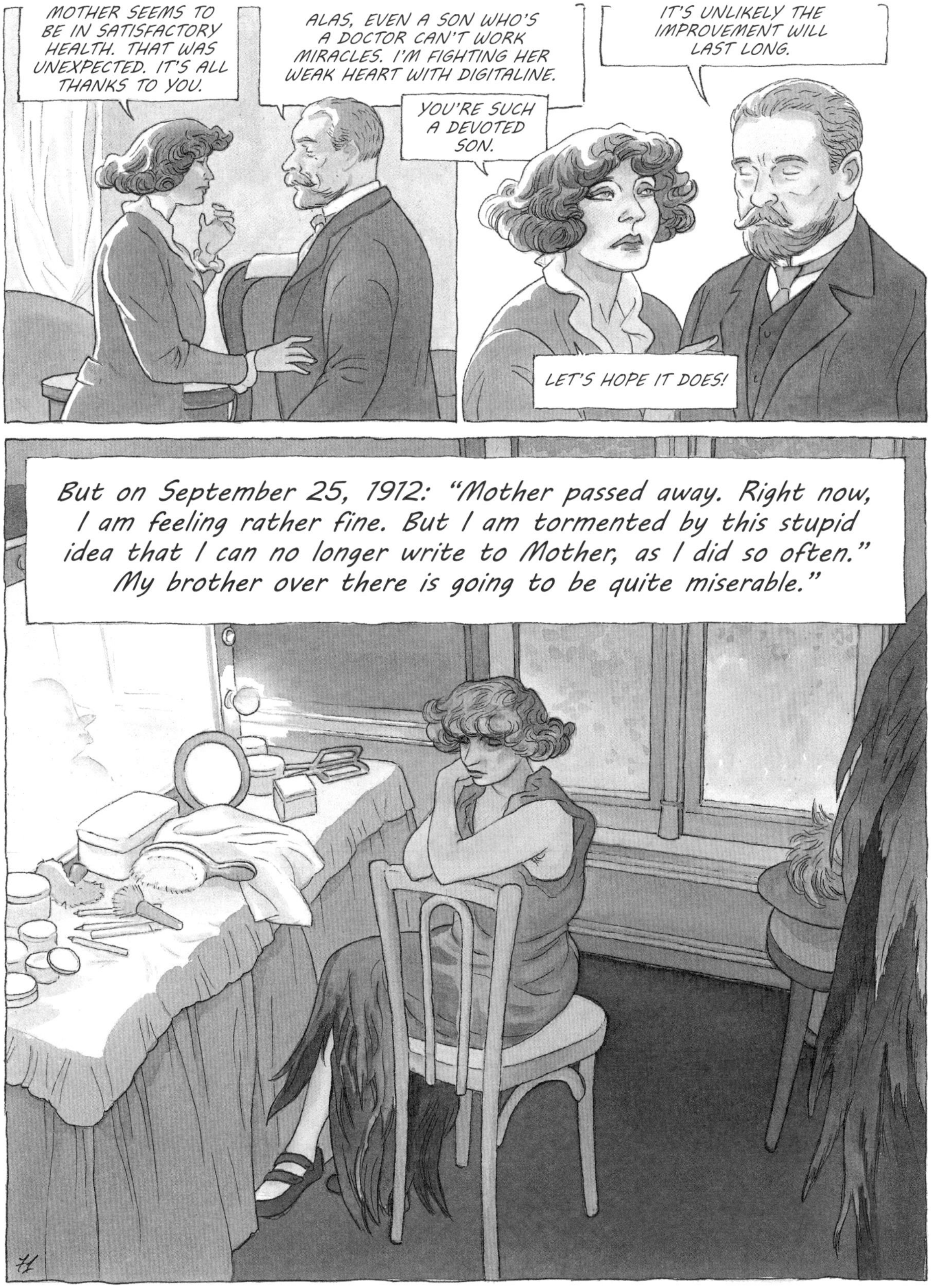

MOTHER SEEMS TO BE IN SATISFACTORY HEALTH. THAT WAS UNEXPECTED. IT'S ALL THANKS TO YOU.
ALAS, EVEN A SON WHO'S A DOCTOR CAN'T WORK MIRACLES. I'M FIGHTING HER WEAK HEART WITH DIGITALINE.
YOU'RE SUCH A DEVOTED SON.
IT'S UNLIKELY THE IMPROVEMENT WILL LAST LONG.
LET'S HOPE IT DOES!
But on September 25, 1912: "Mother passed away. Right now, I am feeling rather fine. But I am tormented by this stupid idea that I can no longer write to Mother, as I did so often." My brother over there is going to be quite miserable."

Her declarations:

"I've only ever wanted to know SIDO alive...

I don't want to go to her funeral or mourn her...

I continue to play The NIGHT BIRD and to live the way I normally do."

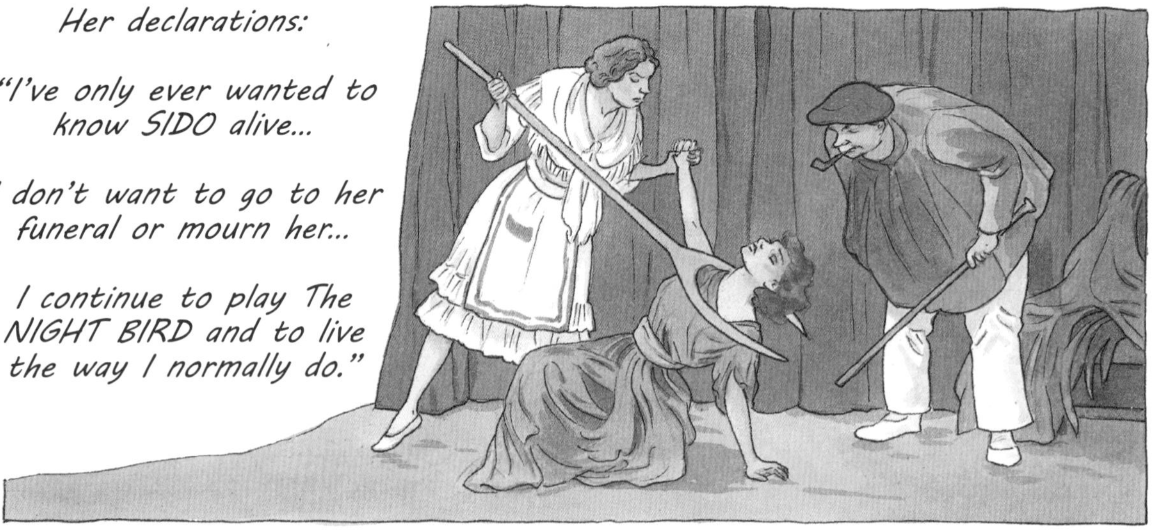

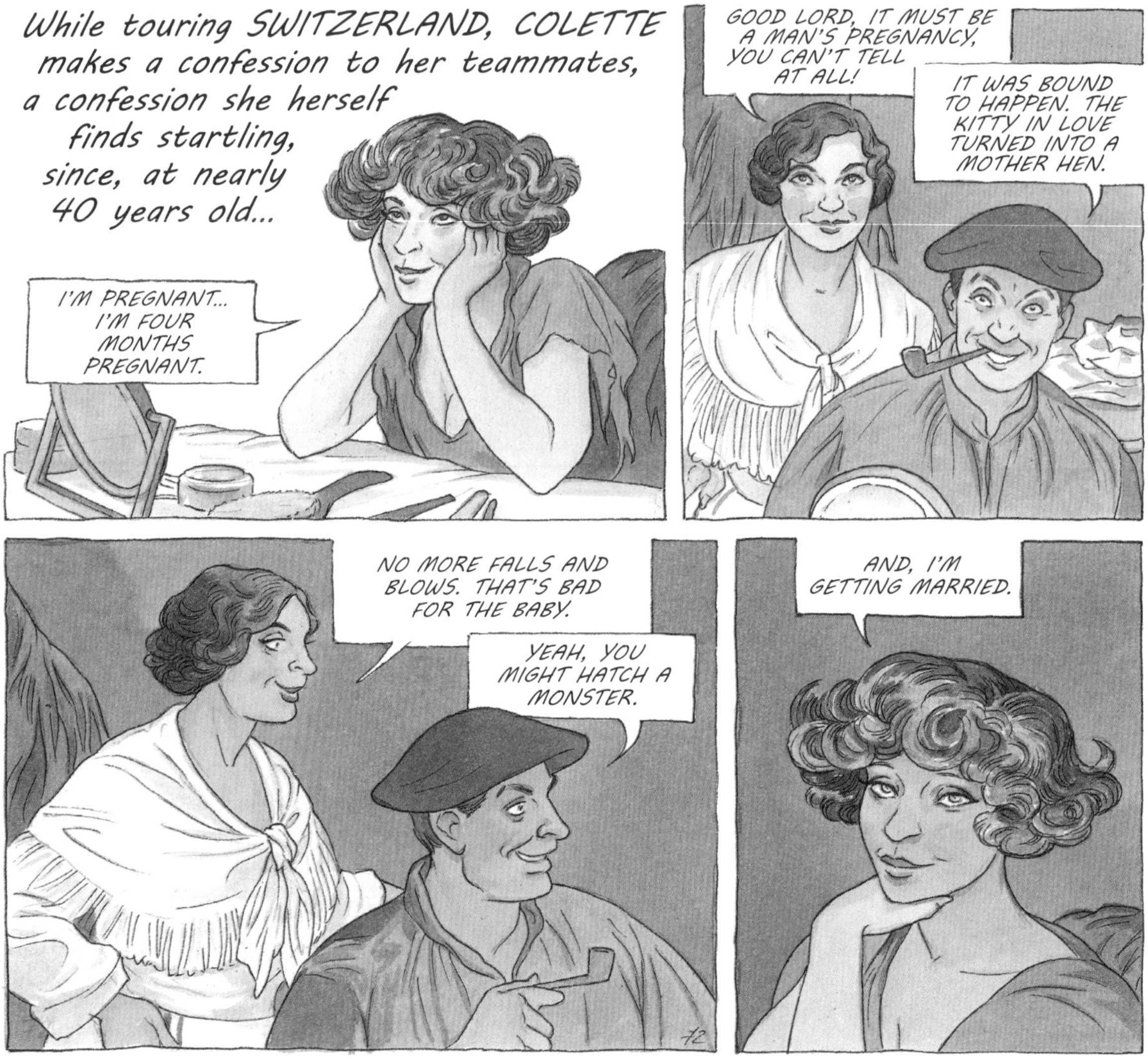
While touring SWITZERLAND, COLETTE makes a confession to her teammates, a confession she herself finds startling, since, at nearly 40 years old...
I'M PREGNANT... I'M FOUR MONTHS PREGNANT.
GOOD LORD, IT MUST BE A MAN'S PREGNANCY, YOU CAN'T TELL AT ALL!
IT WAS BOUND TO HAPPEN. THE KITTY IN LOVE TURNED INTO A MOTHER HEN.
NO MORE FALLS AND BLOWS. THAT'S BAD FOR THE BABY.
YEAH, YOU MIGHT HATCH A MONSTER.
AND, I'M GETTING MARRIED.

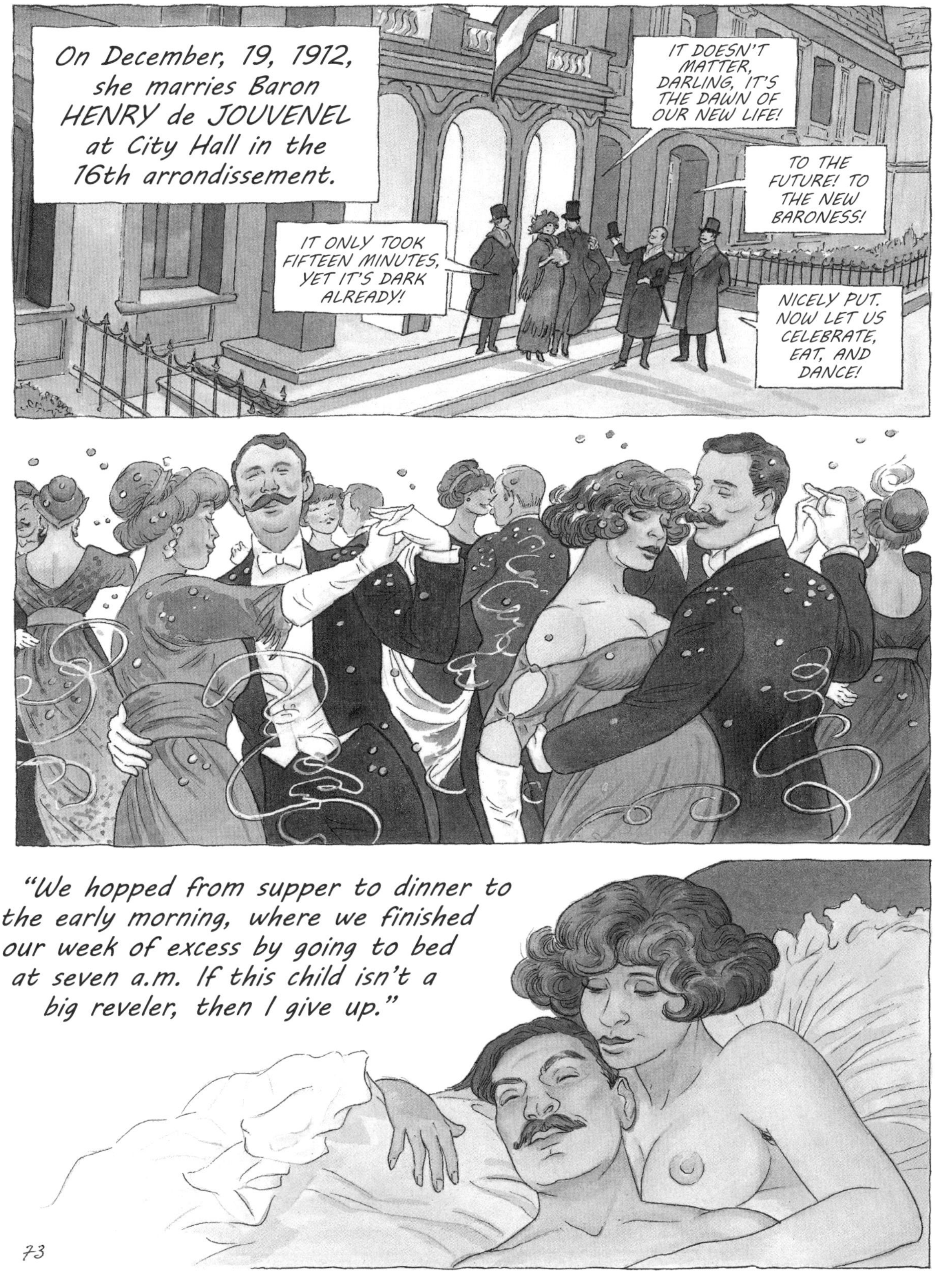
On December, 19, 1912, she marries Baron HENRY de JOUVENEL at City Hall in the 16th arrondissement.
IT ONLY TOOK FIFTEEN MINUTES, YET IT'S DARK ALREADY!
IT DOESN'T MATTER, DARLING, IT'S THE DAWN OF OUR NEW LIFE!
TO THE FUTURE! TO THE NEW BARONESS!
NICELY PUT. NOW LET US CELEBRATE, EAT, AND DANCE!
"We hopped from supper to dinner to the early morning, where we finished our week of excess by going to bed at seven a.m. If this child isn't a big reveler, then I give up."
73

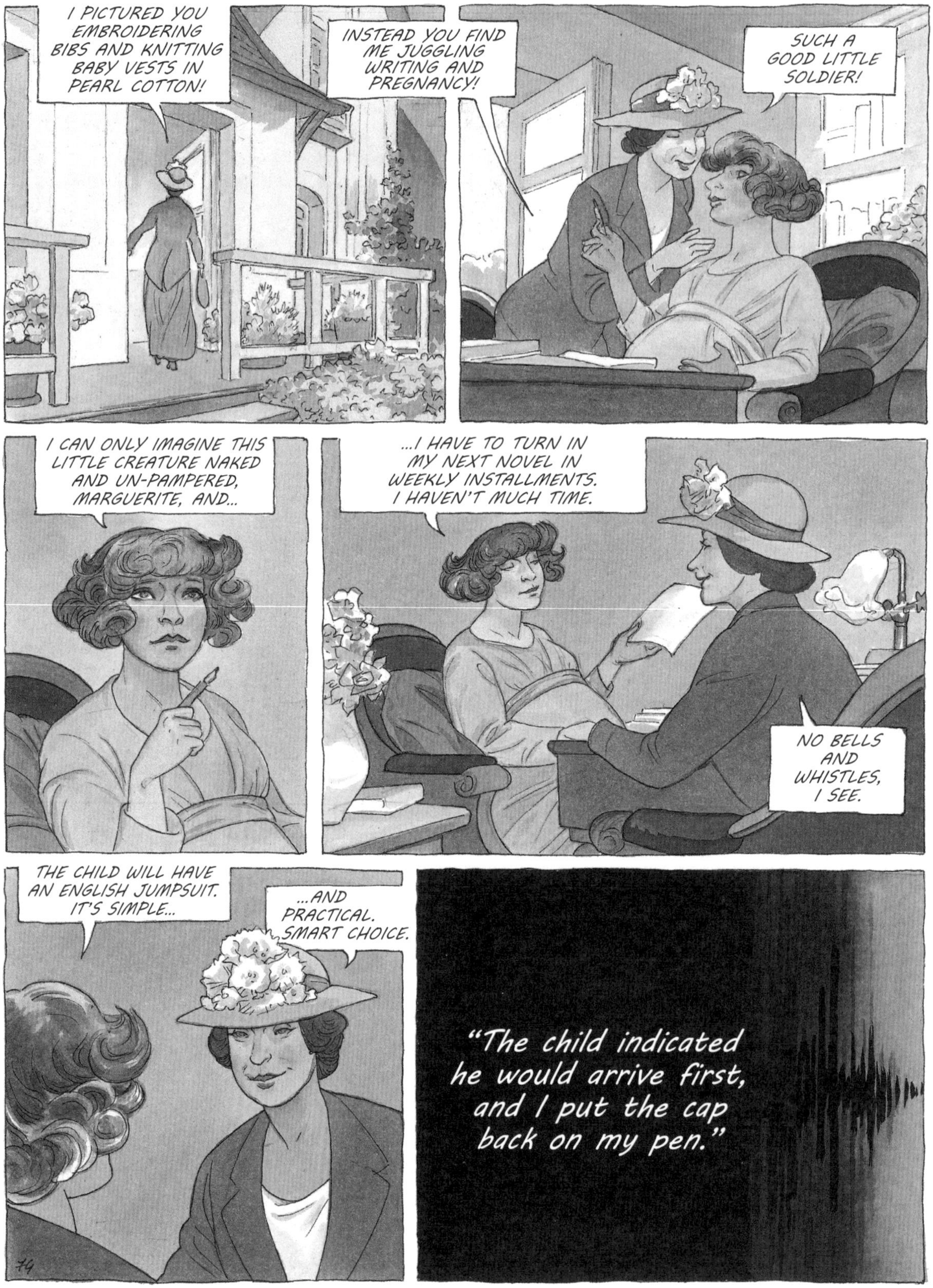
I PICTURED YOU EMBROIDERING BIBS AND KNITTING BABY VESTS IN PEARL COTTON!
INSTEAD YOU FIND ME JUGGLING WRITING AND PREGNANCY!
SUCH A GOOD LITTLE SOLDIER!
I CAN ONLY IMAGINE THIS LITTLE CREATURE NAKED AND UN-PAMPERED, MARGUERITE, AND...
...I HAVE TO TURN IN MY NEXT NOVEL IN WEEKLY INSTALLMENTS. I HAVEN'T MUCH TIME.
NO BELLS AND WHISTLES, I SEE.
THE CHILD WILL HAVE AN ENGLISH JUMPSUIT. IT'S SIMPLE...
...AND PRACTICAL. SMART CHOICE.
"The child indicated he would arrive first, and I put the cap back on my pen."

COLETTE is in labor for 30 hours straight. In the end, the doctor uses chloroform on the mother and forceps on the child.

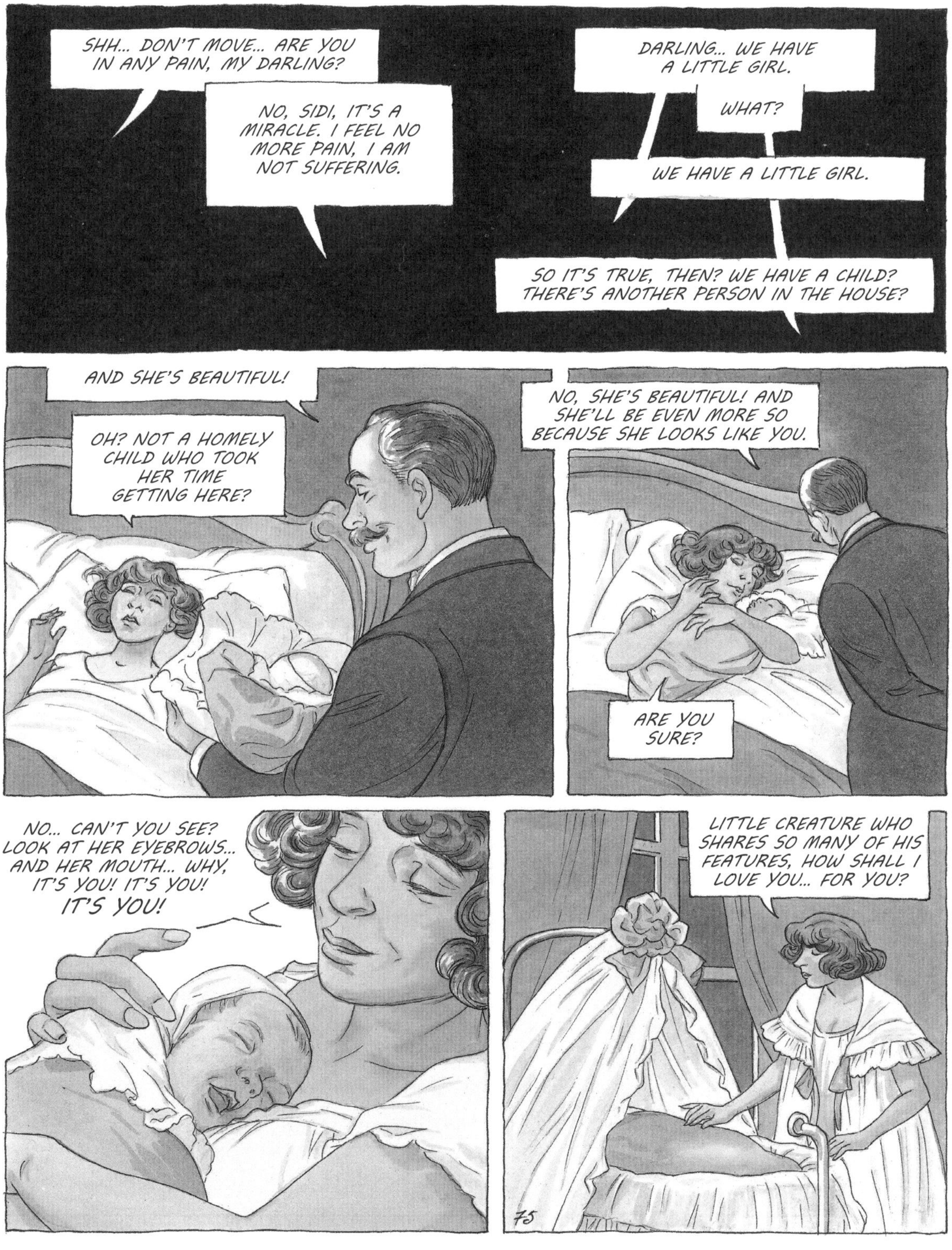
SHH... DON'T MOVE... ARE YOU IN ANY PAIN, MY DARLING?
NO, SIDI, IT'S A MIRACLE. I FEEL NO MORE PAIN, I AM NOT SUFFERING.
DARLING... WE HAVE A LITTLE GIRL.
WHAT?
WE HAVE A LITTLE GIRL.
SO IT'S TRUE, THEN? WE HAVE A CHILD? THERE'S ANOTHER PERSON IN THE HOUSE?
AND SHE'S BEAUTIFUL!
OH? NOT A HOMELY CHILD WHO TOOK HER TIME GETTING HERE?
NO, SHE'S BEAUTIFUL! AND SHE'LL BE EVEN MORE SO BECAUSE SHE LOOKS LIKE YOU.
ARE YOU SURE?
NO... CAN'T YOU SEE? LOOK AT HER EYEBROWS... AND HER MOUTH... WHY, IT'S YOU! IT'S YOU! IT'S YOU!
LITTLE CREATURE WHO SHARES SO MANY OF HIS FEATURES, HOW SHALL I LOVE YOU... FOR YOU?

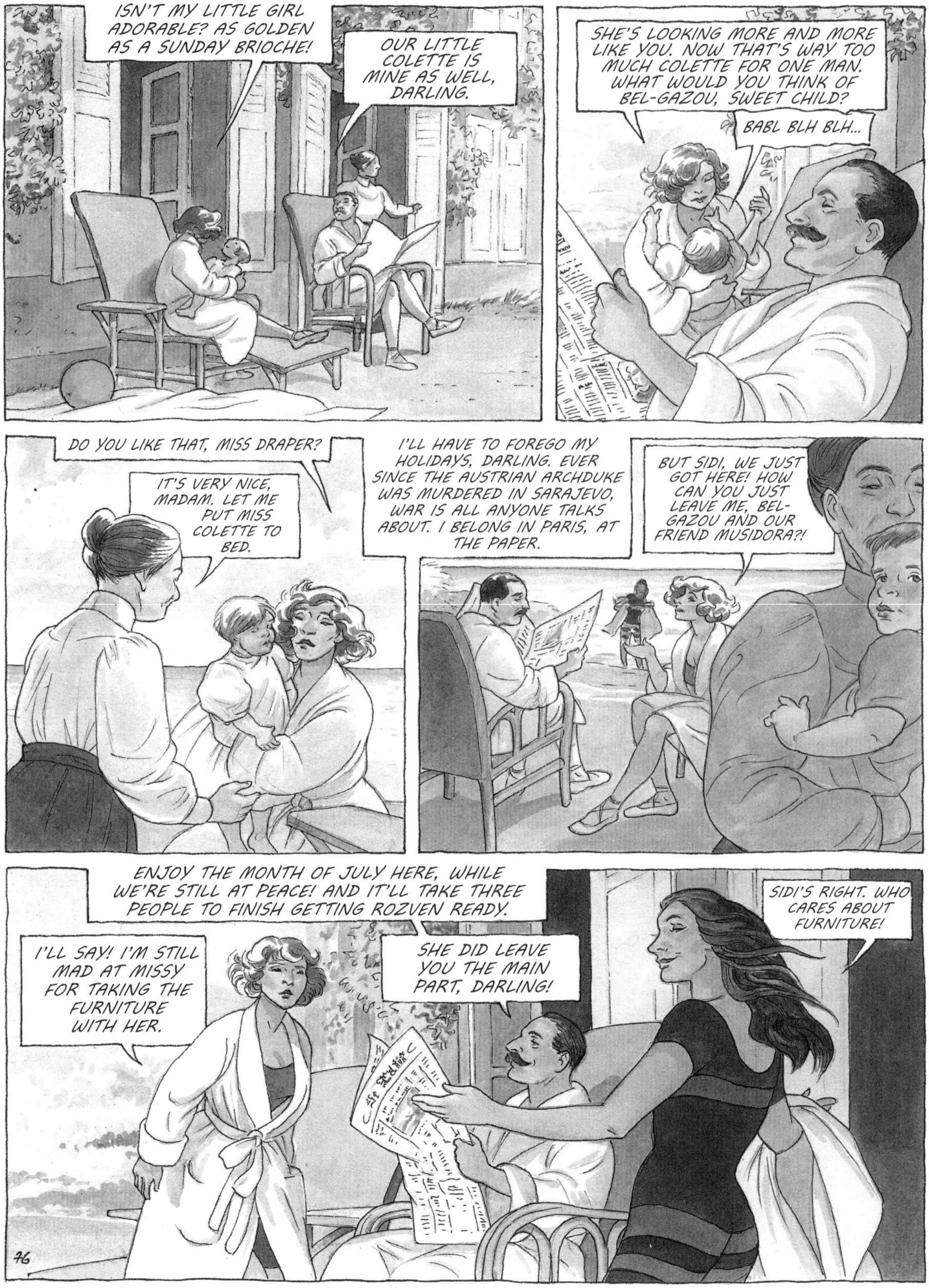
ISN'T MY LITTLE GIRL ADORABLE? AS GOLDEN AS A SUNDAY BRIOCHE!
OUR LITTLE COLETTE IS MINE AS WELL, DARLING.
SHE'S LOOKING MORE AND MORE LIKE YOU. NOW THAT'S WAY TOO MUCH COLETTE FOR ONE MAN. WHAT WOULD YOU THINK OF BEL-GAZOU, SWEET CHILD?
BABL BLH BLH...
DO YOU LIKE THAT, MISS DRAPER?
IT'S VERY NICE, MADAM. LET ME PUT MISS COLETTE TO BED.
I'LL HAVE TO FOREGO MY HOLIDAYS, DARLING. EVER SINCE THE AUSTRIAN ARCHDUKE WAS MURDERED IN SARAJEVO, WAR IS ALL ANYONE TALKS ABOUT. I BELONG IN PARIS, AT THE PAPER.
BUT SIDI, WE JUST GOT HERE! HOW CAN YOU JUST LEAVE ME, BEL-GAZOU AND OUR FRIEND MUSIDORA?!
ENJOY THE MONTH OF JULY HERE, WHILE WE'RE STILL AT PEACE! AND IT'LL TAKE THREE PEOPLE TO FINISH GETTING ROZVEN READY.
I'LL SAY! I'M STILL MAD AT MISSY FOR TAKING THE FURNITURE WITH HER.
SHE DID LEAVE YOU THE MAIN PART, DARLING!
SIDI'S RIGHT. WHO CARES ABOUT FURNITURE!
46

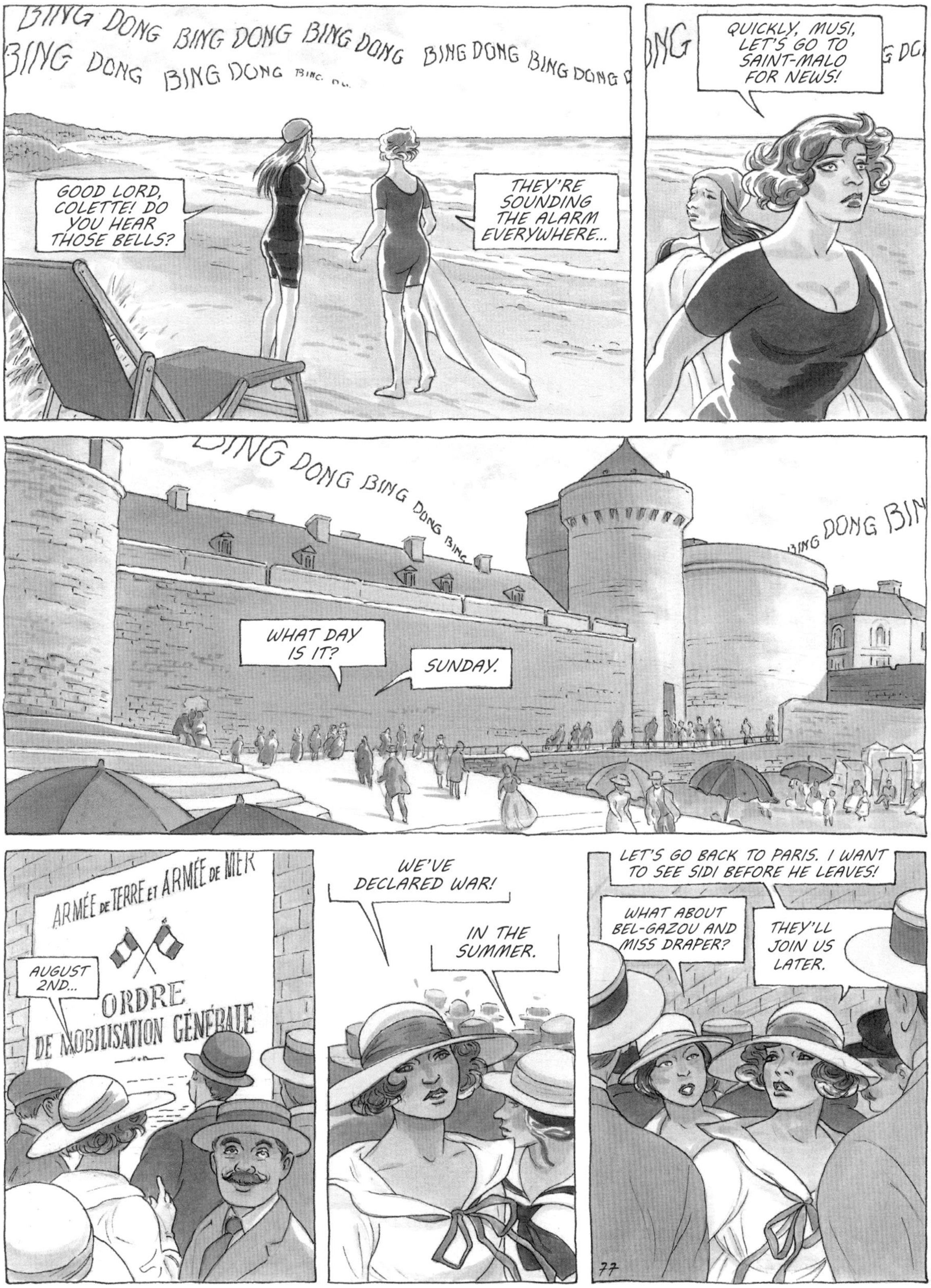
BING DONG BING DONG BING DONG BING DONG BING DONG
BING DONG BING DONG
GOOD LORD, COLETTE! DO YOU HEAR THOSE BELLS?
THEY'RE SOUNDING THE ALARM EVERYWHERE...
QUICKLY, MUSI, LET'S GO TO SAINT-MALO FOR NEWS!
DONG BING DONG BING
BING DONG BIN
WHAT DAY IS IT?
SUNDAY.
ARMÉE DE TERRE ET ARMÉE DE MER
ORDRE DE MOBILISATION GÉNÉRALE
AUGUST 2ND...
WE'VE DECLARED WAR!
IN THE SUMMER.
LET'S GO BACK TO PARIS. I WANT TO SEE SIDI BEFORE HE LEAVES!
WHAT ABOUT BEL-GAZOU AND MISS DRAPER?
THEY'LL JOIN US LATER.
77

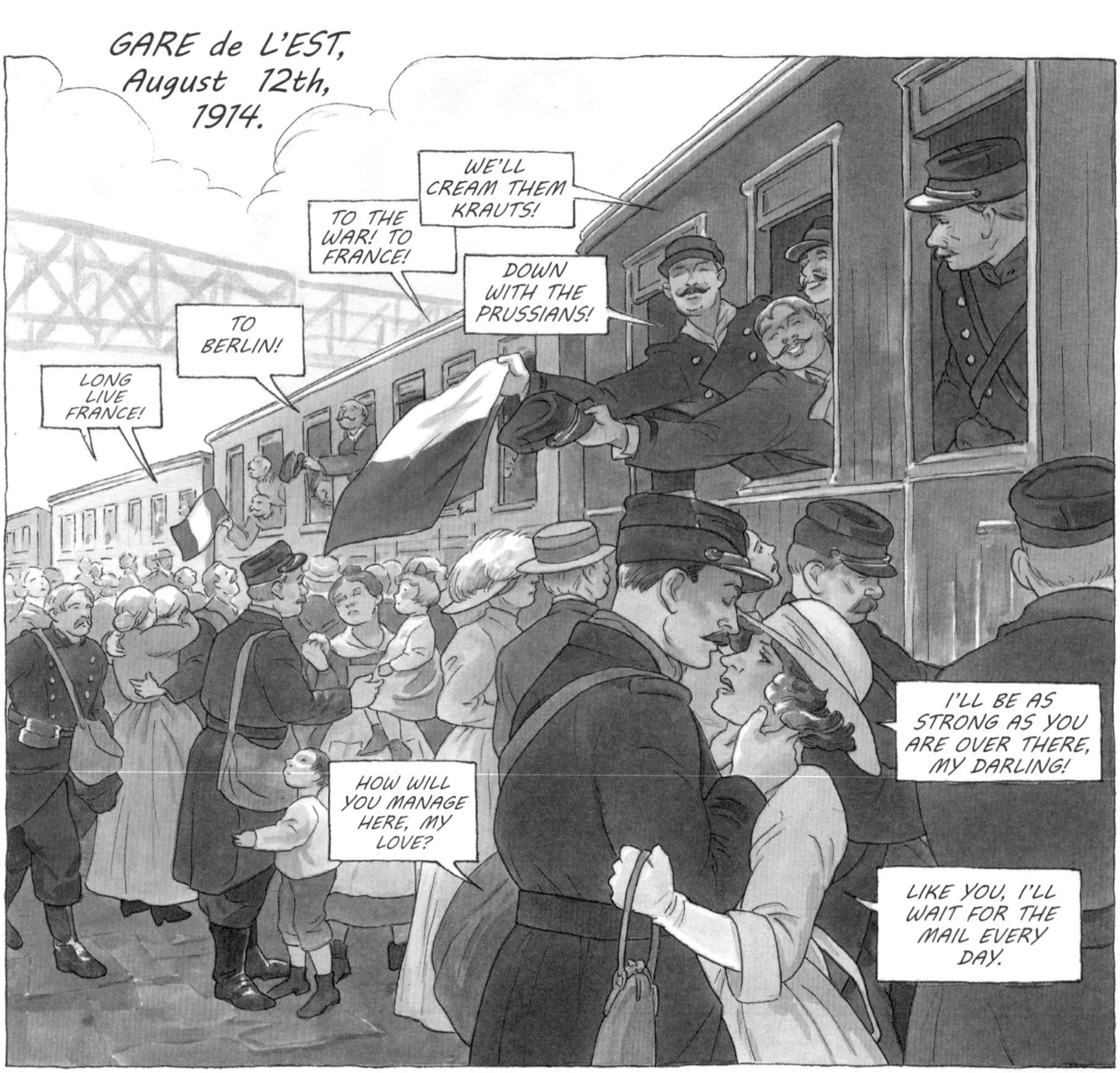
GARE de L'EST, August 12th, 1914.
WE'LL CREAM THEM KRAUTS!
TO THE WAR! TO FRANCE!
DOWN WITH THE PRUSSIANS!
TO BERLIN!
LONG LIVE FRANCE!
I'LL BE AS STRONG AS YOU ARE OVER THERE, MY DARLING!
HOW WILL YOU MANAGE HERE, MY LOVE?
LIKE YOU, I'LL WAIT FOR THE MAIL EVERY DAY.

And I'll ask my girlfriends to pull together our meager resources.

Launched out of bravado, the idea takes the shape of a utopian community made up of MARGUERITE, MORENO and MUSIDORA, both actresses, and writer ANNIE de PÈNE at COLETTE's place in PASSY.

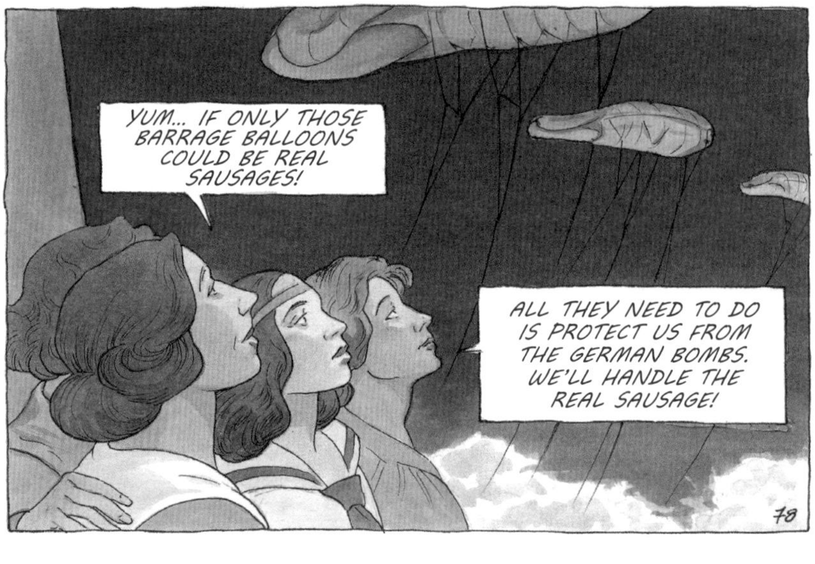
YUM... IF ONLY THOSE BARRAGE BALLOONS COULD BE REAL SAUSAGES!
ALL THEY NEED TO DO IS PROTECT US FROM THE GERMAN BOMBS. WE'LL HANDLE THE REAL SAUSAGE!
78

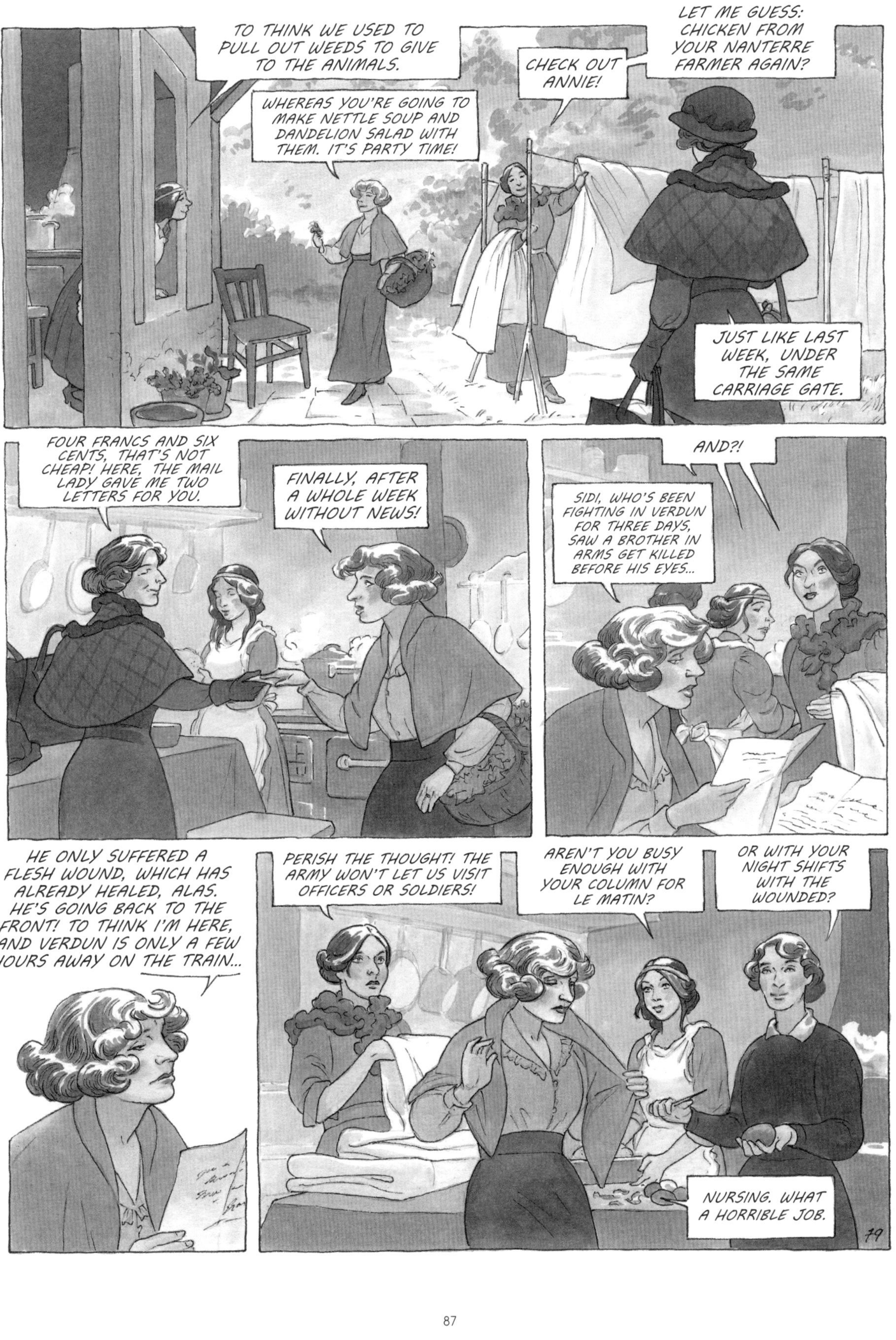

TO THINK WE USED TO PULL OUT WEEDS TO GIVE TO THE ANIMALS.
WHEREAS YOU'RE GOING TO MAKE NETTLE SOUP AND DANDELION SALAD WITH THEM. IT'S PARTY TIME!
CHECK OUT ANNIE!
LET ME GUESS: CHICKEN FROM YOUR NANTERRE FARMER AGAIN?
JUST LIKE LAST WEEK, UNDER THE SAME CARRIAGE GATE.
FOUR FRANCS AND SIX CENTS, THAT'S NOT CHEAP! HERE, THE MAIL LADY GAVE ME TWO LETTERS FOR YOU.
FINALLY, AFTER A WHOLE WEEK WITHOUT NEWS!
AND?!
SIDI, WHO'S BEEN FIGHTING IN VERDUN FOR THREE DAYS, SAW A BROTHER IN ARMS GET KILLED BEFORE HIS EYES...
HE ONLY SUFFERED A FLESH WOUND, WHICH HAS ALREADY HEALED, ALAS. HE'S GOING BACK TO THE FRONT! TO THINK I'M HERE, AND VERDUN IS ONLY A FEW HOURS AWAY ON THE TRAIN...
PERISH THE THOUGHT! THE ARMY WON'T LET US VISIT OFFICERS OR SOLDIERS!
AREN'T YOU BUSY ENOUGH WITH YOUR COLUMN FOR LE MATIN?
OR WITH YOUR NIGHT SHIFTS WITH THE WOUNDED?
NURSING. WHAT A HORRIBLE JOB.
79

The JANSON-de-SAILLY high school, turned into a military hospital...

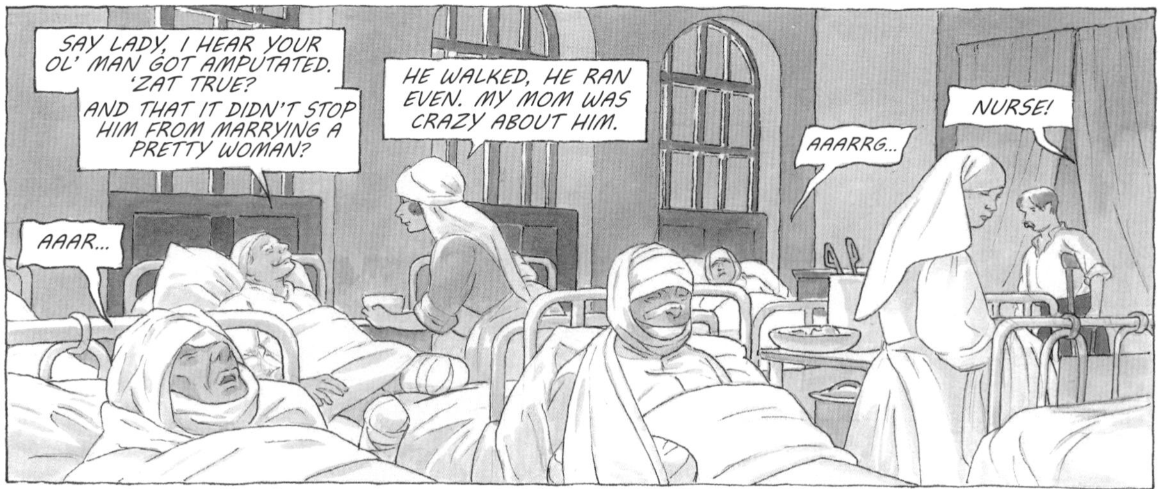
SAY LADY, I HEAR YOUR OL' MAN GOT AMPUTATED. 'ZAT TRUE?
AND THAT IT DIDN'T STOP HIM FROM MARRYING A PRETTY WOMAN?
HE WALKED, HE RAN EVEN. MY MOM WAS CRAZY ABOUT HIM.
AAARRG...
NURSE!
AAAR...

"I haven't seen SIDI in 64 days!" A fake name, borrowed papers and a 13-hour journey later, despite heavy fire between CHÂLONS and VERDUN...

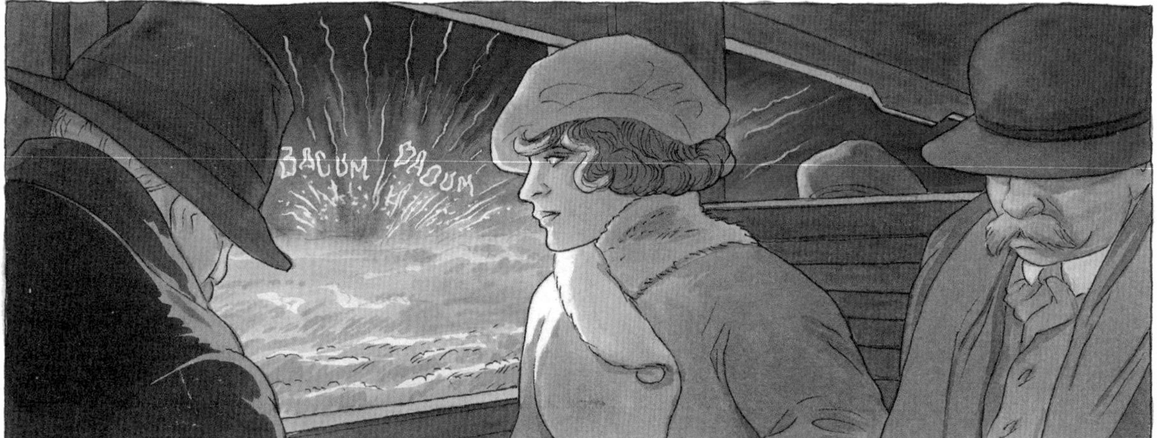
BAOUM
BAOUM

...she is reunited with SIDI in the home of second lieutenant LAMARQUE and his wife LOUISE.

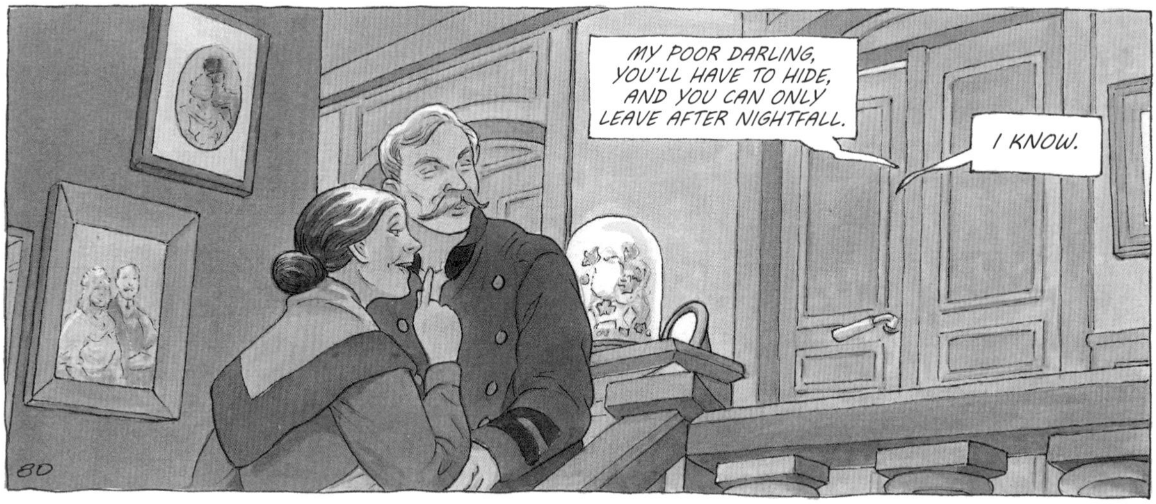
MY POOR DARLING, YOU'LL HAVE TO HIDE, AND YOU CAN ONLY LEAVE AFTER NIGHTFALL.
I KNOW.
BD

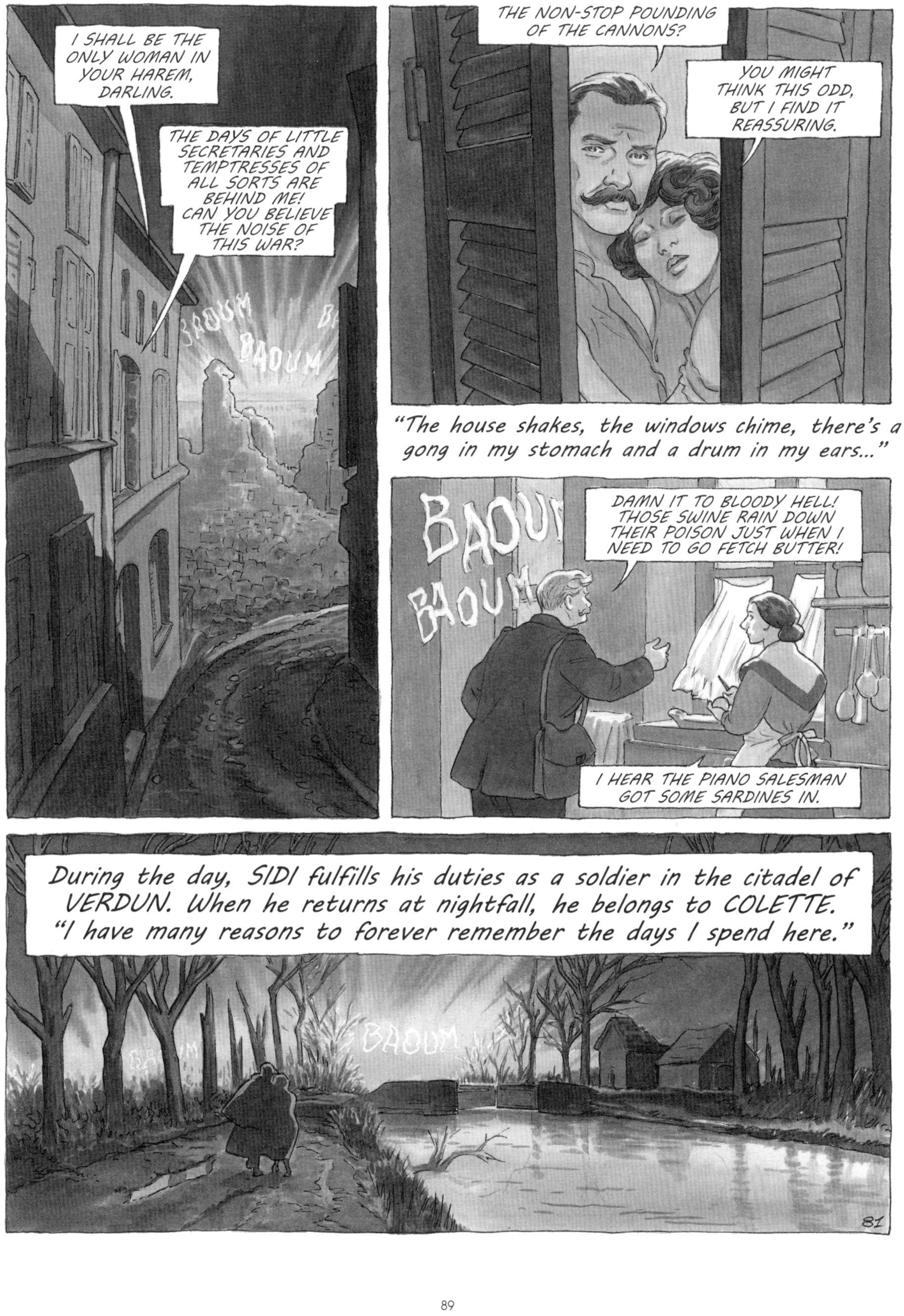
I SHALL BE THE ONLY WOMAN IN YOUR HAREM, DARLING.
THE DAYS OF LITTLE SECRETARIES AND TEMPTRESSES OF ALL SORTS ARE BEHIND ME! CAN YOU BELIEVE THE NOISE OF THIS WAR?
BAOUM
BAOUM
THE NON-STOP POUNDING OF THE CANNONS?
YOU MIGHT THINK THIS ODD, BUT I FIND IT REASSURING.
"The house shakes, the windows chime, there's a gong in my stomach and a drum in my ears..."
BAOUM
BAOUM
DAMN IT TO BLOODY HELL! THOSE SWINE RAIN DOWN THEIR POISON JUST WHEN I NEED TO GO FETCH BUTTER!
I HEAR THE PIANO SALESMAN GOT SOME SARDINES IN.
During the day, SIDI fulfills his duties as a soldier in the citadel of VERDUN. When he returns at nightfall, he belongs to COLETTE. "I have many reasons to forever remember the days I spend here."
BAOUM
81

"I shall write about all this, but not until later." Perhaps after traveling to ITALY on a diplomatic mission with HENRY de JOUVENEL, who knows...

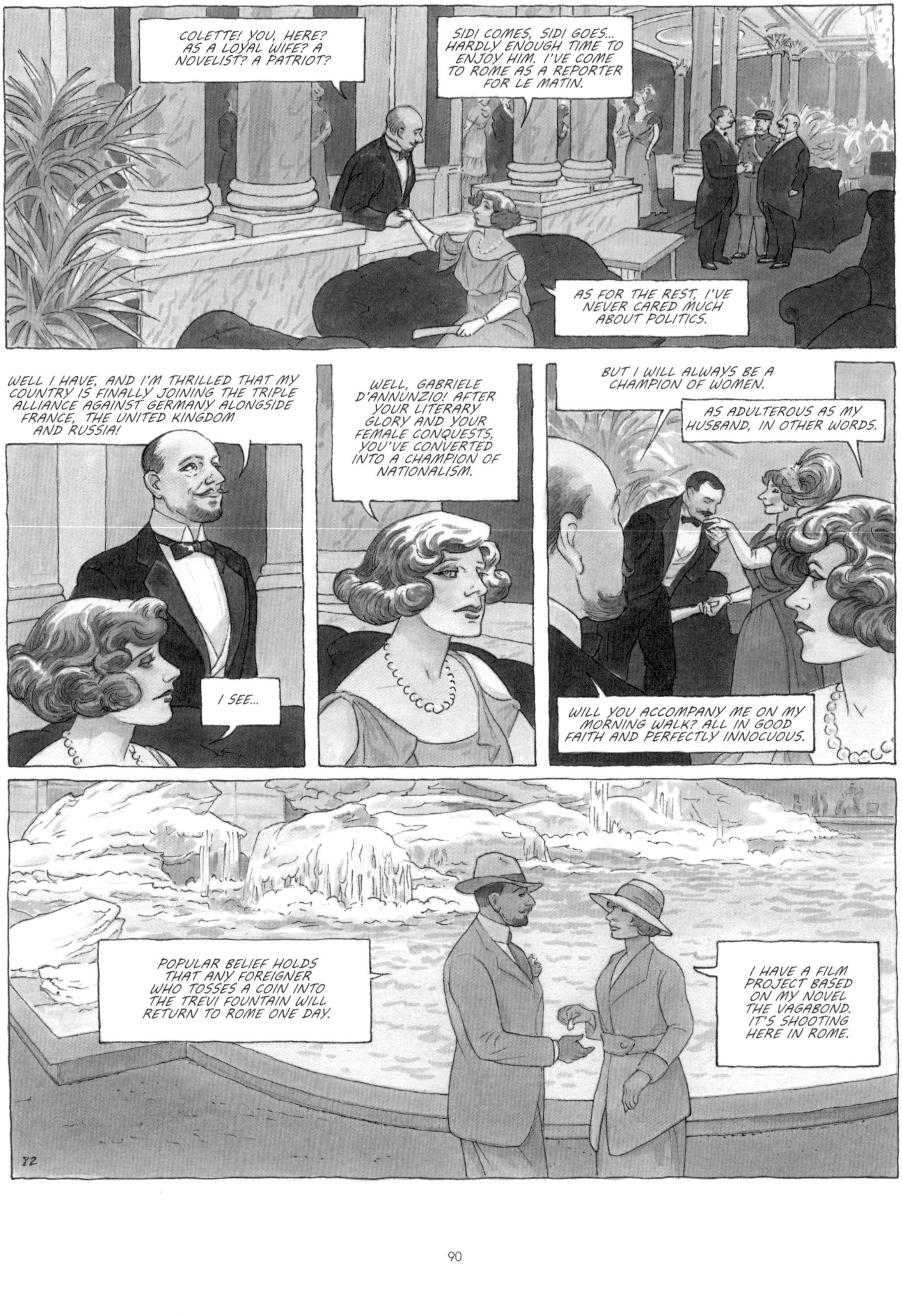
COLETTE! YOU, HERE? AS A LOYAL WIFE? A NOVELIST? A PATRIOT?
SIDI COMES, SIDI GOES... HARDLY ENOUGH TIME TO ENJOY HIM. I'VE COME TO ROME AS A REPORTER FOR LE MATIN.
AS FOR THE REST, I'VE NEVER CARED MUCH ABOUT POLITICS.
WELL I HAVE, AND I'M THRILLED THAT MY COUNTRY IS FINALLY JOINING THE TRIPLE ALLIANCE AGAINST GERMANY ALONGSIDE FRANCE, THE UNITED KINGDOM AND RUSSIA!
I SEE...
WELL, GABRIELE D'ANNUNZIO! AFTER YOUR LITERARY GLORY AND YOUR FEMALE CONQUESTS, YOU'VE CONVERTED INTO A CHAMPION OF NATIONALISM.
BUT I WILL ALWAYS BE A CHAMPION OF WOMEN.
AS ADULTEROUS AS MY HUSBAND, IN OTHER WORDS.
WILL YOU ACCOMPANY ME ON MY MORNING WALK? ALL IN GOOD FAITH AND PERFECTLY INNOCUOUS.
POPULAR BELIEF HOLDS THAT ANY FOREIGNER WHO TOSSES A COIN INTO THE TREVI FOUNTAIN WILL RETURN TO ROME ONE DAY.
I HAVE A FILM PROJECT BASED ON MY NOVEL THE VAGABOND. IT'S SHOOTING HERE IN ROME.

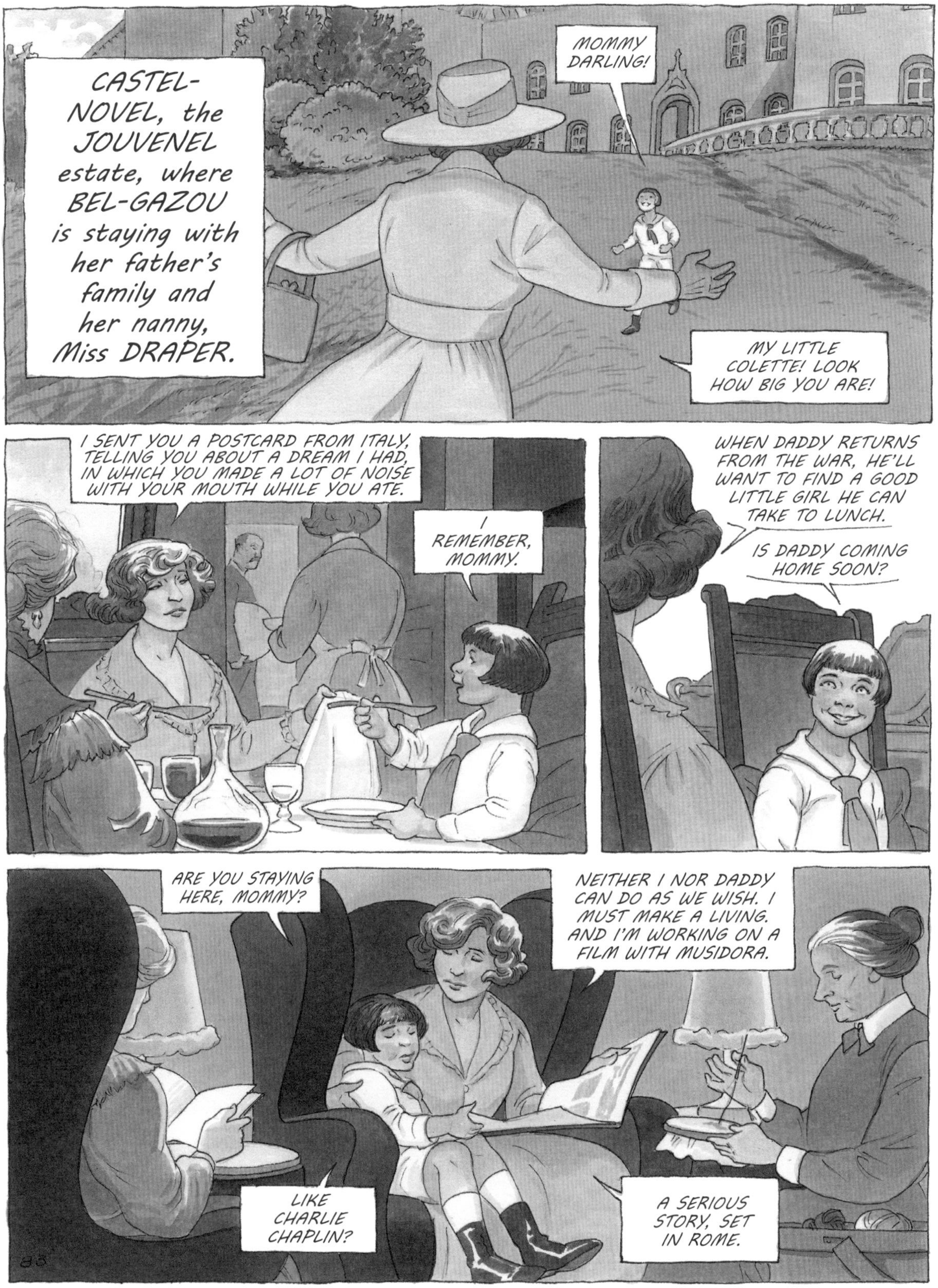
CASTEL-NOVEL, the JOUVENEL estate, where BEL-GAZOU is staying with her father's family and her nanny, Miss DRAPER.
MOMMY DARLING!
MY LITTLE COLETTE! LOOK HOW BIG YOU ARE!
I SENT YOU A POSTCARD FROM ITALY, TELLING YOU ABOUT A DREAM I HAD, IN WHICH YOU MADE A LOT OF NOISE WITH YOUR MOUTH WHILE YOU ATE.
I REMEMBER, MOMMY.
WHEN DADDY RETURNS FROM THE WAR, HE'LL WANT TO FIND A GOOD LITTLE GIRL HE CAN TAKE TO LUNCH.
IS DADDY COMING HOME SOON?
ARE YOU STAYING HERE, MOMMY?
NEITHER I NOR DADDY CAN DO AS WE WISH. I MUST MAKE A LIVING. AND I'M WORKING ON A FILM WITH MUSIDORA.
LIKE CHARLIE CHAPLIN?
A SERIOUS STORY, SET IN ROME.

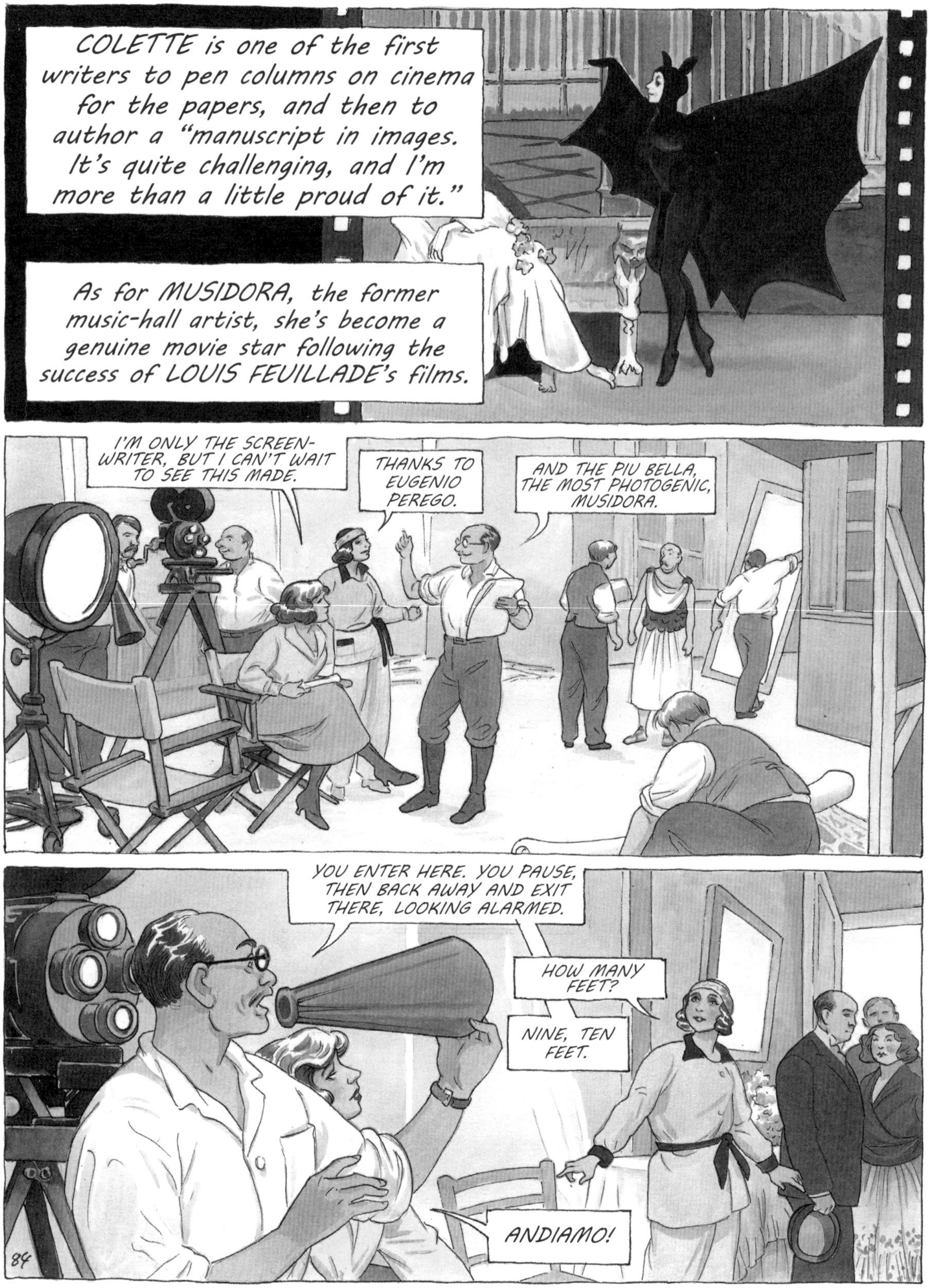
COLETTE is one of the first writers to pen columns on cinema for the papers, and then to author a "manuscript in images. It's quite challenging, and I'm more than a little proud of it."
As for MUSIDORA, the former music-hall artist, she's become a genuine movie star following the success of LOUIS FEUILLADE's films.
I'M ONLY THE SCREEN-WRITER, BUT I CAN'T WAIT TO SEE THIS MADE.
THANKS TO EUGENIO PEREGO.
AND THE PIU BELLA, THE MOST PHOTOGENIC, MUSIDORA.
YOU ENTER HERE. YOU PAUSE, THEN BACK AWAY AND EXIT THERE, LOOKING ALARMED.
HOW MANY FEET?
NINE, TEN FEET.
ANDIAMO!
84

BASTA PER OGGI!
É FINITO!

WHEW! I WENT THROUGH ELEVEN
WARDROBE AND HAIRSTYLE
CHANGES, AND TOMORROW WE'RE
SHOOTING IN THE MOUNTAINS.

DON'T YOU MISS
THE THEATER?
HAVING A LIVE
AUDIENCE?

MAYBE. BUT IN FILM, YOU
SEE YOURSELF. YOU HAVE
A DOUBLE OF YOURSELF, IN
BLACK AND WHITE, FOREVER.

Forever free. Such is the magic of film.

But the return to reality is anything
but magical. The vulnerable house
in PASSY, worm-eaten and humid
through and through, collapsed
under a strong gust of wind
during a summer storm.
"The man in the East,
the child in the field,"
COLETTE goes in
search of a
new address.

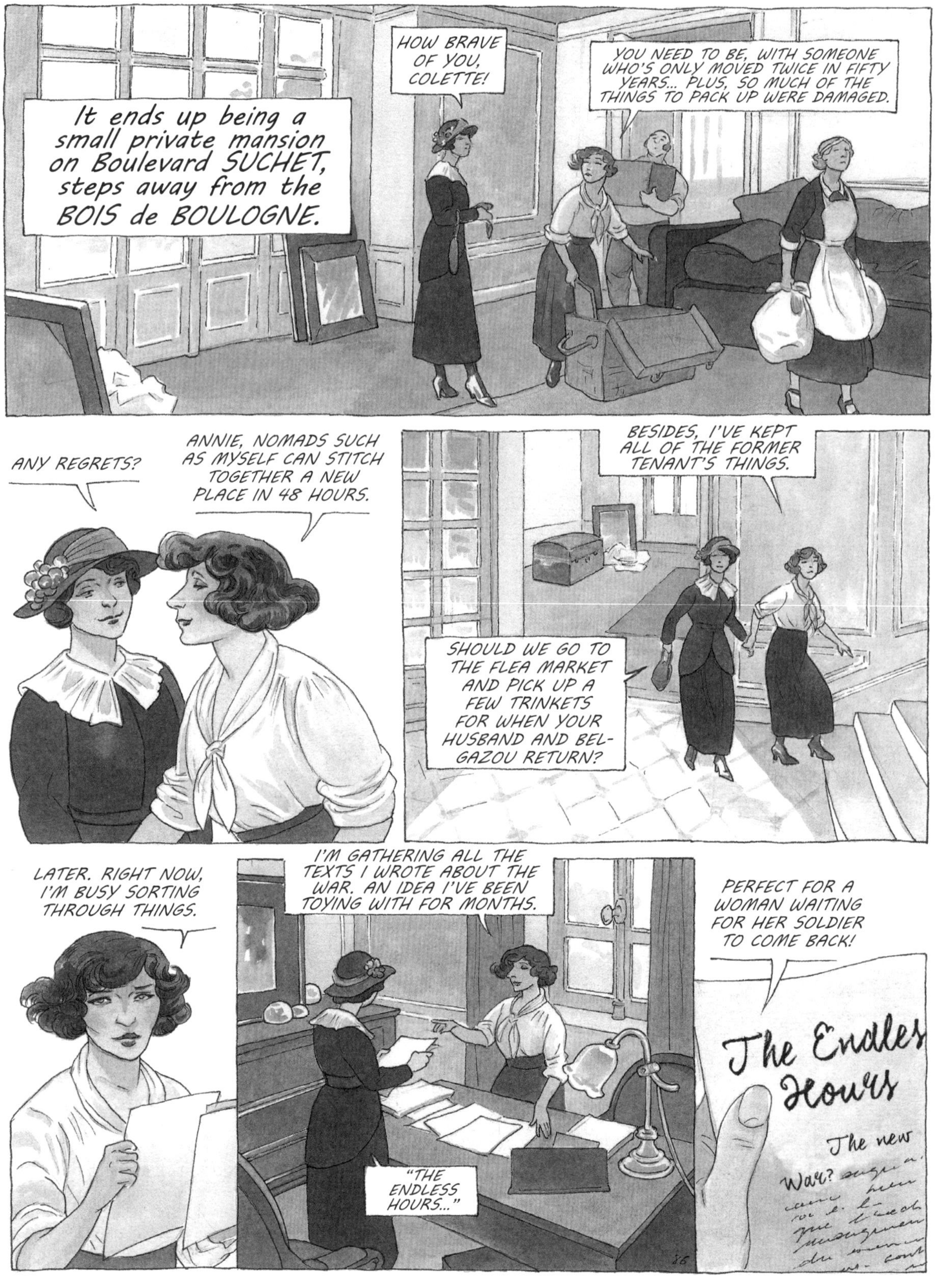

It ends up being a small private mansion on Boulevard SUCHET, steps away from the BOIS de BOULOGNE.
HOW BRAVE OF YOU, COLETTE!
YOU NEED TO BE, WITH SOMEONE WHO'S ONLY MOVED TWICE IN FIFTY YEARS... PLUS, SO MUCH OF THE THINGS TO PACK UP WERE DAMAGED.
ANY REGRETS?
ANNIE, NOMADS SUCH AS MYSELF CAN STITCH TOGETHER A NEW PLACE IN 48 HOURS.
BESIDES, I'VE KEPT ALL OF THE FORMER TENANT'S THINGS.
SHOULD WE GO TO THE FLEA MARKET AND PICK UP A FEW TRINKETS FOR WHEN YOUR HUSBAND AND BEL-GAZOU RETURN?
LATER. RIGHT NOW, I'M BUSY SORTING THROUGH THINGS.
I'M GATHERING ALL THE TEXTS I WROTE ABOUT THE WAR. AN IDEA I'VE BEEN TOYING WITH FOR MONTHS.
"THE ENDLESS HOURS..."
PERFECT FOR A WOMAN WAITING FOR HER SOLDIER TO COME BACK!
The Endles
Hours
The new
War?

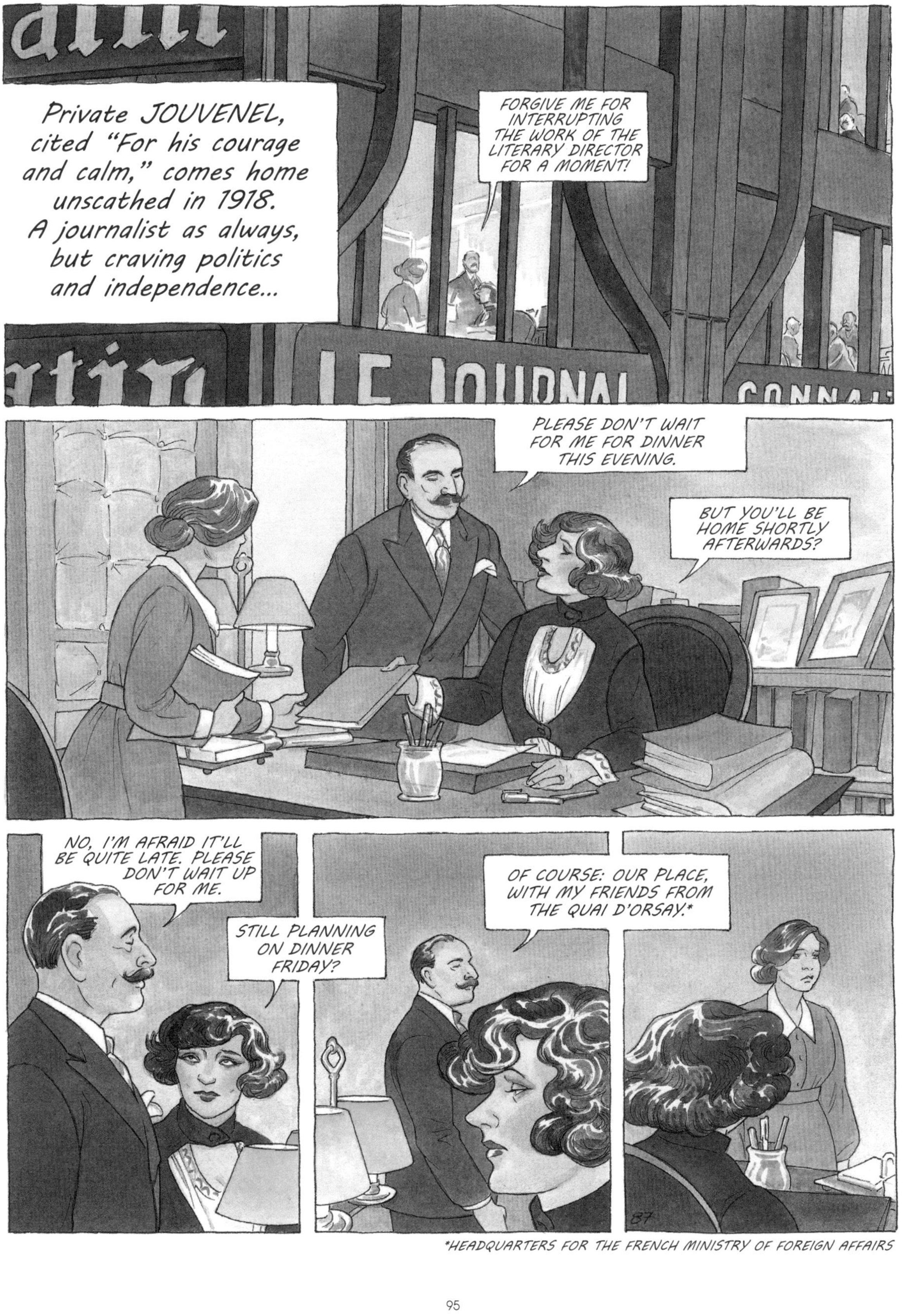

Private JOUVENEL, cited "For his courage and calm," comes home unscathed in 1918. A journalist as always, but craving politics and independence...
FORGIVE ME FOR INTERRUPTING THE WORK OF THE LITERARY DIRECTOR FOR A MOMENT!
PLEASE DON'T WAIT FOR ME FOR DINNER THIS EVENING.
BUT YOU'LL BE HOME SHORTLY AFTERWARDS?
NO, I'M AFRAID IT'LL BE QUITE LATE. PLEASE DON'T WAIT UP FOR ME.
STILL PLANNING ON DINNER FRIDAY?
OF COURSE: OUR PLACE, WITH MY FRIENDS FROM THE QUAI D'ORSAY.*

*HEADQUARTERS FOR THE FRENCH MINISTRY OF FOREIGN AFFAIRS

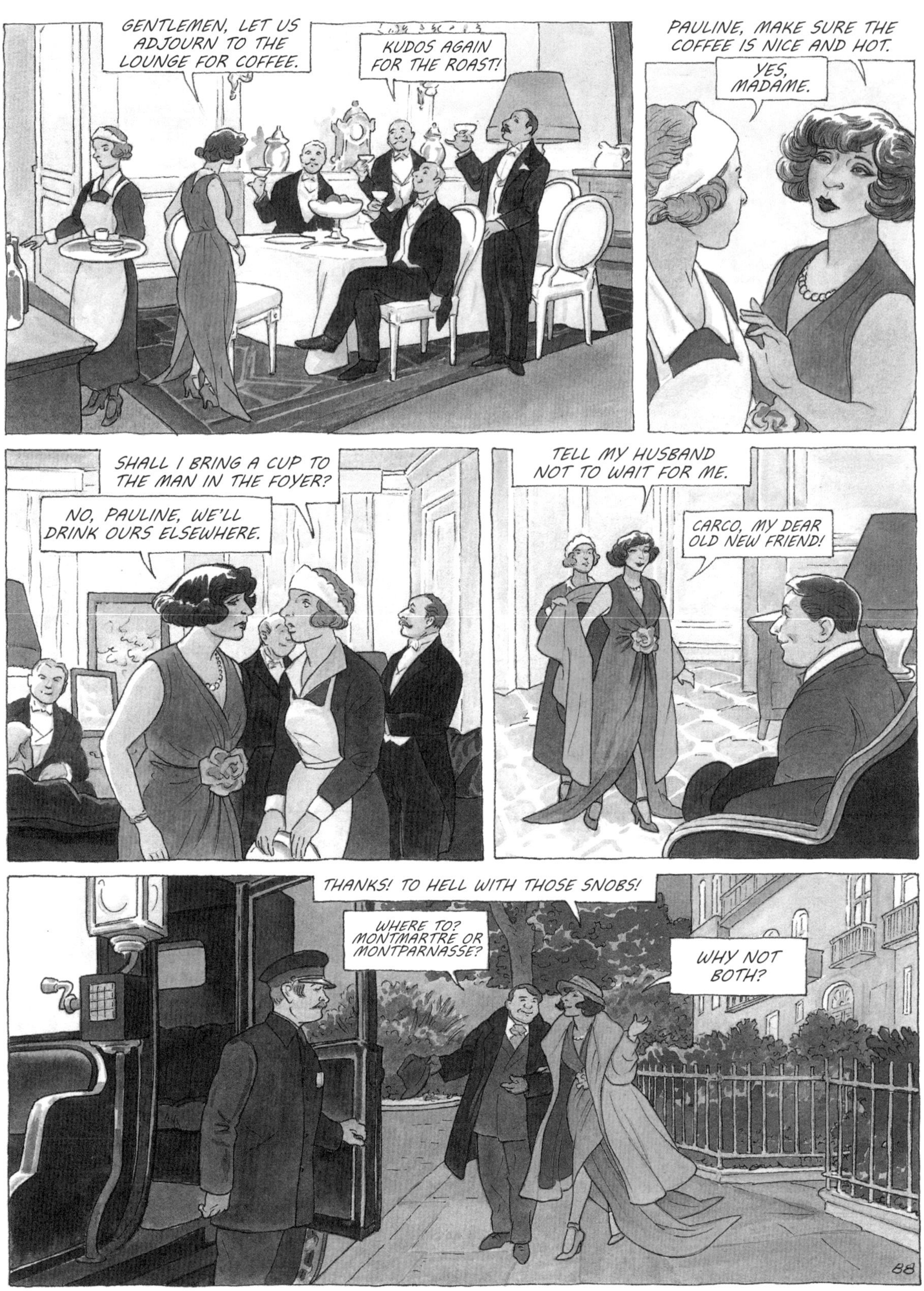
GENTLEMEN, LET US ADJOURN TO THE LOUNGE FOR COFFEE.
KUDOS AGAIN FOR THE ROAST!
PAULINE, MAKE SURE THE COFFEE IS NICE AND HOT.
YES, MADAME.
SHALL I BRING A CUP TO THE MAN IN THE FOYER?
NO, PAULINE, WE'LL DRINK OURS ELSEWHERE.
TELL MY HUSBAND NOT TO WAIT FOR ME.
CARCO, MY DEAR OLD NEW FRIEND!
THANKS! TO HELL WITH THOSE SNOBS!
WHERE TO? MONTMARTRE OR MONTPARNASSE?
WHY NOT BOTH?
88

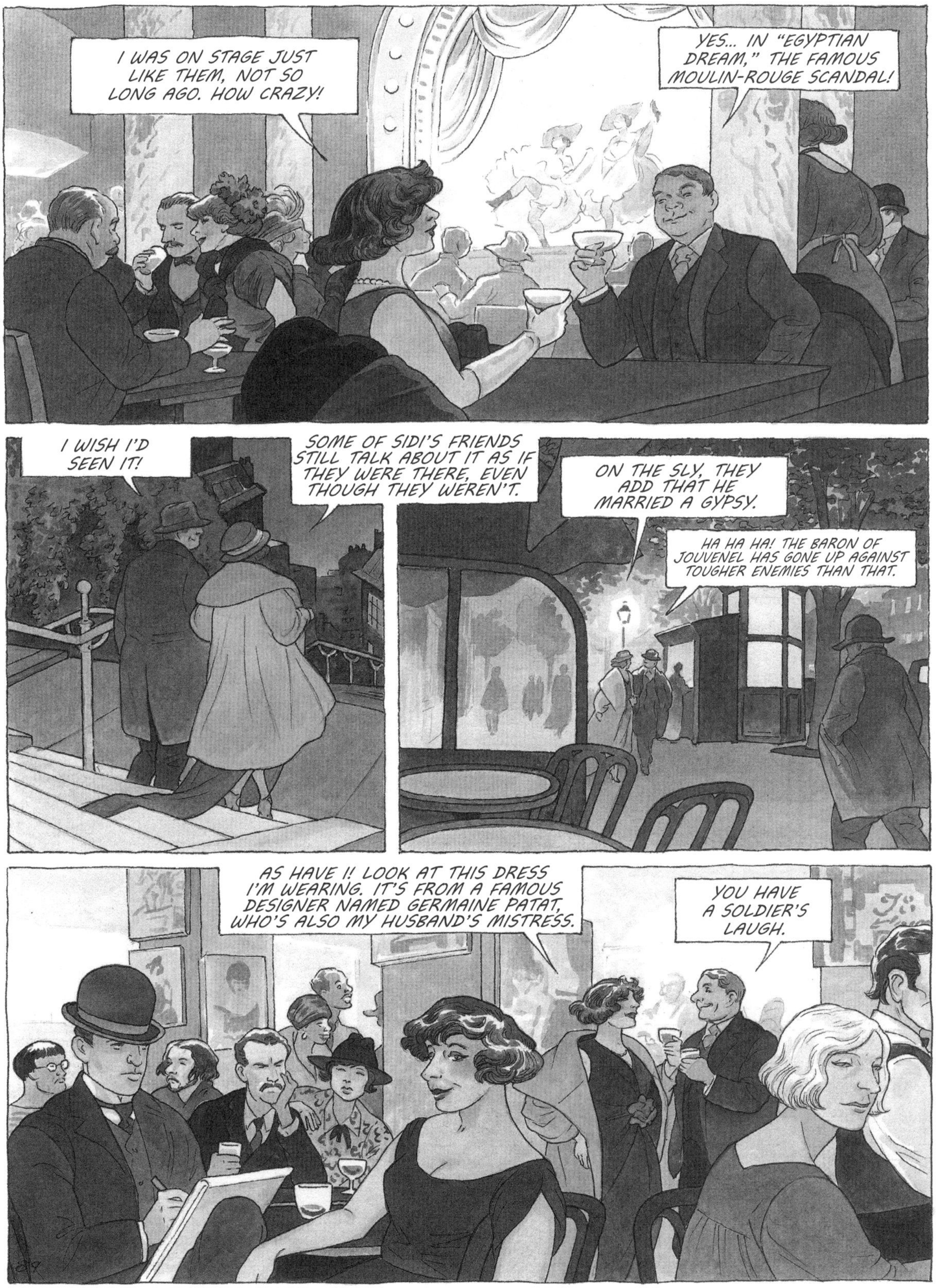
I WAS ON STAGE JUST LIKE THEM, NOT SO LONG AGO. HOW CRAZY!
YES... IN "EGYPTIAN DREAM," THE FAMOUS MOULIN-ROUGE SCANDAL!
I WISH I'D SEEN IT!
SOME OF SIDI'S FRIENDS STILL TALK ABOUT IT AS IF THEY WERE THERE, EVEN THOUGH THEY WEREN'T.
ON THE SLY, THEY ADD THAT HE MARRIED A GYPSY.
HA HA HA! THE BARON OF JOUVENEL HAS GONE UP AGAINST TOUGHER ENEMIES THAN THAT.
AS HAVE I! LOOK AT THIS DRESS I'M WEARING. IT'S FROM A FAMOUS DESIGNER NAMED GERMAINE PATAT, WHO'S ALSO MY HUSBAND'S MISTRESS.
YOU HAVE A SOLDIER'S LAUGH.

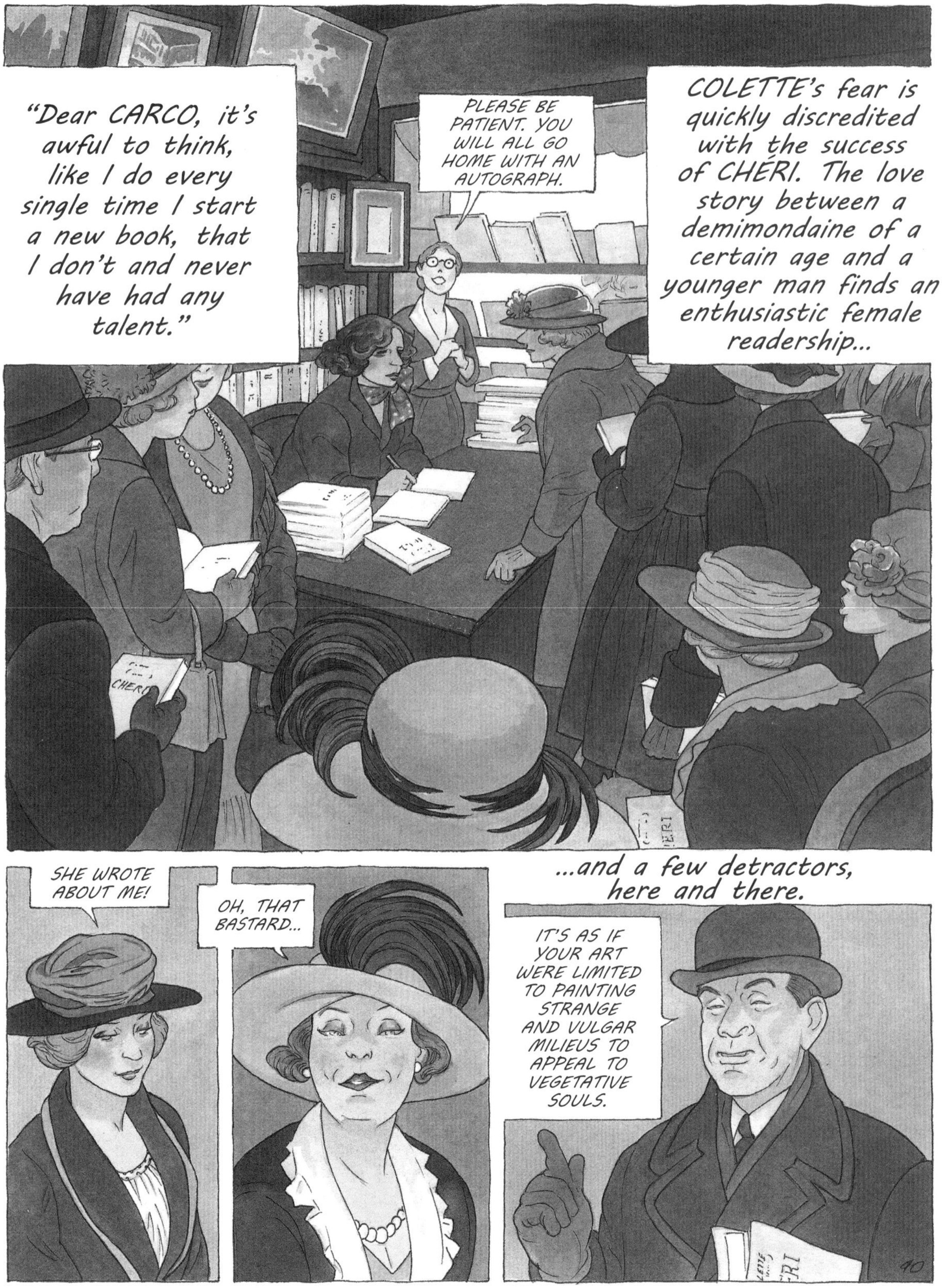
"Dear CARCO, it's awful to think, like I do every single time I start a new book, that I don't and never have had any talent."
PLEASE BE PATIENT. YOU WILL ALL GO HOME WITH AN AUTOGRAPH.
COLETTE's fear is quickly discredited with the success of CHÉRI. The love story between a demimondaine of a certain age and a younger man finds an enthusiastic female readership...
SHE WROTE ABOUT ME!
OH, THAT BASTARD...
...and a few detractors, here and there.
IT'S AS IF YOUR ART WERE LIMITED TO PAINTING STRANGE AND VULGAR MILIEUS TO APPEAL TO VEGETATIVE SOULS.

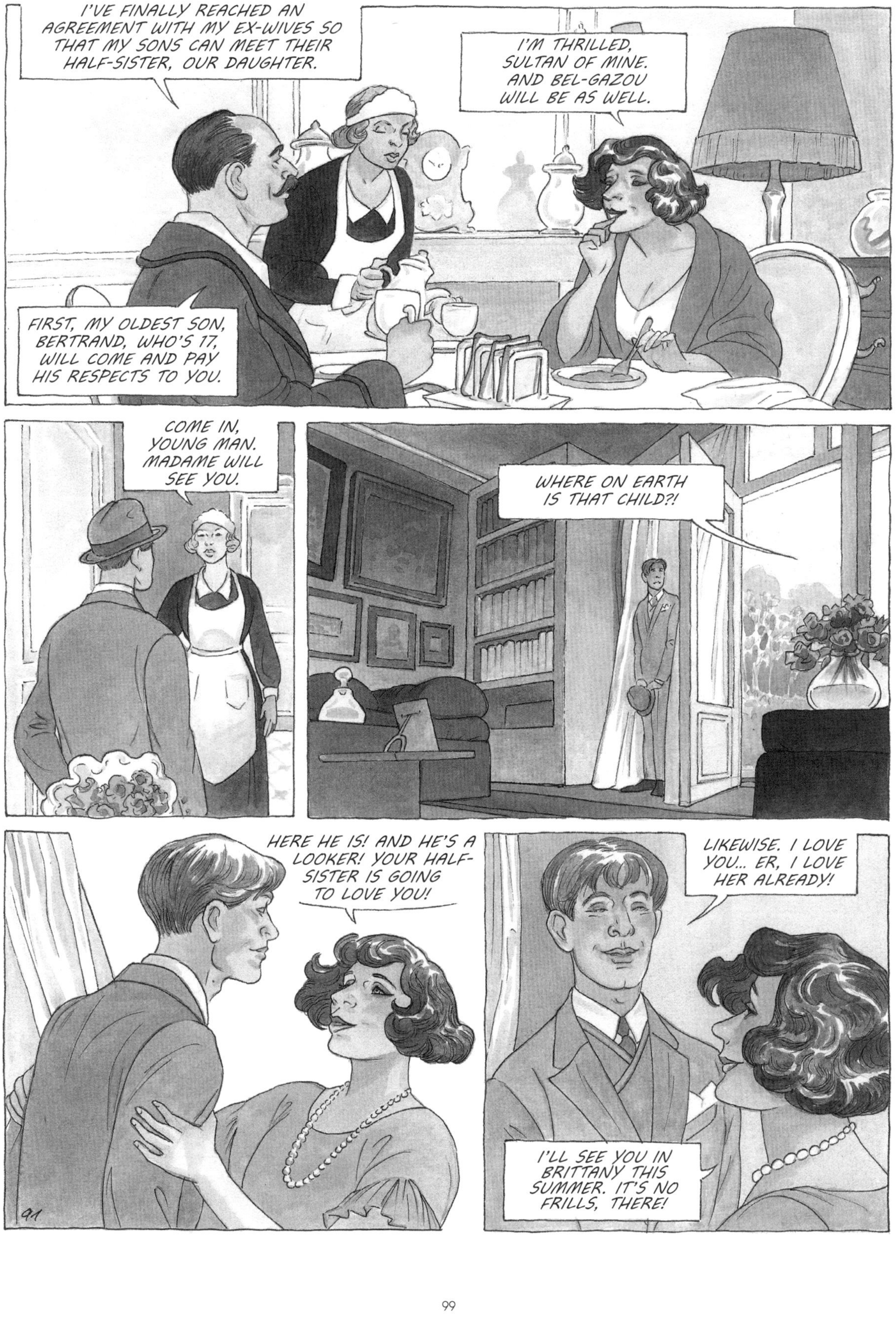
I'VE FINALLY REACHED AN AGREEMENT WITH MY EX-WIVES SO THAT MY SONS CAN MEET THEIR HALF-SISTER, OUR DAUGHTER.
I'M THRILLED, SULTAN OF MINE. AND BEL-GAZOU WILL BE AS WELL.
FIRST, MY OLDEST SON, BERTRAND, WHO'S 17, WILL COME AND PAY HIS RESPECTS TO YOU.
COME IN, YOUNG MAN. MADAME WILL SEE YOU.
WHERE ON EARTH IS THAT CHILD?!
HERE HE IS! AND HE'S A LOOKER! YOUR HALF-SISTER IS GOING TO LOVE YOU!
LIKEWISE. I LOVE YOU... ER, I LOVE HER ALREADY!
I'LL SEE YOU IN BRITTANY THIS SUMMER. IT'S NO FRILLS, THERE!

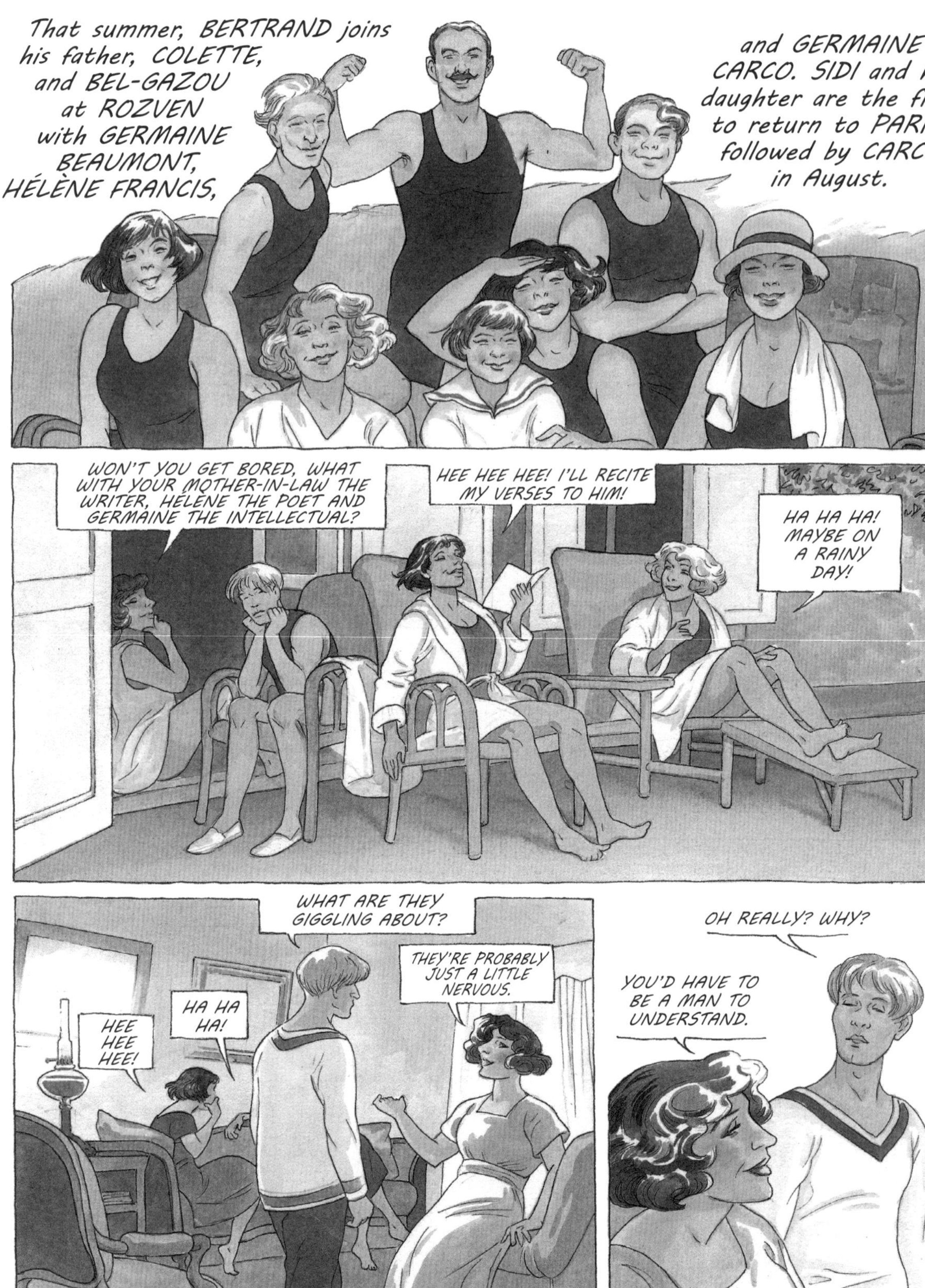

That summer, BERTRAND joins his father, COLETTE, and BEL-GAZOU at ROZVEN with GERMAINE BEAUMONT, HÉLÈNE FRANCIS,
and GERMAINE CARCO. SIDI and his daughter are the first to return to PARIS, followed by CARCO in August.
WON'T YOU GET BORED, WHAT WITH YOUR MOTHER-IN-LAW THE WRITER, HÉLÈNE THE POET AND GERMAINE THE INTELLECTUAL?
HEE HEE HEE! I'LL RECITE MY VERSES TO HIM!
HA HA HA! MAYBE ON A RAINY DAY!
WHAT ARE THEY GIGGLING ABOUT?
HEE HEE HEE!
HA HA HA!
THEY'RE PROBABLY JUST A LITTLE NERVOUS.
OH REALLY? WHY?
YOU'D HAVE TO BE A MAN TO UNDERSTAND.
92

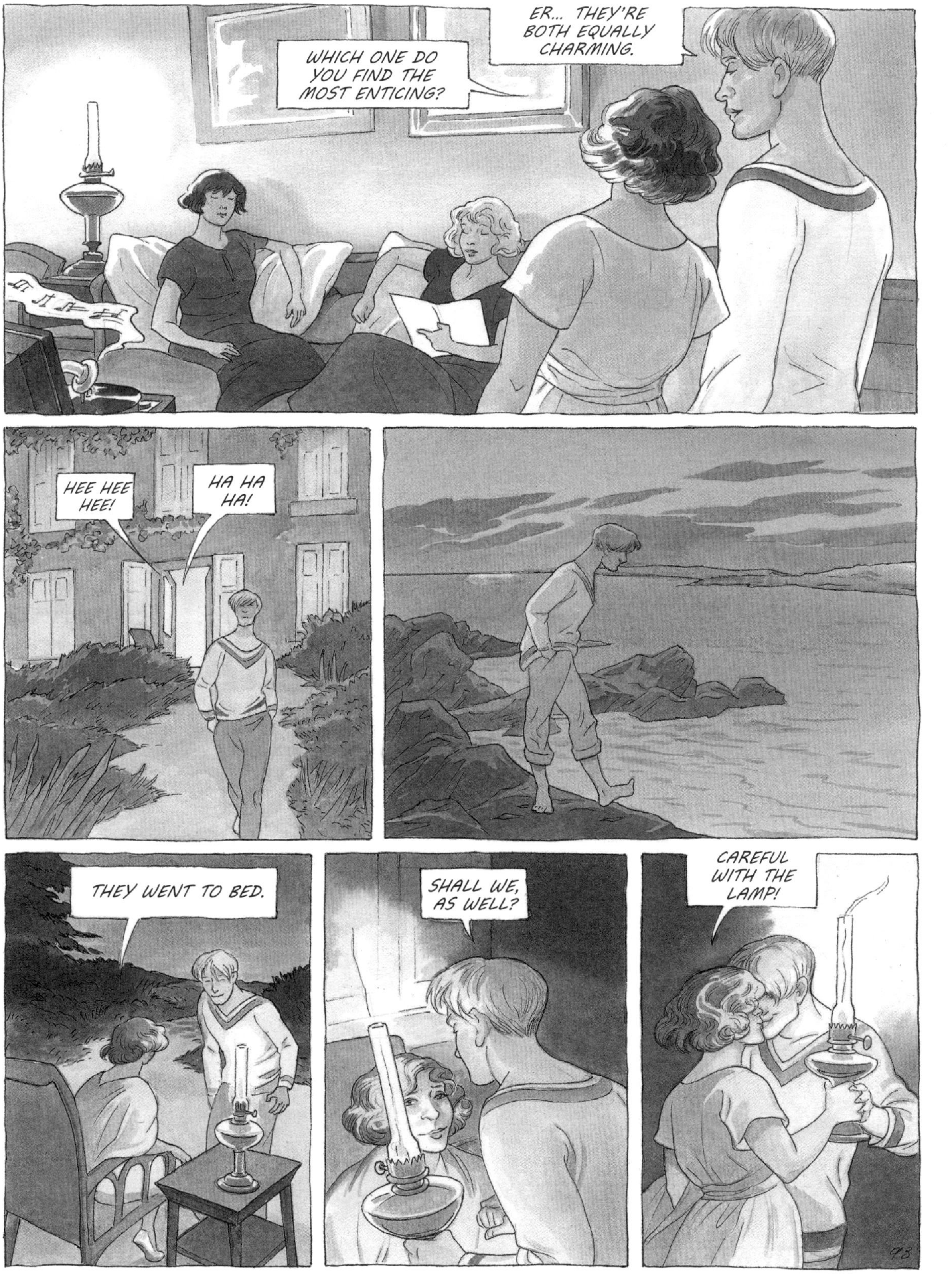
WHICH ONE DO YOU FIND THE MOST ENTICING?
ER... THEY'RE BOTH EQUALLY CHARMING.
HEE HEE HEE!
HA HA HA!
THEY WENT TO BED.
SHALL WE, AS WELL?
CAREFUL WITH THE LAMP!
93

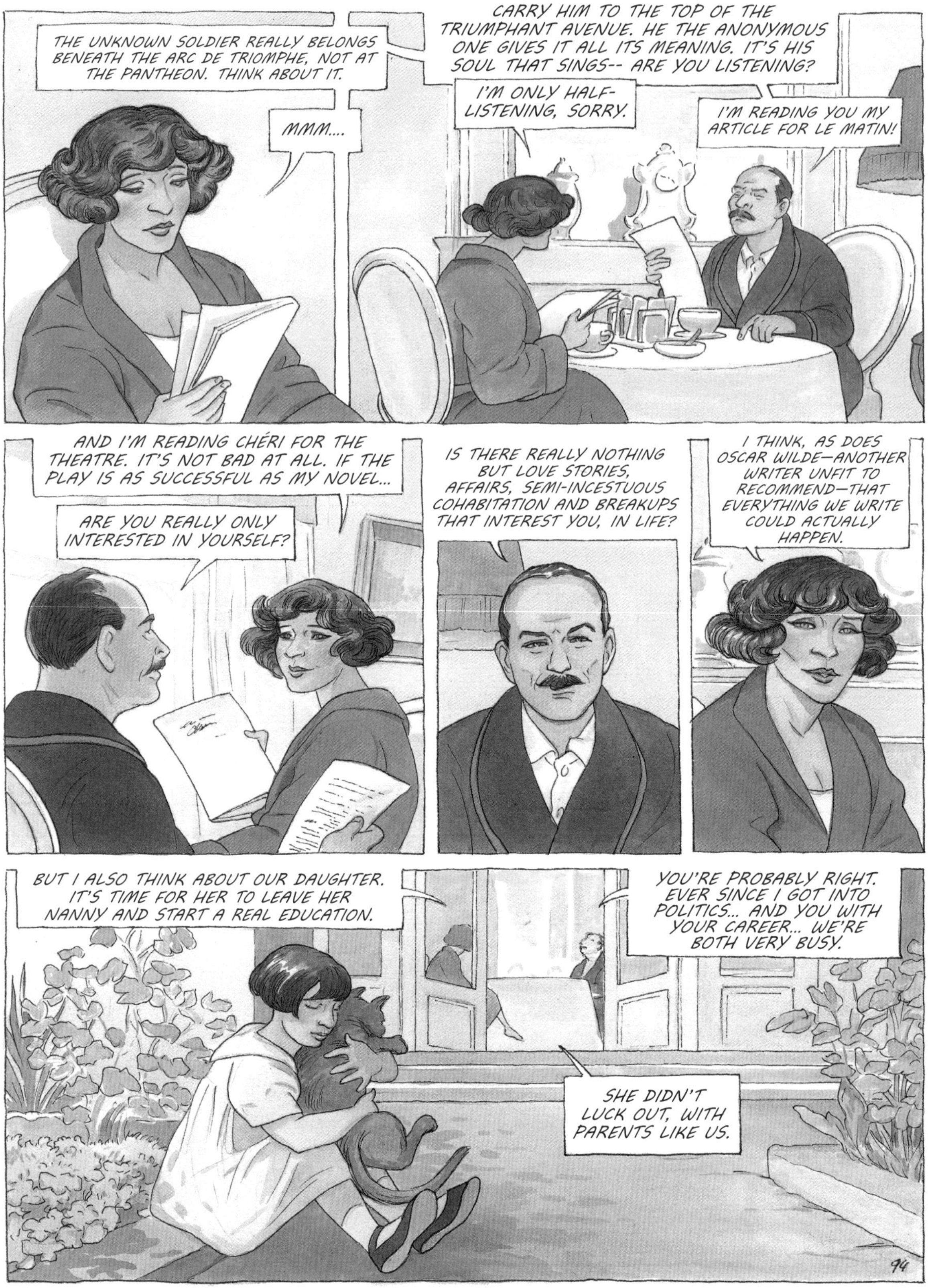
THE UNKNOWN SOLDIER REALLY BELONGS BENEATH THE ARC DE TRIOMPHE, NOT AT THE PANTHEON. THINK ABOUT IT.
MMM....
CARRY HIM TO THE TOP OF THE TRIUMPHANT AVENUE. HE THE ANONYMOUS ONE GIVES IT ALL ITS MEANING. IT'S HIS SOUL THAT SINGS-- ARE YOU LISTENING?
I'M ONLY HALF-LISTENING, SORRY.
I'M READING YOU MY ARTICLE FOR LE MATIN!
AND I'M READING CHÉRI FOR THE THEATRE. IT'S NOT BAD AT ALL. IF THE PLAY IS AS SUCCESSFUL AS MY NOVEL...
ARE YOU REALLY ONLY INTERESTED IN YOURSELF?
IS THERE REALLY NOTHING BUT LOVE STORIES, AFFAIRS, SEMI-INCESTUOUS COHABITATION AND BREAKUPS THAT INTEREST YOU, IN LIFE?
I THINK, AS DOES OSCAR WILDE—ANOTHER WRITER UNFIT TO RECOMMEND—THAT EVERYTHING WE WRITE COULD ACTUALLY HAPPEN.
BUT I ALSO THINK ABOUT OUR DAUGHTER. IT'S TIME FOR HER TO LEAVE HER NANNY AND START A REAL EDUCATION.
YOU'RE PROBABLY RIGHT. EVER SINCE I GOT INTO POLITICS... AND YOU WITH YOUR CAREER... WE'RE BOTH VERY BUSY.
SHE DIDN'T LUCK OUT, WITH PARENTS LIKE US.
94

YOU'RE A GOOD LITTLE GIRL. DON'T BECOME SOMEONE ORDINARY. I'M WAITING TO SEE SOMETHING OF YOUR FATHER AND ME IN YOU.

MAKE SURE YOU DON'T DISAPPOINT US.

YES, MOMMY.

YES, MOMMY DARLING.

My dear Mommy, I'm begging you, please write to me...

I beg of you, please come to see me Thursday, my darling little Mommy..

Daddy says he's coming soon. I would love it if you came with him, but I fear you're not able to...

Daddy campaigns in CORRÈZE to be elected senator. True to her word, Mommy returns to the stage for the 100th performance of CHÉRI, where she plays LÉA, the demimondaine.

95

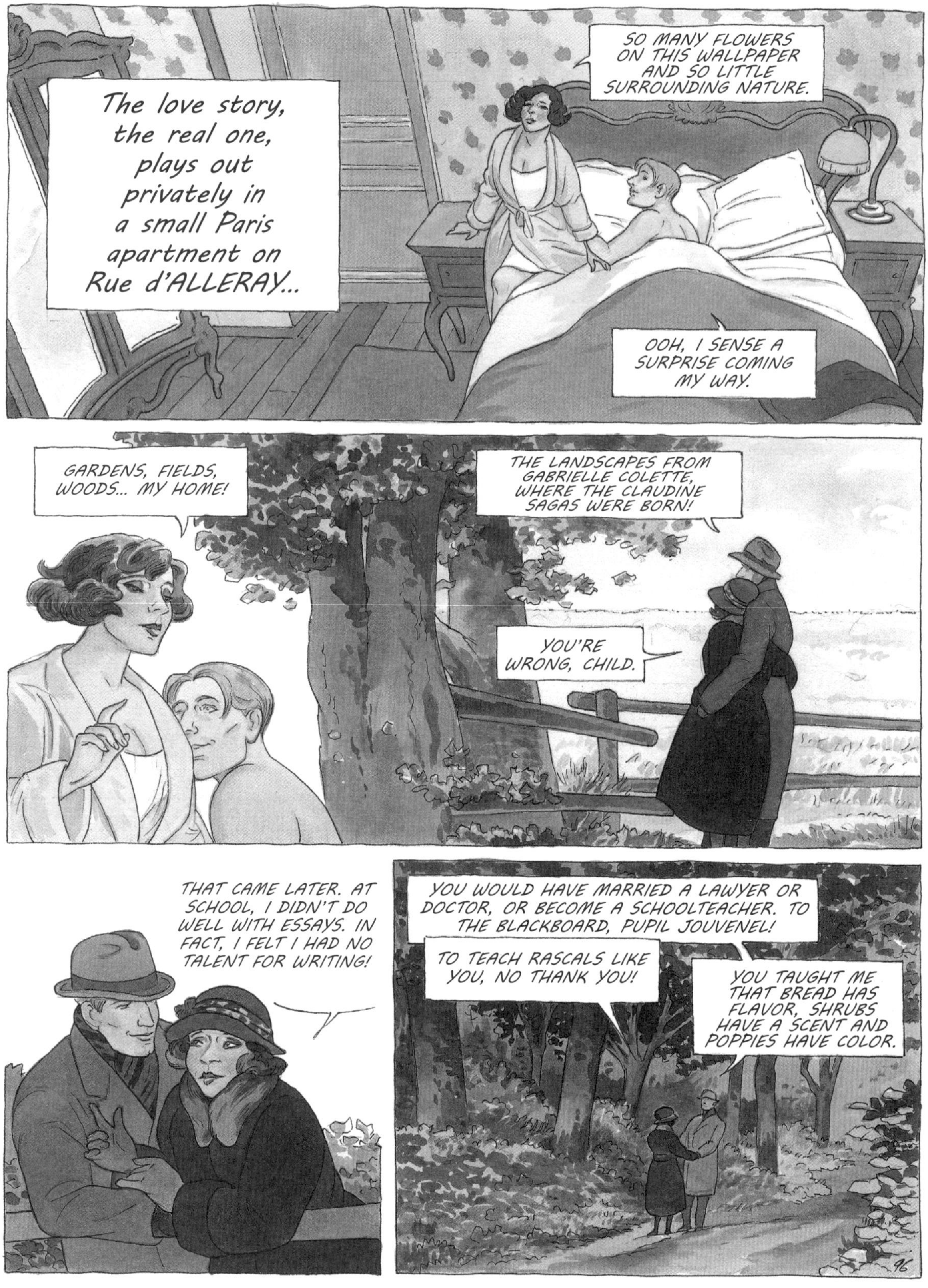
The love story, the real one, plays out privately in a small Paris apartment on Rue d'ALLERAY...
SO MANY FLOWERS ON THIS WALLPAPER AND SO LITTLE SURROUNDING NATURE.
OOH, I SENSE A SURPRISE COMING MY WAY.
GARDENS, FIELDS, WOODS... MY HOME!
THE LANDSCAPES FROM GABRIELLE COLETTE, WHERE THE CLAUDINE SAGAS WERE BORN!
YOU'RE WRONG, CHILD.
THAT CAME LATER. AT SCHOOL, I DIDN'T DO WELL WITH ESSAYS. IN FACT, I FELT I HAD NO TALENT FOR WRITING!
YOU WOULD HAVE MARRIED A LAWYER OR DOCTOR, OR BECOME A SCHOOLTEACHER. TO THE BLACKBOARD, PUPIL JOUVENEL!
TO TEACH RASCALS LIKE YOU, NO THANK YOU!
YOU TAUGHT ME THAT BREAD HAS FLAVOR, SHRUBS HAVE A SCENT AND POPPIES HAVE COLOR.
96

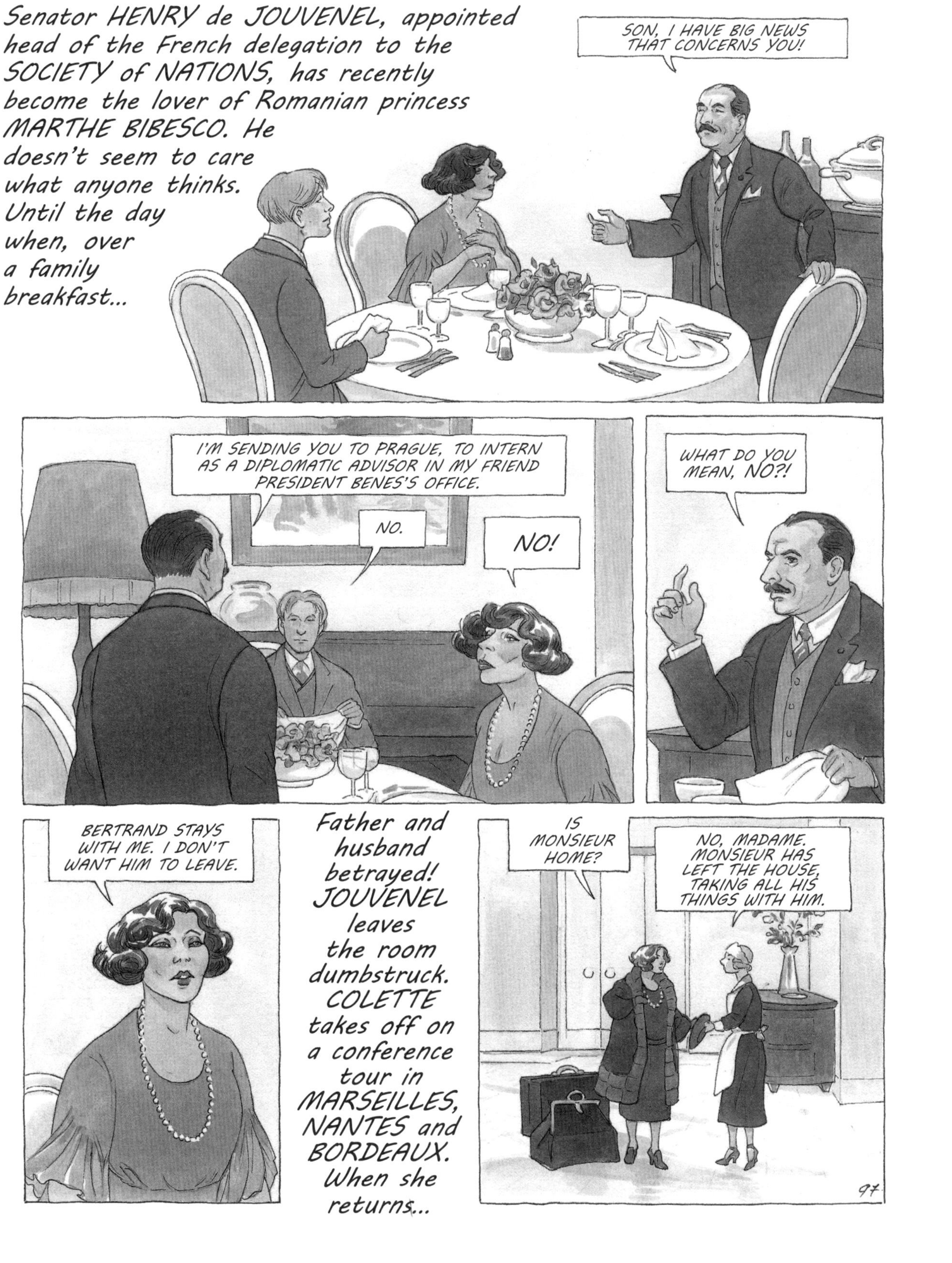
Senator HENRY de JOUVENEL, appointed head of the French delegation to the SOCIETY of NATIONS, has recently become the lover of Romanian princess MARTHE BIBESCO. He doesn't seem to care what anyone thinks. Until the day when, over a family breakfast...
SON, I HAVE BIG NEWS THAT CONCERNS YOU!
I'M SENDING YOU TO PRAGUE, TO INTERN AS A DIPLOMATIC ADVISOR IN MY FRIEND PRESIDENT BENES'S OFFICE.
NO.
NO!
WHAT DO YOU MEAN, NO?!
BERTRAND STAYS WITH ME. I DON'T WANT HIM TO LEAVE.
Father and husband betrayed! JOUVENEL leaves the room dumbstruck. COLETTE takes off on a conference tour in MARSEILLES, NANTES and BORDEAUX. When she returns...
IS MONSIEUR HOME?
NO, MADAME. MONSIEUR HAS LEFT THE HOUSE, TAKING ALL HIS THINGS WITH HIM.
97

Everything works out, but with a few changes...

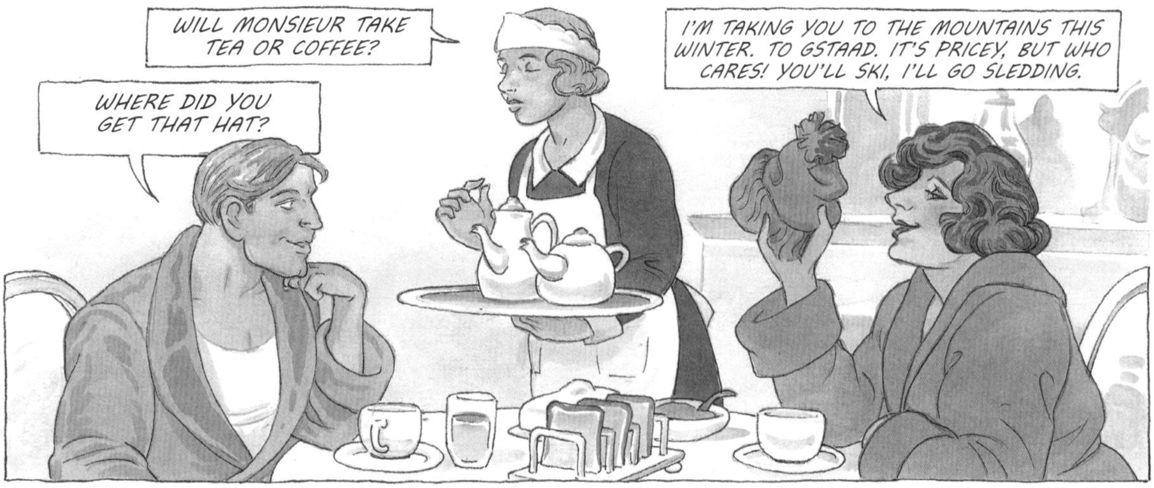
WILL MONSIEUR TAKE TEA OR COFFEE?
I'M TAKING YOU TO THE MOUNTAINS THIS WINTER. TO GSTAAD. IT'S PRICEY, BUT WHO CARES! YOU'LL SKI, I'LL GO SLEDDING.
WHERE DID YOU GET THAT HAT?

COLETTE comes back "broke, in fine spirits, and with a sunburned nose."

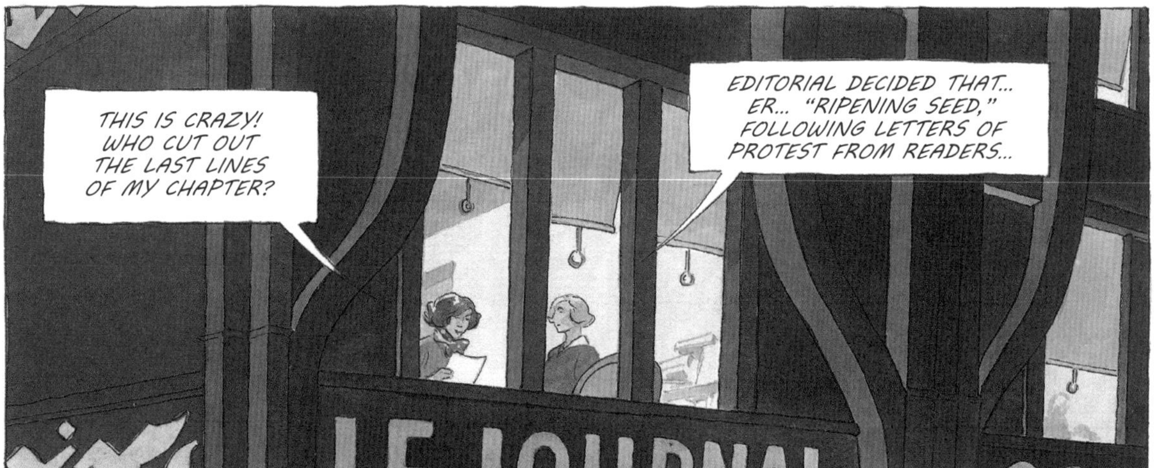
THIS IS CRAZY! WHO CUT OUT THE LAST LINES OF MY CHAPTER?
EDITORIAL DECIDED THAT... ER... "RIPENING SEED," FOLLOWING LETTERS OF PROTEST FROM READERS...

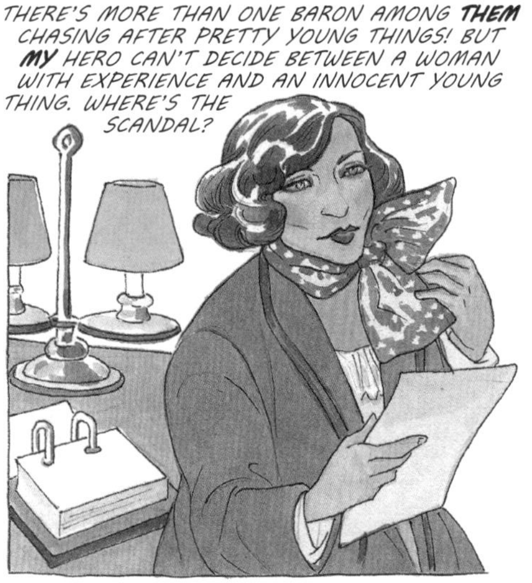
THERE'S MORE THAN ONE BARON AMONG **THEM** CHASING AFTER PRETTY YOUNG THINGS! BUT **MY** HERO CAN'T DECIDE BETWEEN A WOMAN WITH EXPERIENCE AND AN INNOCENT YOUNG THING. WHERE'S THE SCANDAL?

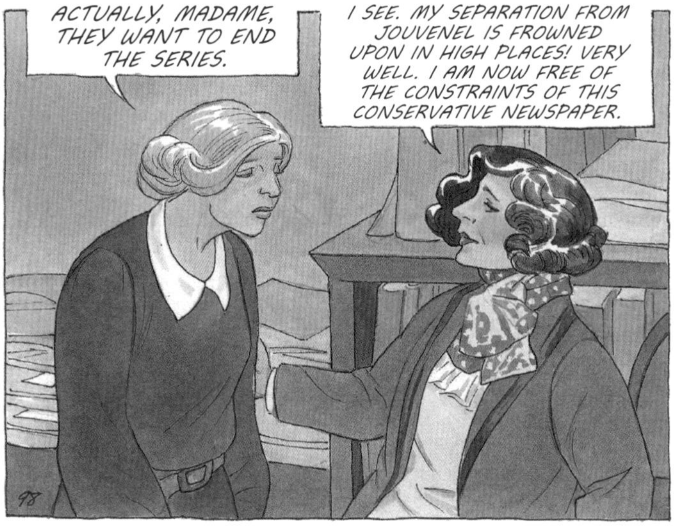
ACTUALLY, MADAME, THEY WANT TO END THE SERIES.
I SEE. MY SEPARATION FROM JOUVENEL IS FROWNED UPON IN HIGH PLACES! VERY WELL. I AM NOW FREE OF THE CONSTRAINTS OF THIS CONSERVATIVE NEWSPAPER.

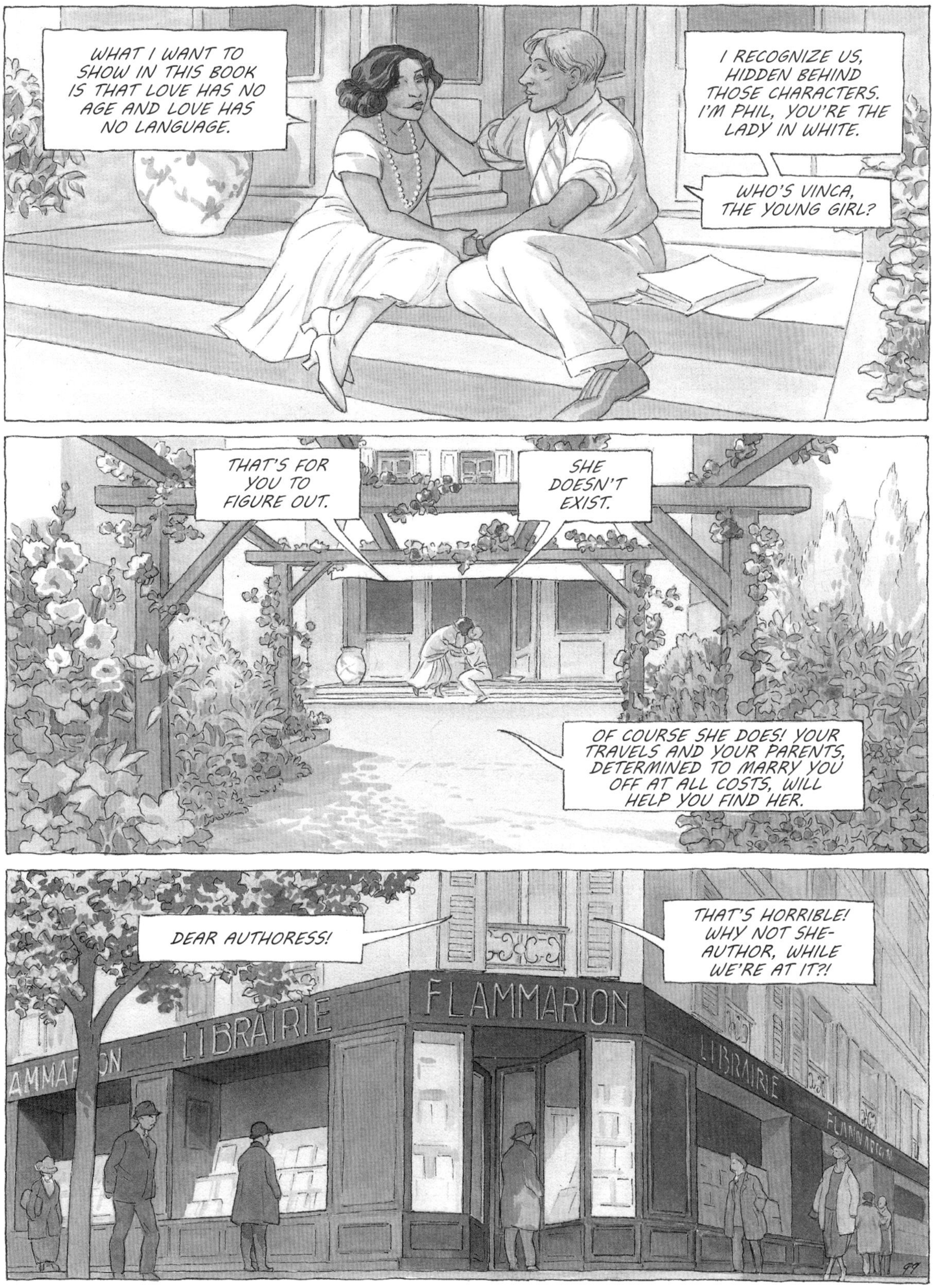
WHAT I WANT TO SHOW IN THIS BOOK IS THAT LOVE HAS NO AGE AND LOVE HAS NO LANGUAGE.
I RECOGNIZE US, HIDDEN BEHIND THOSE CHARACTERS. I'M PHIL, YOU'RE THE LADY IN WHITE.
WHO'S VINCA, THE YOUNG GIRL?
THAT'S FOR YOU TO FIGURE OUT.
SHE DOESN'T EXIST.
OF COURSE SHE DOES! YOUR TRAVELS AND YOUR PARENTS, DETERMINED TO MARRY YOU OFF AT ALL COSTS, WILL HELP YOU FIND HER.
DEAR AUTHORESS!
THAT'S HORRIBLE! WHY NOT SHE-AUTHOR, WHILE WE'RE AT IT?!
FLAMMARION
LIBRAIRIE
AMMARION
LIBRAIRIE
FLAMMARION

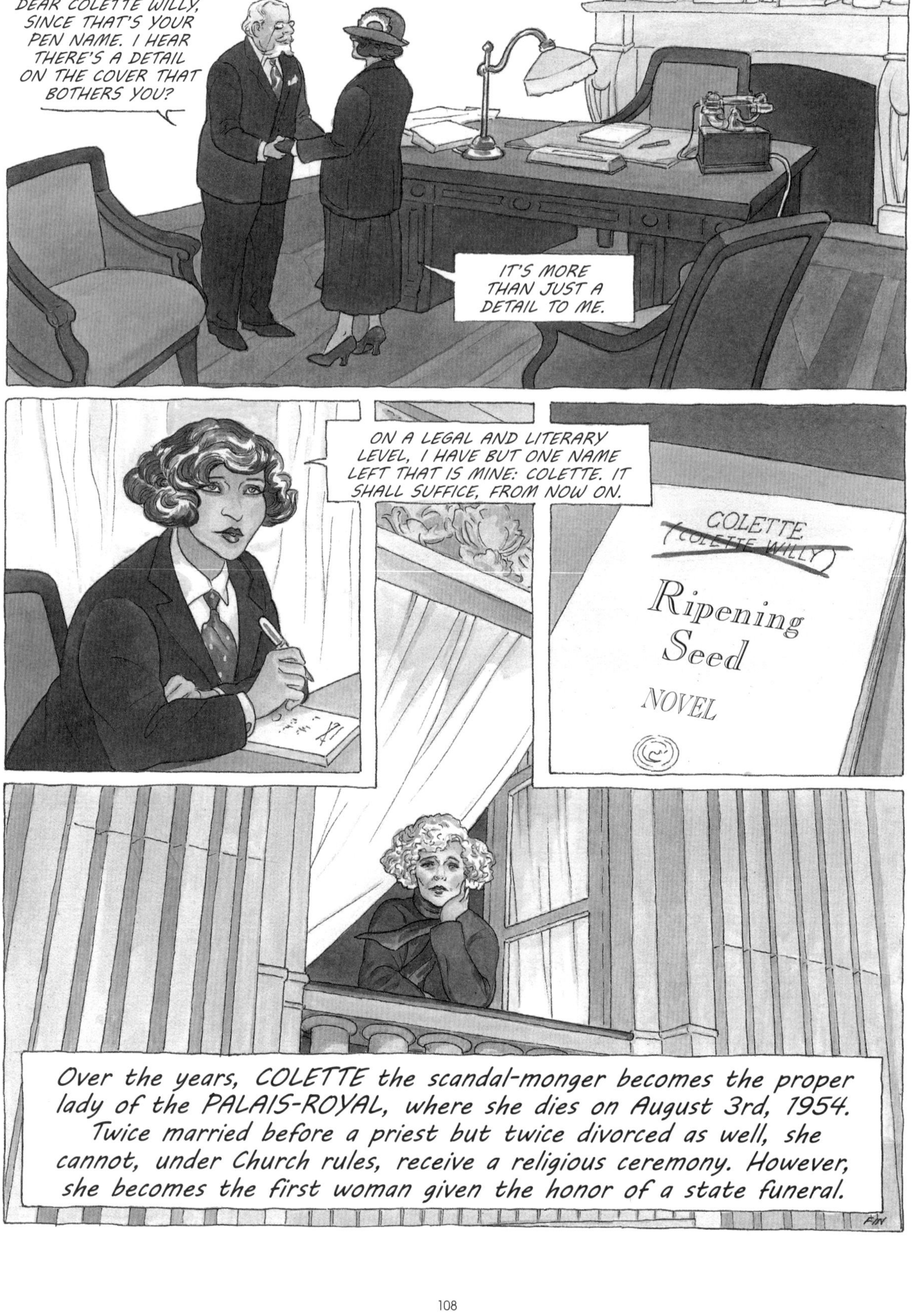
DEAR COLETTE WILLY, SINCE THAT'S YOUR PEN NAME. I HEAR THERE'S A DETAIL ON THE COVER THAT BOTHERS YOU?
IT'S MORE THAN JUST A DETAIL TO ME.
ON A LEGAL AND LITERARY LEVEL, I HAVE BUT ONE NAME LEFT THAT IS MINE: COLETTE. IT SHALL SUFFICE, FROM NOW ON.
COLETTE
(COLETTE WILLY)
Ripening Seed
NOVEL
Over the years, COLETTE the scandal-monger becomes the proper lady of the PALAIS-ROYAL, where she dies on August 3rd, 1954. Twice married before a priest but twice divorced as well, she cannot, under Church rules, receive a religious ceremony. However, she becomes the first woman given the honor of a state funeral.

LITERARY REFERENCES

1865
Sidonie Landoy, widow of Robineau-Duclos, marries a second time, this time to Jules Colette.

1873
Sidonie-Gabrielle Colette is born in Saint-Sauveur.

1885
Colette takes the grade school graduation exam at the Saint-Sauveur school.

1889
Sidonie-Gabrielle Colette receives grade school and secondary education diplomas in Auxerre.

1892
Colette spends two weeks in Paris. She has a life-changing encounter with Henry Gauthier-Villars, pen-named Willy, whom she had met three years earlier on a previous trip.

1893
Colette marries Henry Gauthier-Villars in Châtillon-sur-Loing. The newlyweds move into his apartment at 28, Rue Jacob. Colette makes her debut in the musical and literary salons of Paris.

1894
Colette learns of her husband's infidelities and is gravely ill for more than two months. She convalesces on the island of Belle-Île from June to September, accompanied by Willy and their friend Paul Masson. Following her husband's suggestion, Colette spends this year and the next working on a first draft of what would become *Claudine in School*. Willy dismisses the manuscript but rediscovers it four years later, submitting it to editors unsuccessfully.

1896
Willy and Colette move out of the apartment on Rue Jacob and into their new home at 93, Rue de Courcelles.

1900
Claudine in School is released, with Willy the only accredited author.

1901
Claudine in Paris comes out.

1902
Claudine, a comedy in three acts, opens at the Bouffes-Parisiens theater, preceded by a prologue, *Claudine in School*. Polaire plays the rôle of Claudine. Willy walks around Paris with his "twins" on his arms: Polaire and Colette.
Claudine Married (originally titled *Claudine In Love*) is published.
Near the end of the year, Willy and Colette move into 177 bis, Rue de Courcelles. Colette has a small gymnastics room installed on the second floor.

1903
Claudine and Annie is released.

1904
Creatures Great and Small comes out, under the name Colette Willy. A new edition, with three additional conversations and a preface by Francis Jammes, is released the following year.
Minne is released under Willy's name.

1905
Division of property between Colette and Willy.
Minne's Wanderings comes out under Willy's name.
Death of Jules Colette, the novelist's father.
Near the end of the year, Colette begins taking mime lessons with Georges Wague.

1906

Colette performs in public for the first time at the Théâtre des Mathurins, where she plays the role of a faun in *Love, Desire and the Chimera*, a mimodrama by Francis de Croisset and Jean Nouguès.

Colette makes the acquaintance of Missy at the Victor-Hugo society club.

The debut performances of *The Gypsy*, a pantomime by Paul Franck, take place at the famed Olympia music hall from October 1st to November 2nd.

On November 27 at the Arts and Sports Club, Colette performs in *The Gypsy* opposite Missy, who plays the role of the painter.

Charles Van Lerberghe's *Pan* opens at the Théâtre Marigny on November 28.

Also in November, Willy and Colette separate.

1907

The premiere of *Egyptian Dream* at the Moulin-Rouge, a pantomime by Vuillermoz, Wague and Willy, Missy from causes a riot. Police Commissioner Lépine forbids Missy from appearing on stage again.

In February, Willy's and Colette's separation becomes official.

Retreat from Love is released under the name Colette Willy.

Flesh opens at the Apollo.

1908

Publication of *Coils of the Vine*.

1909

Colette's play in two acts, *As Friends*, opens at the Théâtre des Arts.

Colette learns that Willy sold rights to the *Claudine* series to his editors two years earlier.

Colette and Willy agree that henceforth, the books will be released under both their names and will include a note about authorship.

Colette travels to thirty-two cities in France on the Baret tour for *Claudine in Paris*.

The Innocent Libertine, a rewritten merging of the two *Minne* books, comes out.

1910

Colette starts working at *Paris-Journal*.

In April and May, Colette (and Missy, who comes with her) embarks on a thirty-city French tour for three plays in repertory: Jules Renard's *The Fanatic*, *The Idiot or I'm Sick of Margot* by Georges Courteline and Pierre Wolff, and *Fear of Blows* by Georges Courteline.

The Vagabond is serialized in the weekly magzine *La Vie Parisienne* from May 21st to October 1st.

Publishing house Ollendorff releases the book in November.

Colette and Willy get divorced in June.

That same month, Missy purchases the Rozven manor in Brittany, in Colette's name.

Claudine is produced at the Moulin-Rouge as an operetta in three acts.

Later that year, Colette begins working as a regular contributor to the daily *Le Matin* with an anonymously penned fairytale titled *Poison Woman*.

The following year, she forgoes anonymity and adopts the "Colette Willy" byline for her fifth tale.

1911

The relationship with Missy deteriorates between May and October.

Colette moves in with Henry de Jouvenel, co-editor-in-chief of the daily newspaper *Le Matin*.

1912

Colette plays *The Cat In Love* at the Ba-Ta-Clan.

In June, on assignment for *Le Matin*, she covers the ascension of the Clément-Bayard blimp, followed by the Guillotin trial in Tours.

Sido, the writer's mother, passes away on September 25.

In December, Colette marries Henry de Jouvenel.

1913

The following works are released: *Prrou and Poucette*, *Music-Hall Sidelights* and *The Shackle*.

Colette-Renée de Jouvenel, daughter of Colette and Henry de Jouvenel, is born in Paris on July 3rd.

Achille Robineau-Duclos, Colette's half-brother, passes away on December 13th.

1914

France declares war. Henry de Jouvenel is drafted.
In December, Colette travels to Verdun to be with him.
She makes several more trips in 1915.

1915

Between June and August, Colette travels throughout
Italy as a reporter for *Le Matin*, including Turin, Rome,
Venice, Milan and Lugano.

1916

Publication of *Peace Among the Animals*.
December: film shoot of *Minne*, adapted from
The Innocent Libertine and directed by Jacques de
Baroncelli and Musidora. It was never released.

1917

Mid-April: the film *The Vagabond* starring Musidora
shoots in Rome.
Colette starts writing film reviews.
Children in the Ruins and *Long Hours* come out.

1918

Colette begins writing for the paper L'Éclair where she
does theater reviews until November 14 and where she
meets Francis Carco.
The film *The Hidden Flame*, directed by Musidora and
written by Colette, shoots in Paris.
Publication of *In the Crowd*.

1919

Mitsou, or How Girls Grow Wise comes out. Marcel
Proust, who is a big fan of the book, later sends
Colette a copy of *In the Shadow of Young Girls in Flower*.
In June, Colette begins seeing Léopold Marchand,
then 28 years old.
In December, Colette, who already oversees the Tales
of One Thousand and One Mornings, is now also in
charge of theater reviews for the same daily paper.
Her reviews are later published into five works,
between 1934 and 1949, titled *The Black Twin*.

1920

Publication of *Chéri*. A comedy in four acts from it by
Colette and Léopold Marchand is published two years
later.
On September 25th, Colette is made Knight of the
Legion of Honor. She goes on to be promoted to the
level of Officer in 1928, then to Commander in 1936, and
finally to Grand Officer in 1953.

1921

The Room with Light, *The One Who Came Back From It*
and the first anthology of Colette's texts are released.
Colette and Léopold Marchand finish adapting *Chéri*
for the stage.

1922

Colette plays the role of Léa for the 100th performance
of her play *Chéri*.
The Selfish Voyage and *My Mother's House* come out.
July 20: beginning of the serialized
publication of *Ripening Seed* in the daily
Le Matin, which continues through
Chapter 15 in the book (published in the
March 15, 1923 edition of the paper), after
which letters of protest from readers
put an end to it. The novel is later published
under the sole name of Colette, which the
writer adopts once and for all.
In September, Colette works on the
stage adaptation of *The Vagabond*,
begun at Rozven with Léopold Marchand.

1923

Colette returns to Paris in December
and finds out that Henry de Jouvenel
has left the conjugal home
for good. His son Bertrand
ends up sharing Colette's
life until 1925.

1924

Colette's last theater review for *Le Matin* comes out.

1925
Colette breaks up with Bertrand de Jouvenel; she and
Henry are officially divorced in April.
Colette meets Maurice Goudeket. They end up
marrying ten years later.

1926
The Last of Chéri comes out.
Colette purchases a villa in Saint-Tropez.
It's called Tamaris-les-Pins, but
Colette promptly renames it
"The Climbing Muscat Vine"

1928
Break of Day is released.

1929
The Second One comes out.
Colette writes *Look*, a text that is later
published with illustrations
by Méheut.

1930
Revised edition of *Sido*, with two additional, previously
unpublished sections, Parts 2 and 3: *The Captain* and
The Savages.

1931
Serialized publication of *These Pleasures...*
in the weekly Grimoire, before
letters of protest from readers
put an end to it. The novel is
published in 1932.
The film version of *The Vagabond*
comes out.

1932
Colette's beauty products store opens on June 1st at 6,
Rue de Miromesnil.
Publication of *Prisons and Paradises*.

1933
The Cat comes out.
Colette writes dialogue for the
screenplay for *Lake of Ladies*, adapted
from a novel by Vicki Baum, which
Marc Allégret later directs. The film is
released in 1934.
Colette replaces Claude Farrère as
theater critic for *Le Journal*, where
she stays until 1937.

1934
Duo comes out.

1935
Colette is elected to Belgium's Royal Academy of
Language and French Literature.
Release of the film *Divine*, directed by
Max Ophuls and George Auriol, with
a screenplay by Colette, adapted from
her *Music-Hall Sidelights*.

1936
What I learned. What Claudine Didn't Say comes out.
Cats comes out: text by Colette and etchings by
Jacques Nam.
Publication of *The Splendor of Butterflies*.

1937
Serge de Poligny's film *Claudine in School*, based on
Colette's novel, is released in Paris.
Bella-Vista comes out.
Colette moves into 9, Rue de Beaujolais, where she
remains until her death.

1938
Colette starts writing for the daily paper *Paris-Soir*.
Release of *Toutounier*, the sequel to *Duo*.
Colette starts working for *Marie-Claire* magazine,
where she answers mail from
the female readership.

1939

On assignment for Paris-Soir, Colette attends the trial of Weidmann, a murderer sentenced to death.

1940

The two short stories *Hotel Room* and *Moon Rain* are published under the title of the first one.

1941

The following works are released: *The Backwards Journal*; *My Notebooks* which contains a fairyland ballet which has never been performed, titled *The Decapitated Woman*; and *The Pure and the Impure*.

1942

The following works are released: *From My Window*, the short story collection *The Kepi*, and *From Paw to Wing*.

1943

The following works are released: *Flore and Pomone*, *Nudity*, and *Gigi and Other Short Stories*.

1944

The following works are released: *Paris From My Window*, *Three... Six... Nine...*, and *Ancient Embroidery*.

1945

Colette is unanimously voted into the prestigious literary organization Académie Goncourt. Publication of *Summers*.

1947

The Vesper Star comes out.

1948-1950

A 15-volume comprehensive collection of Colette's work is published.

1949

The following works come out: *Line for Line*, *The Flower of Age*, *Intermittent Journal*, *The Blue Lantern* and *On Familiar Ground*.
Once a week for one whole year, Colette's editor sent her flowers that he asked her to write about, whereby *For an Herbarium* is published.
Colette is appointed president of the Académie Goncourt.
The film *Gigi*, adapted from Colette's novel by Pierre Laroche, with dialogue penned by the writer, is released in Paris.
The following year, the same director adapts two more of her works for the screen: *Chéri* and *Minne, the Depraved Ingenue*.

1951

The film *Colette*, directed by Yannick Bellon, is shown at the Pleyel cinema.
Gigi premieres on Broadway at the Fulton Theatre, starring Audrey Hepburn in the title role.

1953

A special issue of the *The Figaro Littéraire* magazine publishes a feature article in honor of Colette's 84th birthday that includes texts by Proust, Valéry, Mauriac, Gide, Claudel, and Anouilh.

1954

The film *Ripening Seed*, adapted from her novel of the same title, is shown in Paris and later goes on to receive the Grand Prize of French Cinema.
Colette passes away in her home on August 3rd. Four days later, she is given a state funeral in the main courtyard of the Palais-Royal, but the Church won't allow a religious ceremony.
Colette is buried in the famed Père-Lachaise cemetery.

Colette-Renée de Jouvenel, known as Bel-Gazou
(1913-1981)

The only daughter of Colette–who gave birth to her at forty–and Henry de Jouvenel, she owed her nickname (which means "Lovely chirping" in the Provençal dialect) to the one her grandfather gave to her mother when she was a child. She was raised by an English nanny, Miss Draper, until 1922, then went to boarding school in Saint-Germain-en-Laye, during which time she only saw her mother on holiday at Rozven or Castel-Novel. A rebellious teen and a courageous resistance fighter, she hid many refugees in the Corrèze castle of Curemonte, where her mother and her father-in-law, Maurice Goudeket, came to visit. Driven by the same love of writing as her mother, she wrote several articles for the Parisian press after WWII. She also wrote tales, songs, and kept a private diary, of which only a few excerpts have been published to date. She was passionate about issues relating to the role of women in the work world, and used her pen to defend gender equality–a radical position that annoyed her mother. When Colette died, Bel-Gazou discovered that her mother hadn't left her much in her will. She managed to recover moral rights to her mother's body of work, and, began rereleasing her works in 1977.

Jules-Joseph Colette, known as Captain Colette
(1829-1905)

Colette's father. A career officer who trained at the famous Saint-Cyr military school, he retired at just thirty, following a serious injury to his left leg. He then became the tax collector in Saint-Sauveur.

François Carcopino-Tusoli, known as Francis Carco
(1886-1958)

French writer, poet, songwriter and journalist of Corsican origin, born in Nouméa (New Caledonia); also known under the pseudonym Jean d'Aiguières. He began to frequent Montmartre in 1910 and became friends with Apollinaire. He first met Colette at the L'Éclair newspaper in 1917, and the two remained friends until her death. They spent holidays together in Brittany. He produced a significant body of work counting over a hundred titles, from novels, articles, memoirs, collections of poetry, to plays. In 1937, he was elected member of the Academy Goncourt.

Natalie Clifford Barney
(1876-1972)

An American woman of letters, known less for her writing than for turning her life into a veritable work of art, and for her commitment to feminist issues via her literary salon in the 6th Arrondissement, one of the last ones in Paris, which left a lasting imprint. Openly gay, she actively contributed to the development of a women's literary and artistic world for more than half a century, namely through her many romantic conquests, which included Colette.

Gabriele D'Annunzio
(1863-1938)

Prince of Montenevoso, writer and WWI hero, he flirted with fascism in its early days before distancing himself from it. One of the leading representatives of the Italian Decadent movement, he remains famous to this day for two of his seven novels, *The Child of Pleasure* (1889) and *The Maidens of the Rocks* (1899).

Auguste Hériot
(1826-1879)

French businessman who created the stores Galeries du Louvre and then the Grands Magasins du Louvre (1855-1974). He was Émile Zola's chief inspiration for the character of Octave Mouret, hero of the novel *The Ladies' Paradise* (1883).

Bertrand Jouvenel des Ursins
(1903-1987)

A French journalist and writer who wrote his novels under the pseudonym Guillaume Champlitte. Also a lawyer, political scientist and economist associated with the liberal movement, he was, along with Gaston Berger, one of the pioneers and theorists of foresight in France, as well as political ecology. The son of Henry de Jouvenel and his first wife, he began an affair with Colette around 1920, at the age of seventeen, which lasted five years. Colette went on to use this relationship as inspiration for her novel *Ripening Seed*.

Henry Jouvenel des Ursins
(1876-1935)

French journalist and politician. In 1905, he was appointed chief of staff of the Minister of Commerce. After that, he embarked on a career as a journalist, writing for *Le Journal* and other publications before becoming editor-in-chief of the daily newspaper *Le Matin*, which is where he met Colette who went on to become his second wife (the first one being Sarah-Claire Boas). He started a lengthy political career during the post-WWI era:

Senator of Corrèze, Minister of Public Instruction and Fine Arts in the Poincaré Administration, High Commissioner of the French Republic in Syria and Lebanon from November 10, 1925 to June 23, 1926, French Ambassador to Italy from 1932 to 1933, and Minister of France Overseas.

Marguerite Maniez, known as Meg Villars
(1885-1960)

A dancer, actress, singer and novelist born and raised in London, she was Willy's mistress then wife, in 1911. The same year, following in the tradition of *Claudine*, she wrote *Peggy's Recklessness*, which Willy translated.

Mathilde de Morny, known as Missy
(1863-1944)

Born of a prestigious lineage: the last daughter of the Duke of Morny, the half-brother of Napoleon III, and his wife Princess Sophie Troubetzkoi (possibly the biological daughter of Tsar Nicholas I). She was famous for her unusual lifestyle, openly displaying her homosexuality despite her marriage to the Marquis Jacques Godart de Belbeuf, whom she divorced in 1903. Due to her very masculine look (male suit and undergarments, short hair, cigar; hysterectomy and double mastectomy), she was the victim of constant and violent attacks. Her fortune enabled her to keep many women in Paris, including Colette. But she went broke and committed suicide in 1944.

Lucie Marie Marguerite Monceau, known as Marguerite Moreno,
(1871-1948)

French actress. She trained at the Paris Conservatory and then at the famed Comédie-Française. She became "the muse of the

Symbolists" and the confidante of Stéphane Mallarmé. In 1903, she joined Sarah Bernhardt's theater, then the Théâtre Antoine, before heading up the French section of the Buenos Aires Conservatory for seven years. In 1915, she discovered the cinema and acted in many films (though she never gave up the stage).

Jeanne Roques, known as Musidora
(1889-1957)

French actress and director, famous for her role as Irma Vep in the Louis Feuillade series *The Vampires*. She was one of the Surrealists' many muses. At the same time, she got involved in co-directing while working on the screen adaptation of two of Colette's novels, *The Innnocent Libertine*, which became *Minne* (1915); and *La Vagabonda* (1917); then she directed a film from an original screenplay by Colette, *The Hidden Flame* (1918), before writing and directing *Vicenta* (1919). In 1944, she began working with Henri Langlois on the development of the french Cinémathèque Française.

Émilie Marie Bouchaud, known as Polaire
(1874-1939)

French singer and actress born in Algiers, Algeria. Famous for her unbelievably thin waist, which stood out among all others at a time when women were subjected to the tyranny of the corset, she was cast in the role of Claudine in the play *Claudine in Paris* and was also a model for Henri de Toulouse-Lautrec.

Achille Robineau-Duclos
(1863-1913)

Colette's half-brother. A doctor in Châtillon-Coligny, he opened his home to the entire family when the Colettes left Saint-Sauveur-en-Puisaye. "A full brother in terms of heart, choice, and likeness," Colette said of him. He passed away a few months after his mother.

Eugénie Sidonie Landoy, known as Sido
(1835-1912)

Colette's mother. Born in Paris, she lived with her brothers, in Belgium, in a milieu of intellectual journalists until her first marriage to Jules Robineau-Duclos, with whom she had two children: Héloïse-Émilie-Juliette and Edmé-Jules-Achille. After her husband died, she married Captain Colette and gave birth to Leopold and Colette. Despite the strong bond they shared, Colette didn't attend her mother's funeral.

Henry Gauthier-Villars, known as Willy
(1859-1931)

French journalist, music critic and novelist, and one of the most prominent men on the Paris scene during the Belle Epoque. Using several pseudonyms–Henry Maugis, Robert Parville, and Henry Willy–he had a whole team of ghostwriters working for him. A notorious womanizer, one of his many lovers was Marie-Louise Servat, wife of Émile Cohl, with whom he had a son, Jacques Henry Gauthier-Villars. He was Colette's first husband and her great love.

Books by Colette published in English

The Complete Claudine (*Claudine at School; Claudine in Paris; Claudine Married; Claudine and Annie* (1900-1903)); Farrar, Straus and Giroux, 2001
The Vagabond (1910); Farrar, Straus and Giroux, 2001
The Ripening Seed (1923); Farrar Straus and Giroux, 1955
Gigi, Julie de Carneilhan, and Chance Acquaintances: Three Short Novels, (1944); Farrar, Straus and Giroux, 2001
Cheri and The Last of Cheri (1920 and 1926); Farrar, Straus and Giroux, 2001
Break of Day (1928); Farrar, Straus and Giroux, 2002
The Other Woman (1929); Signet Classics, 1975
My Mother's House & Sido, (1922 and 1930); Farrar, Straus and Giroux, 2002
The Pure and the Impure (1932); NYRB Classics, 2000
The Shackle (1913); Ballantine Books, 1982
The Innocent Libertine (1909); Farrar Straus & Giroux, 1978
The Collected Stories (1958); Farrar Strauss and Giroux, 1984

Books on Colette

Benstock, Shari. *Women of the Left Bank: Paris, 1900-1940.* University of Texas Press, 1986
Francis, Claude and Gontier, Fernand. *Creating Colette: Volume 1: From Ingenue to Libertine, 1873-1913; Volume 2: From Baroness to Woman of Letters, 1912-1954.* Steerforth Press, 1999-
Jouve, Nicole Ward, *Colette.* Indiana University Press, 1987
Ladimer, Bethany. *Colette, Beauvoir, and Duras: Age and Women Writers.* University Press of Florida, 1999
Richardson, Joanna. *Colette*, Methuen, London, 1983
Thurman, Judith. *Secrets of the flesh: a Life of Colette*, Bloomsbury, London, 1999

Articles

Hopkin, James: "Colette has more punch than Proust," The Guardian, March 25, 2011.
Shilling, Jane. "The Life of Colette," The Telegraph, May 14, 2009.

Films about Colette

Colette (2018); directed by Wash Westmoreland; starring Keira Knightley and Dominic West.

Films based on Colette's work

Gigi (1958); directed by Vincente Minnelli; adapted from the novella written by Colette; starring Leslie Caron, Maurice Chevalier, and Louis Jourdan.
La Vagabonda (1918); co-directed by Musidora and Eugenio Perego; adapted from the novel The Vagabond written by Colette; starring Musidora, Ettore Baccani, Luisa Cansalvo.
Cheri (1950); directed by Pierre Billon; adapted from the novel by Colette; starring Jean Desailly, Marcelle Chantal, Jane Marken.
Cheri (2009); directed by Stephen Frears; starring Michelle Pfeiffer, Rupert Friend, Kathy Bates.

ACKNOWLEDGEMENTS

The end of a book means that the time has come to detach yourself
from it. Everything has been said, drawn, done. The notes, sketches,
and reproductions become paperwork to throw away.

But it pulls at the heartstrings, because though it was done alone,
this story owes much to the kindness of those around me.

And so, I would like to especially thank Pierre and Anne Lebedel,
Stéphane Lutz-Sorg, Nathalie Crom, Marie-Noëlle Pichard and
Éric Lahirigoyen, not to mention the support of the CNL, including
Laurence Pisicchio.

These pages would be just a story without all the work contributed
by Elise Borel, Philippe Ravon and Christophe Boisset, who
meticulously went over a thousand details to make the work shine.

Lastly, I would like to thank Pauline Mermet and Anaïs Aubert, my
patient and enthusiastic editors.

Annie Goetzinger

also available by Annie Goetzinger:
Girl in Dior, quarterbound embossed hardcover.
The story of Dior as seen through the eyes of a cub fashion reporter.
"Rendered in beautiful detail."
-Vogue UK
"A whimsical tale."
-ELLE
Marie Antoinette, The Phantom Queen
The ghost of the queen will not rest before she is properly buried, based on a real account.
Booklist starred review
"A sprightly tale told with lavish scenes and witty dialogue"
-Richard Pachter, Miami Herald

Annie Goetzinger
Girl in
Dior

Marie Antoinette
Rodolphe & Annie Goetzinger
Phantom Queen
nbm

Other biographies from NBM:
Niki de Saint Phalle, The Garden of Secrets
Sartre
Monet, Itinerant of Light

See previews, get exclusives and order from:
NBMPUB.COM

we have over 200 titles available
Catalog upon request
NBM
160 Broadway, Suite 700, East Wing,
New York, NY 10038

Niki
de Saint Phalle
The Garden of Secrets
nbm

SARTRE
nbm

MONET
nbm

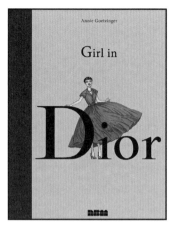

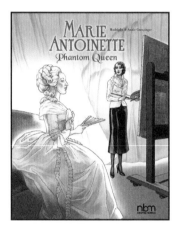

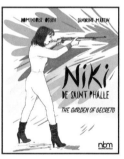

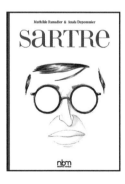

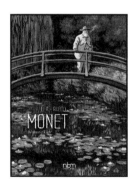